Scottish Mountaineering Club
District Guidebooks

MUNRO'S TABLES

Series Editor: D.J. BENNET

Published by
The Scottish Mountaineering Trust

MUNRO'S TABLES
AND OTHER TABLES OF LOWER HILLS

Revised and Edited by
Derek A. Bearhop

Scottish Mountaineering Club District Guidebook

PUBLISHED BY THE SCOTTISH MOUNTAINEERING TRUST: 1997
© THE SCOTTISH MOUNTAINEERING CLUB (PARTS 1, 2, 3, 5)
and ALAN DAWSON (PART 4)

First Published 1891
Revised and Republished 1921
Enlarged and Republished 1933
New Edition 1953
1953 Edition Revised 1969
First Metric Edition 1974
Reprinting history excluded
New Edition 1981
Revised and Reprinted 1984
Revised and Reprinted 1990
New Edition 1997

British library Cataloguing in Publication Data
ISBN 0 907521 - 53 - 3

A catalogue record of this book is available from
The British Library

Book design by Donald Bennet
Maps by Donald Bennet and David Langworth
Production by Scottish Mountaineering Trust (Publications) Limited
Typeset by Just Design, Glasgow
Colour separations and graphic work by Arneg, Glasgow
Printed by GNP Booth Limited, Yoker, Glasgow
Bound by Hammond Bindery Limited, Wakefield
Distributed by Cordee, 3a DeMontfort Street, Leicester LE1 7HD

Contents

PART 1. MUNRO'S TABLES

Introduction   1
Table 1. The Munros and Tops by District   13
Table 2. The Munros and Tops in Order of Height   58
Index to Munro's Tables   70
List of Munroists   75
The Furths   92

PART 2. CORBETT'S TABLES

Introduction   94
Table 3. The Corbetts by District   97
Index to Corbett's Tables   109

PART 3. DONALD'S TABLES

Introduction   112
Table 4. The Donalds by District   114
Table 5. The Donalds in Order of Height   120
Index of Donald's List of 2000ft Hills   124

PART 4. THE GRAHAMS

Introduction   127
Table 6. The Grahams by Region   129
The Highest Grahams   139

PART 5. A GAELIC GUIDE

Introduction   141
The Meaning and Pronunciation of the Munros, Tops and Corbetts   148

The Climber and the Mountain Environment   166

List of Illustrations

View south-west from Stob Choire a'Mhail in the Mamores   *Grahame Nicoll*   Front Cover
Looking towards Ben Lui from the summit of Beinn Eunaich   *Donald Bennet*   Title Page
Sir Hugh T. Munro, Bart., of Lindertis   viii
The Inaccessible Pinnacle   *Donald Bennet*   4
Rev. A.E.Robertson   6
Ben Lomond from Ben Vorlich   *Peter Hodgkiss*   16
Ben Lawers from Beinn Ghlas   *Ruaridh Pringle*   17
Beinn Dorain   *Matthew Baker*   17
The peaks of Bidean nam Bian   *Donald Bennet*   21
Aonach Eagach   *Derek Bearhop*   21
Looking north-east from Binnein Mor to Binnein Beag and the Grey Corries   *Niall Ritchie*   25
Ben Nevis and Carn Mor Dearg from Aonach Beag   *Alastair Matthewson*   25
Looking north-east from Geal-charn to Meall Chuaich and Carn na Caim   *Rab Anderson*   27
Beinn a'Ghlo from Ben Vrackie   *Scott Johnstone*   29
Lochnagar   *Niall Ritchie*   30
Cairn Toul and Sgor an Lochain Uaine from Ben Macdui   *Niall Ritchie*   35
Garbh Chioch Mhor and Sgurr na Ciche from Sgurr nan Coireachan   *Jim Renny*   40
Ladhar Bheinn from Sgurr nan Eugallt   *Grahame Nicoll*   41
Spidean Mialach and Gleouraich from the South Glen Shiel ridge   *Peter Hodgkiss*   41
Sgurr na Lapaich, Glen Affric   *Scott Johnstone*   45
The Five Sisters of Kintail from Loch Duich   *Niall Ritchie*   45
Lurg Mhor   *Jim Renny*   47
Spidean a'Choire Leith from Stuc a'Choire Dhuibh Bhig   *Donald Bennet*   49
Mullach Coire Mhic Fhearchair and
Beinn Tarsuinn from the east ridge of Beinn Dearg Mor   *Peter Hodgkiss*   52
An Teallach   *Andy Cunningham*   52
Ben Hope across Loch Eriboll from Beinn Spionnaidh   *Scott Johnstone*   55
Sgurr Alasdair and Sgurr Dearg from Sgurr a'Ghreadaidh   *Alastair Matthewson*   56
Cul Beag from Stac Pollaidh   *Donald Bennet*   95
The summit of The Cobbler, Ben Lomond beyond   *Alex Keith*   96
Stob Dubh from the head of Loch Etive   *Jim Renny*   99
Ben Rinnes and Corryhabbie Hill from the northern slopes of Ben Avon   *Jim Renny*   101
Garbh Bheinn   *Jas Hepburn*   103
Streap and Streap Comhlaidh from Sgurr Thuilm   *Ruaridh Pringle*   105
Beinn Damh from the south-east   *Alex Keith*   107
Caisteal Abhail from North Goatfell   *Ken Andrew*   108
Ben Ever in the Ochil Hills   *Jim Renny*   112
Looking towards Saddle Yoke from Hart Fell in the Moffat Hills   *Ken Andrew*   116
Kirriereoch Hill and Merrick from Rowantree Toll   *Ken Andrew*   118
View south-west from Beinn Fhionnlaidh across cloud-covered
Loch Etive to Ben Cruachan   *Alex Keith*   Back Cover

PART 1

Munro's Tables

All the Scottish Mountains of 3000 feet height and above

Compiled and Revised by
Sir Hugh T. Munro, Bart.,
of Lindertis

Rearranged by
J. Gall Inglis F.R.S.E.

Later Revisions by
James C. Donaldson
Hamish M. Brown
Derek A. Bearhop

Sir Hugh T. Munro, Bart.,
of Lindertis

INTRODUCTION

Sir Hugh Munro

Hugh Thomas Munro was born in London in 1856, the eldest of the nine children of Sir Campbell Munro of Lindertis. The family were Scottish and split their time equally between London and the family estate near Kirriemuir, which Munro first managed and then inherited. As a child he was an enthusiastic collector; from shells and fossils to eggs and butterflies. This passion was to continue into later life and it is well recorded that he returned from one spell in South Africa with a collection of Basuto curios, antelope heads, a black boy and a monkey. Travel played an enormous part in his life both professionally and for pleasure. His introduction to the mountains came in his late teens when he was a student in Stuttgart and was able to climb in the Alps. He subsequently undertook a business training in London which is thought to have given him the ordered yet inquiring mind which led to his enthusiasm for the meticulous classification of Scottish peaks for which he is best known. Munro was unquestionably an enthusiast and showed a degree of proficiency in most things he tackled. He was an accomplished flautist, dancer and orator; although not renowned for his brevity or reticence! As a Queen's Messenger, he acted as a professional courier carrying foreign despatches for diplomats. In 1880, while still only 24, he joined Sir George Colley, Governor of Natal, as his private secretary; eventually playing a part in the Basuto War when he served with an irregular cavalry corps.

Back in Britain after a bout of pleurisy, Munro spent much more of his time at Lindertis which he now came to regard as his home no matter how far his travels took him. In 1885 he stood as a Conservative candidate for Kirkcaldy Burghs in Fife, but the cause was a forlorn one and he never stood again although he was active behind the scenes in his local Forfar seat. Munro did marry, but his wife Selina died after ten years and he lived most of his life as a widower. When they were old enough, his children often accompanied him on his various ventures to Germany, Greece, Morocco, America, Japan and other corners of the globe.

Munro was an original member of the Scottish Mountaineering Club at its inception in 1889, by which time he had already amassed considerable experience of climbing the Scottish hills. He became the Club's third President in 1894 and contributed over 80 entries to the Club Journal. Many of his entries describe topographical detail which was not present on the maps of the time: indeed, the Ordnance Survey took another 80 years to produce reliable maps of parts of the north-west of the country! The first volume of the Club Journal speculated that there were possibly 300 hills in Scotland over 3000 feet in height although the exact number was unknown and some of the peaks had perhaps never been ascended. It is generally believed that when Sir Hugh Munro's *Tables of Heights over 3000 Feet* was published in the 1891 edition of the Scottish Mountaineering Club Journal this was the first serious attempt to catalogue Scotland's principal peaks. This is not strictly true as in 1882 a volume entitled *The Highland Sportsman and Tourist* was produced by Robert Hall. This publication was a fascinating pot-pourri of opinion, geographical data and instruction on sporting etiquette which incorporated a list of no fewer than 236 heights of 3000 feet or more. Although this publication was widely circulated among the sporting and landowning establishment at the time, it is clear that Munro's work was his own as there is considerable variation of hill names and heights (as well as the level of detail) from Hall's list. Munro's Tables caused quite a stir amongst the small but active circle of mountaineers at the time. The challenge of climbing all the hills on the list was seen as a sufficiently demanding, yet feasible, proposition in a lifetime given the conditions of the time. Many rose to this challenge. Munro disliked eponymous mountain names so it is a quirk of fate that the mountains which he listed were quickly to become known as 'Munros' and thus make his name probably better known than any of his contemporaries.

While not renowned for his technical climbing ability, Munro was no slouch and would be active in the hills whatever the weather, summer and winter. There are many tales of the feats of Munro in pursuit of his ambition to scale all of the 3000-foot peaks. He would often undertake his walks alone and at night; as a landowner he had a fanatical belief in the exclusive rights of proprietors in land and went out of his way to avoid any disturbance. In the age before nylon he would tackle whatever the weather could throw at him in his standard 'uniform' of cape, knickerbockers (or kilt) and Balmoral bonnet, usually carrying a long axe and his aneroid for the record-taking which was a part of every trip. His real passion was for long through-routes across wild country, often lasting several days. He did not carry a tent and the mountain bothies of today were either occupied by families, used by the estate or in ruins. For shelter he often had to rely upon the goodwill of the Highland people and by all accounts this was particularly forthcoming. One example illustrates a typical Munro foray. In February 1889 he took the boat to Inverie in Knoydart where the local laird put him up in the lodge, although he had intended to stay at the Inn. The following day he crossed over the high Mam Barrisdale to Skiary on the shores of Loch Hourn where he could do no better for his accommodation than a grimy hut which could provide only oatmeal and bad whisky. He then walked up to Loch Quoich Lodge (now submerged beneath the raised waters of the dammed Loch Quoich) where he had lunch with the factor and accepted a lift to Fort Augustus. The next day, the Loch Ness steamer took him up the loch to Drumnadrochit and he continued west on foot to Glen Cannich where he had an overnight at Guisachan. From there he traversed the Mam Sodhail range and descended to the Shiel Inn on Loch Duich *via* the Glomach Falls. As a February outing, this must have been an exceptionally long day! After a day on the Five Sisters of Kintail above the Inn, he crossed the Mam Ratagan and climbed Beinn Sgritheall before catching the Clansman steamer to Glasgow and then the overnight sleeper to London. In an age before the motor car would revolutionise our approach to the outdoors, Munro's enthusiasm and commitment puts many of our modern comforts in perspective.

The human side of the man is demonstrated by a less than auspicious trip to the north-west the following March. After successfully climbing four summits in the Fannaich group with H. Lawson, the pair were descending northwards to Loch a' Bhraoin when they had difficulty fording a stream. In failing light they made a navigational error and were benighted. The three matches in their possession offered little help and they blundered about all night in freezing conditions attempting to locate the road. Finally, they reached the road at 7am where Munro's driver was still waiting with a fire lit and hot cocoa ready!

Munro was past military age at the time of the Great War in 1914 but he went out to Malta to work with the Red Cross. In 1918 he and two of his daughters organised a canteen for troops in Tarascon near Avignon in Provence. The following spring a chill developed into pneumonia and he died, aged 63. Munro never quite completed the ascent of all the peaks on his list. There has been much speculation as to whether his ultimate objective was the completion of the Tops or if it was the Munros. All of the evidence points to the former. Accounts of his exploits are plentiful in the Club Journal and these make it clear that he would never miss an opportunity to visit a Top, however humble or downright dubious it might be. Munro never succeeded on the Inaccessible Pinnacle (despite several attempts, mostly thwarted by bad weather), but if his objective had been the Munros this would not have presented a problem as the 'In Pinn' was not listed as a full 'Munro' in the original tables. This bizarre situation where the lower peak of Sgurr Dearg was classified as a separate summit and the higher 'In Pinn' was shown as a subsidiary Top was only corrected in the 1921 edition, although Munro's own notes made clear that he himself would have proposed such a change. In his original tables it has been suggested that the presence of a name on the popular map sheet was an important consideration for Munro in determining whether a mountain should be classed as distinct or separate. In a number of instances, such as the 'In Pinn', this consideration seems to have outweighed the presence of a higher but unnamed top nearby. Munro never climbed Carn Cloich-mhuilinn above the Dee as this was being left specially for his last ascent. Its relative ease of access from Lindertis would have made it a pleasant outing for the gathering which he planned for the occasion. It has come to light, however, that there was one other Top which evaded Munro's attentions. In 1917 he wrote that he still aspired to stand on the summits of the only three tops in Scotland exceeding 3000 feet in height which he had not climbed. In addition to the two tops already mentioned, Munro's personal copy of the Tables indicates that Carn an Fhidhleir at the head of Glen Feshie was also unclimbed. He had failed on the mountain in extraordinary circumstances in July 1908. The account is told by his companion William Garden and is worth repetition.

"I accompanied Munro through Glen Tilt. Dining early at Blair Lodge, we drove to Forest Lodge, arriving there at 7.40pm. The threatening afternoon had settled down to a night of persistently heavy rain. By the time we reached the Belford Memorial Bridge (9.40pm) we were thoroughly soaked, and the Tarf and Tilt were already in high flood. From the bridge we followed the Tarf, taking advantage of innumerable sheep tracks when we could strike them in the rapidly increasing

The Inaccessible Pinnacle

darkness. At 11pm we reached the remains of an old shepherd's bothy, where we rigged up a tent with a mackintosh, under which we took our bearings by aid of compass, map and matches. From the bothy we bore away in a north-west direction over gently rising moorland. The rain poured harder than ever. As we ascended we got into dense fog and at 1.05am(!) we reached the large cairn on the summit of An Sgarsoch with some difficulty as the summit is very flat and extensive. It was now quite chilly, very dark, and, what was worse, we had been unable to keep our powder dry, and so could neither read our compasses nor see our maps. We dropped down by the side of the Allt a'Chaoruinn and struck the Geldie. Carn an Fhidhleir, originally included in the programme, had to be abandoned, which was more regretted by Munro than I, because in consequence it still remains one of the few three-thousanders undone by him".

Sir Hugh Munro is buried alongside his wife and his mother in a modest, private graveyard a short distance from the family house near Kirriemuir. His legacy, however, is very much alive today although what Sir Hugh would have made of it all can only be imagined.

Rev A. E. Robertson

The first person to climb all the Munros was the Rev Archibald Eneas Robertson when he ascended Meall Dearg on the Aonach Eagach on 28 September 1901. It is reported that on reaching the summit, he kissed the cairn and his wife - in that order.

Robertson was a gentleman and a fine mountaineer. Like Munro, his talents were many and the SMC Journal is full of his writings and photographs. He was a skilled craftsman and made a table for the Charles Inglis Clark Hut on Ben Nevis which is there to this day. He had the advantage of a Rannoch parish and was often able to take breaks of up to three months at a time. In successive holidays in 1898 and 1899, therefore, he was able to "knock off" 75 and 72 Munros respectively. He climbed and had many other interests and did not devote all of his time to the pursuit of Munros. It took what he called "a desultory campaign of about 10 years" to complete them. Robertson, of course, used the original 1891 Tables and it seems apparent that he had not ascended the Inaccessible Pinnacle (which was only a Top at that time) when he completed in 1901. This assertion is based upon Robertson's own account of his achievement wherein he wrote that "looking back over the hills of Scotland as a whole, I only wish I could tell of some faraway unknown peak bristling with difficulties on all sides, but in fact there are none. The only hills where there are no easy ways to the top are certain of the Coolins of Skye, Sgurr Dubh for example or Mhadaidh or perhaps Sgurr Alasdair". There is no mention of the Pinnacle which surely "bristles with difficulties on all sides" if any peak does! His skills were certainly up to the task and it is more than likely that he attained this elusive summit during a visit to Skye in 1906.

Rev A. E. Robertson

Robertson was Chairman of the Scottish Rights of Way Society and a Fellow of the Royal Scottish Geographical Society (as was Munro). He was President of the Scottish Mountaineering Club from 1930 - 1932 and was later made an Honorary Member in recognition of his prolonged service to mountaineering. When he died in 1958 at the age of 88, a bridge was built over the River Elchaig on the way to the Falls of Glomach as a memorial to him.

It wasn't until 1923 that the second completion was reported when the Rev A. R. G. Burn not only repeated the Munros but added the subsidiary Tops as well. Burn certainly succeeded on the Inaccessible Pinnacle and his obituary has an account of the heartless leg-pulling which he endured at the hands of the young climbers who dragged him up. How many others have had to endure such treatment since? J. A. Parker became Munroist number three in 1929 and added the Furths - the three-thousanders of England, Wales and Ireland. With the coming of better roads, more leisure time and readily available and more accurate information for hill-walkers, the boom period was just around the corner. Even in 1933 it was written that "the ascent of all the Munros under modern road conditions is far from being a feat". How much more so today? It wasn't long before multiple rounds were being completed, rounds were being undertaken in single expeditions and even marathon runs over the hills in ever-faster times. The Munros may have diminished as a lifetime challenge but they still offer the same rewards to those who are willing to succumb to their unquestionable appeal.

Editor's Notes

Munros   In his notes accompanying the first edition of his Tables in 1891, Munro wrote 'The decision as to what are to be considered distinct and separate mountains, and what may be counted as 'Tops', although arrived at after careful consideration, cannot be finally insisted upon'. Munro left no definition and his own uncertainty was illustrated by the substantive changes which he had proposed to his original list but which he was unable to publish before his death in 1919.   While recognising the subjective nature of any judgement as to what constitutes a separate 'Munro', the editor has made a few changes to the list published in previous editions which remove some anomalies without altering the basic character of the Tables as Munro left them.

Tops   An effort has been made to rationalise the many elevations above the 3000 - foot contour. Many have been removed following close scrutiny of large scale maps and observation on the ground which have revealed that the point was of insufficient rise or definition to merit classification. A few additional summits have been added following the same process. All of these alterations are listed at the end of these notes.

Lay-out   The lay-out is that used in the previous edition of this volume. Within the Sections, the hills have been re-organised in a few instances to follow more closely the convention of a south-west to north-east progression.

Column Explanations in Table 1

Column 1. Name   The Ordnance Survey 1:50,000 series names/spellings are used wherever possible as this is the standard walkers' map. These names/spellings are not always correct, or there may be variations or local differences. Larger scale maps or other sources have been used where the present OS sheet has not given a name. In a few cases names have been changed to conform with alterations on the latest OS maps. One significant change of name has been made (in the Carn Mairg range) which is explained in the relevant section.

Column 2. Height   The practice has been to take the height in metres from the most recent published OS sheet at either 1:50,000 or 1:25,000 scale. In many cases this produces a height different from that shown on the more frequently used 1:50,000 series. In the case of Knight's Peak (Sgurr nan Gillean), the largest scale OS sheets were insufficient to determine the exact altitude and observations had to be made on the ground using a precision altimeter. 914.4metres is taken as the metric equivalent of 3000 feet although the OS does not provide spot height data to other than the nearest metre. c indicates that a contour has been used to determine the height.

Columns 3 and 4. Mountains/Tops   These are listed in order of altitude (see Table 2). The separate mountains (more commonly referred to as 'Munros') are listed in column 3 and the hills without separate status (referred to as 'Tops') in column 4.

Column 5. OS Map Sheet   This shows the number of the OS 1:50,000 series map on which the summit appears. Where a summit appears on more than one sheet, this is shown.

Column 6. Map Reference   The 6 figure map reference pinpoints the location of the summit of a hill to within 100 metres. The national alphabetic prefix is shown in each case. Details of how to use the map (or grid) reference appear on most maps.

The Geographical Sections

Section 1.   The country south of a line from Oban, Dalmally, Strath Fillan, Loch Tay and on to the A9.

Section 2.   The area bounded by the West Highland Railway, Loch Rannoch, the A9, Loch Tay, Glen Dochart, Strathfillan to Bridge of Orchy.

Section 3.   The area bounded by Loch Linnhe, Loch Leven, Blackwater Reservoir, the West Highland Railway, Bridge of Orchy, Tyndrum and Oban.

Section 4.   The area bounded by upper Loch Linnhe, Glen Spean, Loch Ericht, Blackwater Reservoir and Loch Leven.

Section 5.   The hills on either side of the A9 at the Drumochter Pass.

Section 6.   The area bounded by Glen Tromie, Glen Geldie, Braemar, the A93 to Perth, the A9 through Blair Atholl and the Gaick Pass.

Section 7.   The country east of the A93 Perth-Braemar road and south of the River Dee from Braemar to Aberdeen.

Section 8.   The country east and north of the Glen Feshie, Glen Geldie, Braemar-Aberdeen line.

Section 9.   The area bounded by the Great Glen, the A9 from Inverness to Newtonmore and the A86 from Newtonmore to Spean Bridge.

Section 10.   The mainland south of Glen Shiel and Glen Moriston and west of the Great Glen.

Section 11.   The area north of Glen Shiel and Glen Moriston, and south of Loch Mullardoch; bounded in the west by the coast and in the east by the Great Glen.

Section 12.   The area south of the Kyle of Lochalsh-Beauly railway and north of a line from Kyle of Lochalsh to Loch Mullardoch to Cannich.

Section 13.   The area west of the Kyle of Lochalsh-Achnasheen railway and south of a line from Achnasheen to Poolewe.

Section 14.   The area north of the road from Garve through Achnasheen to Poolewe and south of the road from Garve to Loch Broom.

Section 15.   The country between the Inverness-Garve-Ullapool road and a line from Ullapool to Lairg.

Section 16.   The country north of the Lochinver-Lairg road.

Section 17.   The Islands.

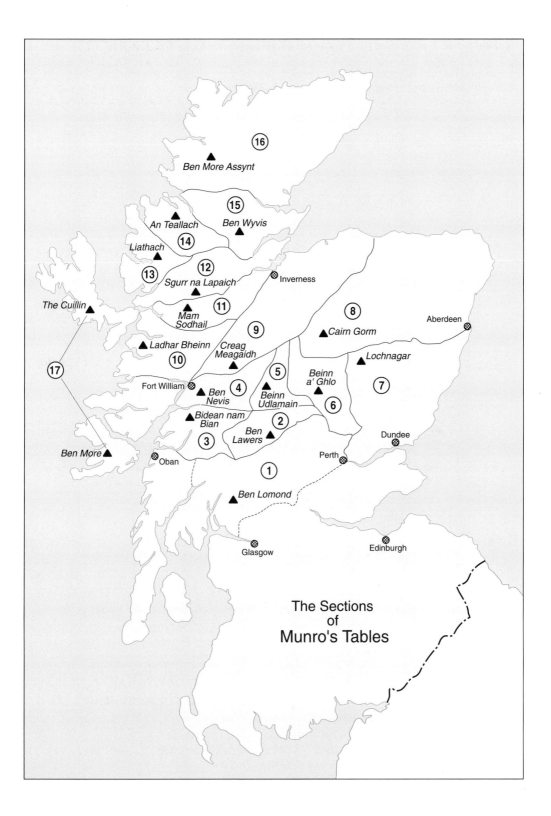

The Sections
of
Munro's Tables

Details of Changes to Munros and Tops in this Edition

The 1990 edition of Munros Tables listed 277 Munros and 517 Tops. The corresponding numbers in this edition are 284 and 511.

Munros

Number listed in 1990			277
Add	Section 2	An Stuc (Ben Lawers)	
	3	Stob na Broige (Buachaille Etive Mor)	
	3	Stob Coire Raineach (Buachaille Etive Beag)	
	3	Stob Coire Sgreamhach (Bidean nam Bian)	
	8	Sgor an Lochain Uaine (Cairn Toul)	
	11	Sgurr na Carnach (Five Sisters of Kintail)	
	13	Tom na Gruagaich (Beinn Alligin)	
	13	Spidean Coire nan Clach (Beinn Eighe)	8
Deduct	4	Sgor an Iubhair (Mamores)	<u>1</u>
			284

Tops

Number listed in 1990			517
Add	Section 2	Meall nan Tarmachan - South-east Top	
	3	Stob an Duine Ruaidh (Ben Starav)	
	7	Little Pap (Lochnagar)	
	10	Druim Shionnach - West Top (Cluanie Ridge)	
	11	Stob Coire na Cloiche (Sgurr nan Ceathreamhnan)	
	11	Stob Fraoch Choire (Sgurr nan Ceathreamhnan)	
	11	Stob Coire Dhomhnuill (Carn Eighe)	
	13	Stuc a'Choire Dhuibh Bhig (Liathach)	
	17	Knight's Peak (Sgurr nan Gillean)	9
Deduct	1	Ben Lui - North-west Top	
	3	Sron nan Giubhas (Stob Ghabhar)	
	3	Aonach Eagach (Stob Ghabhar)	
	7	Cac Carn Mor (Lochnagar)	
	8	Ben Macdui - North Top	
	8	Beinn Mheadhoin - South-west Top	
	9	Stob Poite Coire Ardair - East Top	
	10	The Saddle - Trig Point	
	10	The Saddle - West Top	
	10	The Saddle - East Top	
	11	Stob Coire nan Dearcag (Sgurr nan Ceathreamhnan)	
	12	An Riabhachan - North-east Top	
	14	Slioch - Trig Point	
	14	An Teallach - Corrag Bhuidhe Buttress	
	17	Sgurr Dearg (Cuillin)	<u>15</u>
			511

Some further explanation of the changes in this edition to the number of peaks achieving separate Munro status is called for. As has been mentioned previously, Munro himself was unhappy with his original classification and was in the process of updating his 1891 Tables at the time of his death. The 1921 edition, although published posthumously, was essentially the work of Munro and represented his view of what constituted a separate peak, just as did the 1891 edition. Those who maintain that the historical Tables should remain unchanged must face up to this paradox. The 1981 edition made a determined attempt to address the inconsistencies in the Tables as they stood at that time. As well as taking account of the changes made necessary by metrication and the continuing improvement of the Ordnance Survey coverage of parts of Scotland, the 1981 edition sought to overcome the principal anomaly whereby some large mountain ranges in the north-west were only awarded one Munro while long chains of hills elsewhere were adorned with several. These changes, although the subject of much comment at the time, have become accepted as being sympathetic to Munro's philosophy.

The changes presented in the current edition seek to take this approach to its natural conclusion. There were many who felt that the 1981 changes did not go far enough and, indeed, introduced a number of further inconsistencies. It is this editor's view that the new Munros on Beinn Alligin and Beinn Eighe, for example, cannot be ignored when other lesser summits are included. Indeed, all of the new Munros have a distinct character which sets them apart from adjoining summits (either because of their reascent or physical characteristics) and gives them that intangible sense of 'separateness' which Munro strived to classify. It is acknowledged that no precise definition of a Munro exists but the current Tables have been arrived at on the basis of close adherence to Munro's original ideals, while seeking to make any subsequent alterations consistent with one another. The one deletion in this edition is made on the basis that the grounds for this summit's elevation in a previous edition were much weaker than those for a number of more worthy summits which remain as Tops.

The Editor wishes to acknowledge his indebtedness to Sir Hugh Munro and all subsequent editors of these Tables, his admiration for whom has grown as the preparation of this edition has progressed. Thanks are due to all those who have offered advice and constructive comment but in particular to Donald Bennet, Chris Huntley, Robin Campbell, Alan Dawson, Dave Hewitt, Alec Keith and Matthew Shaw. Appreciation is also expressed to the many people who have written pointing out errors in previous editions or expressing views as to the inclusion or deletion of summits from these Tables. The staff in the Map Room of the National Library of Scotland were always helpful and greatly assisted in ensuring that these Tables have been prepared using the latest cartographical information available. Thanks to David Langworth for the new-look maps and to everyone who has contributed photographs to help the overall appearance of this publication

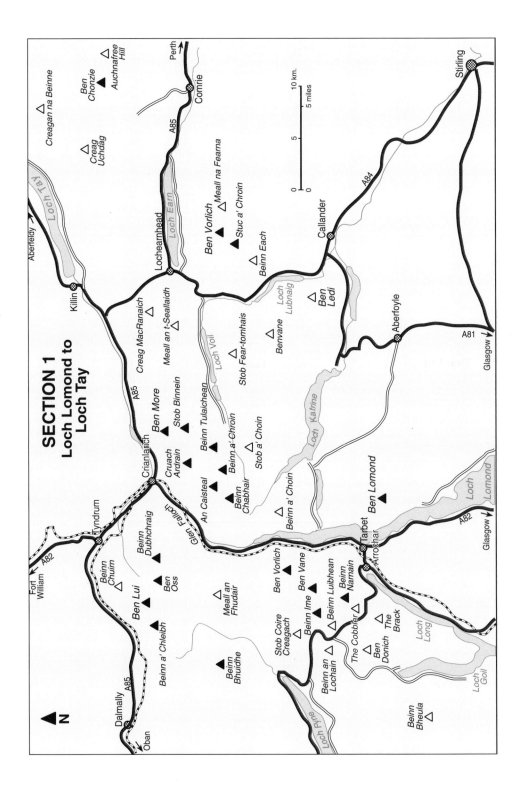

SECTION 1
Loch Lomond to
Loch Tay

N

TABLE 1. The Munros and Tops by District

SECTION 1
Loch Lomond to Loch Tay

Name	Height (metres)	No. in order of height Mtn.	Top	O.S. Map Sheet	Map Ref.
BEN LOMOND and the ARROCHAR ALPS					
1 Ben Lomond	974	184	297	56	NN367028
2 Beinn Narnain	926	259	454	56	NN271066
3 Beinn Ime	1011	118	190	56	NN255084
4 Ben Vane	915	283	507	56	NN277098
5 Ben Vorlich	943	229	391	56/50	NN295124
6 North Top	931		434	56/50	NN294130
7 Beinn Bhuidhe	948	216	371	56/50	NN203187
BEN LUI GROUP					
8 Beinn a'Chleibh	916	281	502	50	NN250256
9 Ben Lui	1130	28	42	50	NN266263
10 Ben Oss	1029	101	161	50	NN287253
11 Beinn Dubhchraig	978	175	282	50	NN307254
BALQUHIDDER					
12 Beinn Chabhair	933	244	426	50/56	NN367179
13 An Caisteal	995	147	238	50/56	NN378193
14 Beinn a'Chroin	940	233	403	50/56	NN394186
15 West Top	938		410	50/56	NN385185
16 Beinn Tulaichean	946	220	380	56	NN416196
17 Cruach Ardrain	1046	87	138	51/56	NN409212
18 Stob Garbh	959		341	51/56	NN411221
19 Stob Binnein	1165	18	27	51	NN434227
20 Stob Coire an Lochain	1068		109	51	NN438220
21 Meall na Dige	966		317	51	NN450225
22 Ben More	1174	16	24	51	NN432244
CRIEFF and LOCH EARN					
23 Stuc a'Chroin	975	182	295	57	NN617174
24 Ben Vorlich	985	165	264	57	NN629189
25 Ben Chonzie	931	250	433	51/52	NN773308

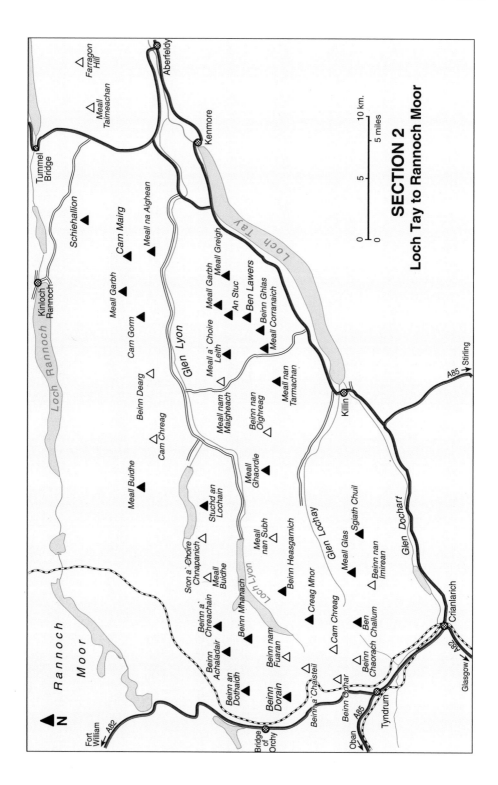

SECTION 2
Loch Tay to Rannoch Moor

SECTION 2

Loch Tay to Rannoch Moor

Name	Height (metres)	No. in order of height Mtn.	Top	O.S. Map Sheet	Map Ref.
GLEN LOCHAY HILLS					
1 Ben Challum	1025	106	170	50	NN386322
2 South Top	998		226	50	NN386315
3 Meall Glas	959	199	340	51	NN431321
4 Beinn Cheathaich.	937		413	51	NN444326
5 Sgiath Chuil	921	270	476	51	NN462317
6 Meall a'Churain.	918		486	51	NN463325
7 Creag Mhor	1047	84	134	50	NN391361
8 Stob nan Clach.	956		354	50	NN387351
9 Beinn Heasgarnich	1078	62	96	51	NN413383
10 Meall Ghaordie.	1039	93	149	51	NN514397
BRIDGE OF ORCHY HILLS					
11 Beinn Dorain.	1076	64	98	50	NN325378
12 Beinn an Dothaidh	1004	129	206	50	NN331408
13 Beinn Achaladair	1038	94	150	50	NN344432
14 South Top	1002		211	50	NN342420
15 Beinn a'Chreachain	1081	61	93	50	NN373440
16 Meall Buidhe	978		284	50	NN359438
17 Beinn Mhanach.	953	211	363	50	NN373411
18 Beinn a'Chuirn.	923		466	50	NN360409
THE LAWERS GROUP					
19 Meall nan Tarmachan.	1044	89	141	51	NN585390
20 South-east Top	923		468	51	NN589385
21 Meall Garbh	1026		169	51	NN578383
22 Beinn nan Eachan	1000		221	51	NN570383
23 Creag na Caillich	916		504	51	NN562377
24 Meall Corranaich	1069	68	105	51	NN615410
25 Meall a'Choire Leith	926	261	457	51	NN612439
26 Beinn Ghlas.	1103	47	72	51	NN625404
27 Ben Lawers	1214	10	13	51	NN635414
28 Creag an Fhithich	1047		133	51	NN635422
29 An Stuc.	1118	34	50	51	NN639431
30 Meall Garbh	1118	35	51	51	NN644436
31 Meall Greigh	1001	136	217	51	NN674438

Ben Lomond from Ben Vorlich

SECTION 2 (continued)

Name	Height (metres)	No. in order of height Mtn.	No. in order of height Top	O.S. Map Sheet	Map Ref.
GLEN LYON					
32 **Stuchd an Lochain**	960	197	338	51	**NN483448**
33 Sron Chona Choirein	927		452	51	NN493445
34 **Meall Buidhe**	932	248	430	51	**NN498499**
35 **Carn Gorm**	1029	103	163	51	**NN635500**
36 An Sgorr	924		461	51	NN640509
37 **Meall Garbh**	968	186	311	51	**NN647517**
38 **Carn Mairg**	1041	91	144	51	**NN684512**
39 Meall Liath	1012		189	51	NN693512
40 Meall a'Bharr	1004		208	51	NN668515
41 **Meall nan Aighean***	981	169	271	51	**NN694496**
42 **Schiehallion**	1083	59	90	51/52	**NN713547**

* Creag Mhor in previous editions. The 1:25,000 sheet makes clear that the earlier name refers to a feature some distance from the summit.

Ben Lawers from Beinn Ghlas

Beinn Dorain

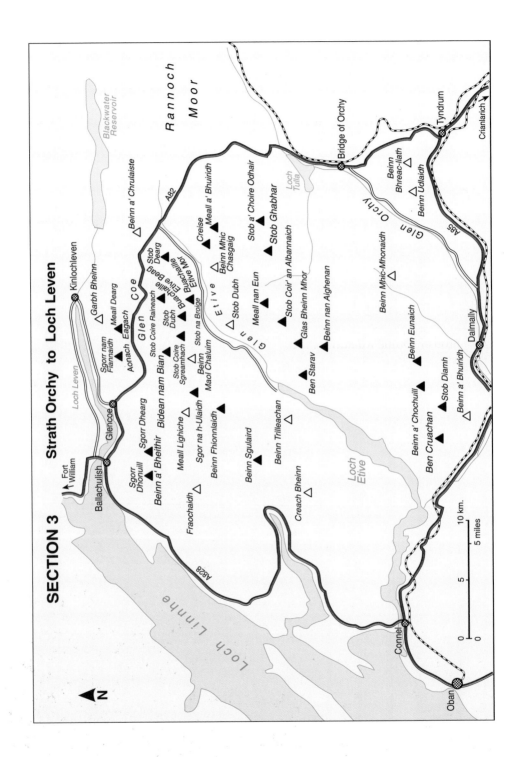

SECTION 3   Strath Orchy to Loch Leven

SECTION 3

Strath Orchy to Loch Leven

Name	Height (metres)	No. in order of height Mtn.	No. in order of height Top	O.S. Map Sheet	Map Ref.
CRUACHAN GROUP					
1 **Ben Cruachan**	**1126**	31	45	50	NN069304
2 Stob Dearg (Taynuilt Peak)....	1104		71	50	NN062307
3 Meall Cuanail...............	918		487	50	NN069295
4 Drochaid Ghlas	1009		197	50	NN083306
5 **Stob Diamh**	998	143	231	50	NN094308
6 Stob Garbh	980		278	50	NN095302
7 Sron an Isean	966		318	50	NN099311
8 **Beinn a'Chochuill**...........	980	172	275	50	NN109328
9 **Beinn Eunaich**..............	989	156	253	50	NN135328
ETIVE HILLS					
10 **Beinn nan Aighenan**	960	196	333	50	NN148405
11 **Ben Starav**	1078	63	97	50	NN125427
12 Stob an Duine Ruaidh........	918		492	50	NN124410
13 Meall Cruidh	930		436	50	NN129415
14 Stob Coire Dheirg	1028		166	50	NN131426
15 **Glas Bheinn Mhor**	997	145	233	50	NN153429
16 **Stob Coir'an Albannaich**......	1044	90	142	50	NN169443
17 **Meall nan Eun**..............	928	254	445	50	NN192449
BLACKMOUNT					
18 **Stob Ghabhar**	1090	55	83	50	NN230455
19 Stob a'Bhruaich Leith	941		401	50	NN208459
20 Sron a'Ghearrain	990		251	50	NN220457
21 **Stob a'Choire Odhair**.........	945	226	387	50	NN257459
22 **Creise**	**1100**	50	75	41	NN238506
23 Clach Leathad	1099		77	50	NN240493
24 Stob a'Ghlais Choire	996		237	41	NN240516
25 **Meall a'Bhuiridh**............	**1108**	45	65	41	NN250503

SECTION 3 (continued)

Name	Height (metres)	No. in order of height Mtn.	Top	O.S. Map Sheet	Map Ref.
APPIN					
26 **Beinn Sgulaird**	937	237	414	50	NN053460
27 **Beinn Fhionnlaidh**	959	198	339	50	NN095497
28 **Sgor na h-Ulaidh.**	994	149	240	41	NN111518
29 Stob an Fhuarain	968		312	41	NN118523
Beinn a'Bheithir -					
30 **Sgorr Dhonuill**	1001	137	219	41	NN040555
31 **Sgorr Dhearg**	1024	107	171	41	NN056558
32 Sgorr Bhan	947		377	41	NN062560
GLEN COE					
33 **Bidean nam Bian.**	1150	23	32	41	NN143542
34 Stob Coire nam Beith.	1107		67	41	NN139545
35 Stob Coire nan Lochan	1115		56	41	NN148548
36 **Stob Coire Sgreamhach**	1072	65	101	41	NN154536
37 Beinn Fhada	952		367	41	NN159540
38 Beinn Fhada - North-east Top. .	931		432	41	NN164543
Buachaille Etive Beag -					
39 **Stob Dubh**	958	201	345	41	NN179535
40 **Stob Coire Raineach**	925	263	460	41	NN191548
Buachaille Etive Mor -					
41 **Stob na Broige**	956	207	353	41	NN190525
42 Stob Coire Altruim	941		402	41	NN197530
43 **Stob Dearg**	1021	110	175	41	NN222542
44 Stob na Doire	1011		192	41	NN207532
Aonach Eagach -					
45 **Sgorr nam Fiannaidh**	967	188	315	41	NN140583
46 Stob Coire Leith	940		404	41	NN149584
47 **Meall Dearg.**	953	212	364	41	NN161583
48 Am Bodach.	943		390	41	NN168580

Bidean nam Bian peaks. Stob Coire Sgreamhach (left) and Stob Coire nan Lochan (right)

Aonach Eagach

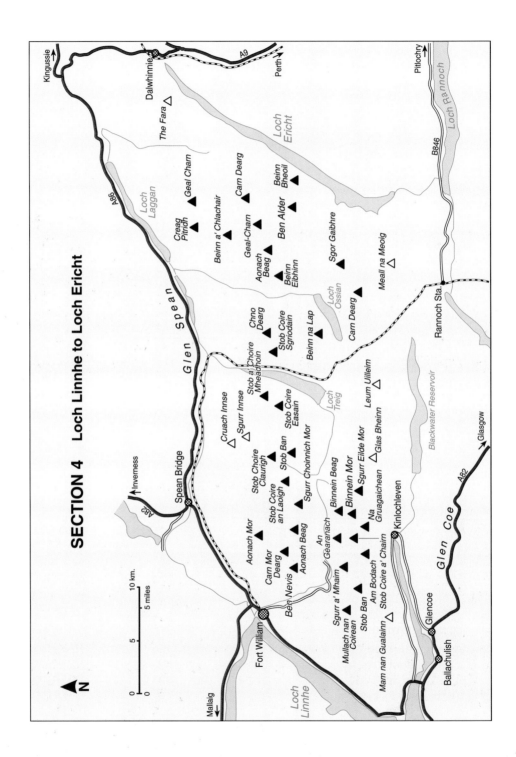

SECTION 4   Loch Linnhe to Loch Ericht

SECTION 4

Loch Linnhe to Loch Ericht

Name	Height (metres)	No. in order of height Mtn.	Top	O.S. Map Sheet	Map Ref.
THE MAMORES					
1 **Mullach nan Coirean**	**939**	**236**	**407**	**41**	**NN122662**
2 South-east Top	917		499	41	NN131654
3 **Stob Ban**....................	**999**	**140**	**225**	**41**	**NN147654**
4 **Sgurr a'Mhaim**	**1099**	**51**	**78**	**41**	**NN164667**
5 Sgor an Iubhair	1001		218	41	NN165655
6 Stob Choire a'Mhail.........	990		252	41	NN163659
7 **Am Bodach**	**1032**	**99**	**156**	**41**	**NN176650**
8 **Stob Coire a'Chairn**	**981**	**171**	**274**	**41**	**NN185660**
9 **An Gearanach**	**982**	**166**	**268**	**41**	**NN187669**
10 An Garbhanach	975		292	41	NN188665
11 **Na Gruagaichean**	**1056**	**74**	**116**	**41**	**NN203652**
12 North-west Top	1041		145	41	NN201654
13 **Binnein Mor**	**1130**	**27**	**41**	**41**	**NN212663**
14 South Top	1062		113	41	NN211656
15 Sgor Eilde Beag	956		351	41	NN219652
16 **Binnein Beag**...............	**943**	**230**	**392**	**41**	**NN221677**
17 **Sgurr Eilde Mor**	**1010**	**123**	**196**	**41**	**NN230657**
BEN NEVIS and THE AONACHS					
18 **Ben Nevis**..................	**1344**	**1**	**1**	**41**	**NN166712**
19 Carn Dearg (South-west)	1020		176	41	NN155701
20 Carn Dearg (North-west)	1221		10	41	NN559719
21 **Carn Mor Dearg**	**1220**	**9**	**11**	**41**	**NN177721**
22 Carn Dearg Meadhonach	1179		21	41	NN176726
23 **Aonach Beag**	**1234**	**7**	**8**	**41**	**NN196715**
24 Stob Coire Bhealaich	1100c		76	41	NN202709
25 Sgurr a'Bhuic	963		322	41	NN204701
26 **Aonach Mor**................	**1221**	**8**	**9**	**41**	**NN192729**
27 Stob an Cul Choire	1068		108	41	NN203731
28 Tom na Sroine	918		495	41	NN207748
GREY CORRIES					
29 **Sgurr Choinnich Mor**........	**1094**	**52**	**80**	**41**	**NN227714**
30 Sgurr Choinnich Beag	963		323	41	NN220710
31 **Stob Coire an Laoigh**	**1116**	**38**	**54**	**41**	**NN239725**
32 Stob Coire Easain............	1080		94	41	NN234727

SECTION 4 (continued)

	Name	Height (metres)	No. in order of height Mtn.	No. in order of height Top	O.S. Map Sheet	Map Ref.
33	Caisteil	1106		68	41	NN246729
34	Beinn na Socaich	1007		200	41	NN236734
35	Stob Coire Cath na Sine	1079		95	41	NN252730
36	**Stob Choire Claurigh**	**1177**	**15**	**22**	**41**	**NN262738**
37	Stob a'Choire Leith	1105		69	41	NN256736
38	Stob Coire na Ceannain.	1123		46	41	NN267745
39	Stob Coire na Gaibhre	958		343	41	NN261757
40	**Stob Ban**.	**977**	**178**	**287**	**41**	**NN266723**
	LOCH TREIG and LOCH OSSIAN					
41	**Stob Coire Easain**	**1115**	**39**	**55**	**41**	**NN308730**
42	**Stob a'Choire Mheadhoin**	**1105**	**46**	**70**	**41**	**NN316736**
43	**Beinn na Lap**	**935**	**241**	**419**	**41**	**NN376695**
44	**Chno Dearg**	**1046**	**86**	**137**	**41**	**NN377741**
45	Meall Garbh	976		290	41	NN371727
46	**Stob Coire Sgriodain**	**979**	**174**	**281**	**41**	**NN356743**
47	South Top	958		344	41	NN359739
48	**Carn Dearg**.	**941**	**231**	**399**	**42**	**NN417661**
49	**Sgor Gaibhre**	**955**	**208**	**356**	**42**	**NN444674**
50	Sgor Choinnich	929		437	42	NN443683
	LOCH ERICHT to LOCH LAGGAN					
51	**Ben Alder**.	**1148**	**25**	**35**	**42**	**NN496718**
52	**Beinn Bheoil**	**1019**	**112**	**178**	**42**	**NN516717**
53	Sron Coire na h-Iolaire	955		357	42	NN513704
54	**Beinn Eibhinn**.	**1102**	**48**	**73**	**42**	**NN449733**
55	Mullach Coire nan Nead.	922		474	42	NN430734
56	Meall Glas Choire	924		463	42	NN436727
57	**Aonach Beag**	**1116**	**37**	**53**	**42**	**NN457741**
58	**Geal-Charn**	**1132**	**26**	**39**	**42**	**NN469746**
59	Sgor Iutharn	1028		165	42	NN489743
60	**Carn Dearg**.	**1034**	**98**	**155**	**42**	**NN504764**
61	Diollaid a'Chairn	922		471	42	NN488758
62	**Beinn a'Chlachair**	**1087**	**56**	**85**	**42**	**NN471781**
63	**Geal Charn**[†]	**1049**	**81**	**129**	**42**	**NN504811**
64	**Creag Pitridh**	**924**	**264**	**462**	**42**	**NN487814**

† also shown as Mullach Coire an Iubhair on some maps

Looking north-east from Binnein Mor to Binnein Beag and the Grey Corries

Ben Nevis and Carn Mor Dearg from Aonach Beag

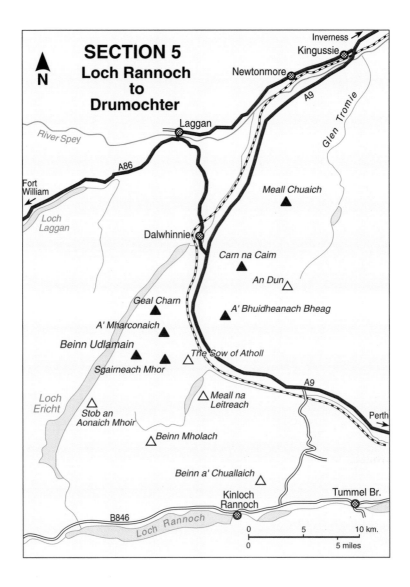

SECTION 5
Loch Rannoch
to
Drumochter

N

Inverness
Kingussie
Newtonmore
A9
Glen Tromie

River Spey
Laggan
A86
Fort William
Loch Laggan

Meall Chuaich ▲

Dalwhinnie

Carn na Caim ▲
An Dun △

Geal Charn ▲
A' Mharconaich ▲
A' Bhuidheanach Bheag ▲
Beinn Udlamain ▲
Sgairneach Mhor ▲
The Sow of Atholl △

Loch Ericht
Stob an Aonaich Mhoir △
Meall na Leitreach △

A9

Perth

Beinn Mholach △

Beinn a' Chuallaich △

Tummel Br.
Kinloch Rannoch

B846
Loch Rannoch

0   5   10 km.
0   5 miles

Looking north-east from Geal-charn to Meall Chuaich and Carn na Caim

SECTION 5

Loch Rannoch to Drumochter

	Name	Height (metres)	No. in order of height Mtn.	Top	O.S. Map Sheet	Map Ref.
	THE DRUMOCHTER HILLS					
1	Sgairneach Mhor............	991	155	249	42	NN598731
2	Beinn Udlamain	1011	119	191	42	NN579739
3	A'Mharconaich	975	179	291	42	NN604762
4	Geal-charn.................	917	279	498	42	NN596782
5	A'Bhuidheanach Bheag	936	240	418	42	NN660776
6	Glas Mheall Mor	928		443	42	NN680769
7	Carn na Caim...............	941	232	400	42	NN677821
8	Meall Chuaich..............	951	214	368	42	NN716878

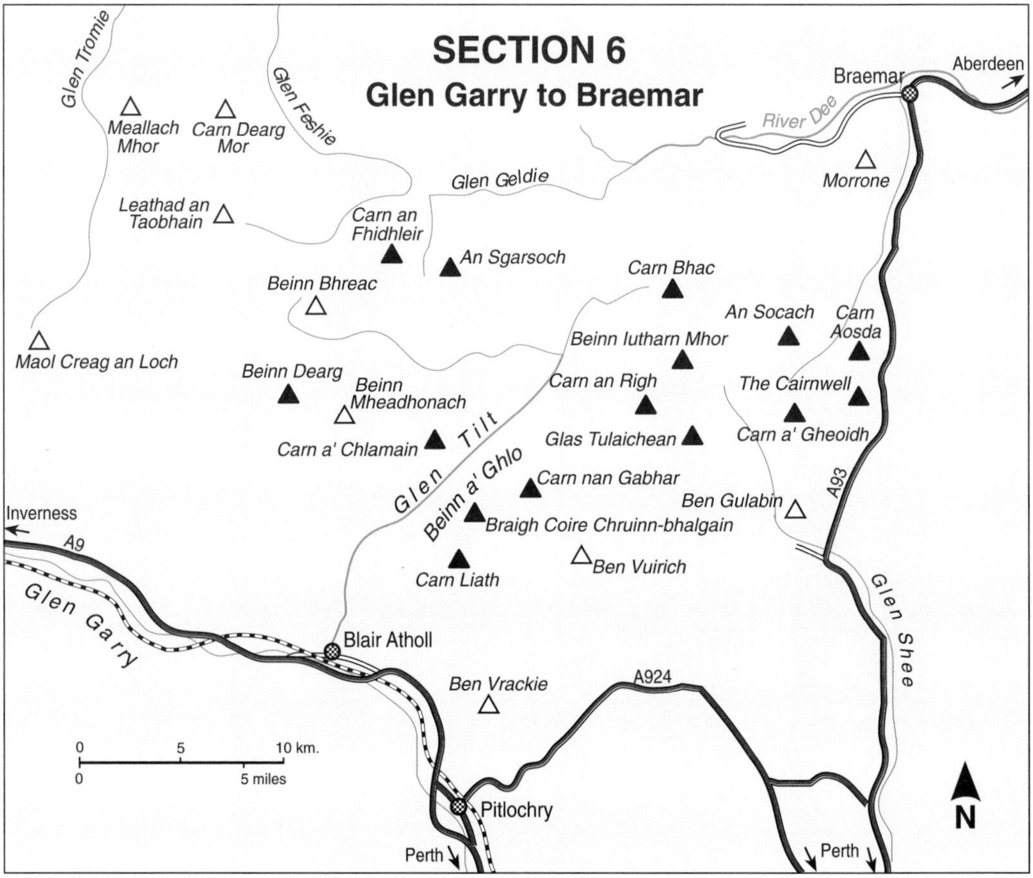

SECTION 6

Glen Garry to Braemar

	Name	Height (metres)	No. in order of height Mtn.	Top	O.S. Map Sheet	Map Ref.
	TARF AND TILT					
1	**Beinn Dearg**	**1008**	**124**	**198**	**43**	**NN852777**
2	**Carn a'Chlamain**	**963**	**192**	**321**	**43**	**NN915758**
3	**Carn an Fhidhleir (Carn Ealar)**	**994**	**148**	**239**	**43**	**NN904842**
4	**An Sgarsoch**	**1006**	**126**	**202**	**43**	**NN933836**
	Beinn a'Ghlo -					
5	**Carn Liath**	**975**	**181**	**294**	**43**	**NN936698**
6	**Braigh Coire Chruinn-bhalgain**	**1070**	**66**	**103**	**43**	**NN945724**
7	**Carn nan Gabhar**	**1121**	**32**	**47**	**43**	**NN971733**
8	Airgiod Bheinn	1061		114	43	NN961720

Beinn a' Ghlo from Ben Vrackie

SECTION 6 (continued)

Name	Height (metres)	No. in order of height Mtn.	Top	O.S. Map Sheet	Map Ref.
	WEST of the CAIRNWELL PASS				
9	**Glas Tulaichean**.	**1051**	**79**	**126**	**43**	**NO051760**
10	**Carn an Righ**	**1029**	**102**	**162**	**43**	**NO028772**
11	**Beinn Iutharn Mhor**	**1045**	**88**	**139**	**43**	**NO045792**
12	Mam nan Carn.	986		262	43	NO049779
13	Beinn Iutharn Bheag	953		362	43	NO065791
14	**Carn Bhac**.	**946**	**221**	**381**	**43**	**NO051832**
15	South-west Top	920		478	43	NO041827
16	**An Socach**	**944**	**227**	**388**	**43**	**NO079799**
17	East Top	938		409	43	NO099805
18	**Carn a'Gheoidh**.	**975**	**180**	**293**	**43**	**NO107767**
19	Carn Bhinnein	917		497	43	NO091762
20	**The Cairnwell**	**933**	**245**	**427**	**43**	**NO134773**
21	**Carn Aosda**	**917**	**278**	**496**	**43**	**NO091762**

Lochnagar

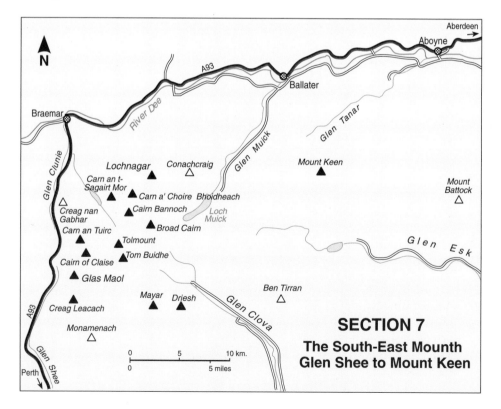

SECTION 7

Glen Shee to Mount Keen

Name	Height (metres)	No. in order of height Mtn.	Top	O.S. Map Sheet	Map Ref.
GLAS MAOL HILLS					
1	**Creag Leacach**	987	159	256	43	**NO154745**
2	South-west Top	943		393	43	NO149741
3	**Glas Maol**	1068	69	107	43	**NO167765**
4	Meall Odhar	922		473	43	NO156773
5	Little Glas Maol	973		302	43	NO175758
6	**Cairn of Claise**	1064	71	111	43	**NO185788**
7	Druim Mor	961		332	43	NO190771
8	**Carn an Tuirc**	1019	113	179	43	**NO174804**
GLEN DOLL HILLS					
9	**Driesh**	947	219	376	44	**NO271735**
10	**Mayar**	928	253	444	44	**NO240737**
11	**Tom Buidhe**	957	204	348	44	**NO213787**
12	**Tolmount**	958	202	346	44	**NO210800**
13	Crow Craigies	920		480	44	NO221798
14	**Broad Cairn**	998	142	228	44	**NO240815**
15	Creag an Dubh-loch	983		265	44	NO233822
16	**Cairn Bannoch**	1012	117	188	44	**NO222825**
17	Fafernie	1000		222	44	NO215823
18	Cairn of Gowal	991		248	44	NO226820
19	Craig of Gowal	927		450	44	NO232809
LOCHNAGAR					
20	**Carn an t-Sagairt Mor**	1047	83	131	44	**NO208843**
21	**Carn a'Choire Bhoidheach**	1110	42	60	44	**NO226845**
22	Creag a'Ghlas-uillt	1068		106	44	NO242842
23	Eagle's Rock	1051		125	44	NO237838
24	Carn an t-Sagairt Beag	1044		140	44	NO216848
25	**Lochnagar - Cac Carn Beag**	1155	21	30	44	**NO243861**
26	Meall Coire na Saobhaidhe	974		298	44	NO242872
27	Cuidhe Crom	1083		89	44	NO259849
28	Little Pap	956		349	44	NO265844
29	Meikle Pap	980		276	44	NO259860
30	**Mount Keen**	939	235	406	44	**NO409869**

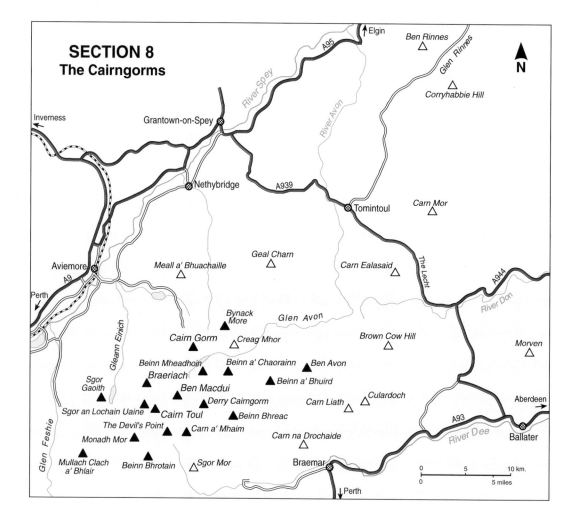

SECTION 8
The Cairngorms

SECTION 8

The Cairngorms

Name	Height (metres)	No. in order of height Mtn.	Top	O.S. Map Sheet	Map Ref.
GLEN FESHIE HILLS					
1 **Mullach Clach a'Bhlair**	**1019**	114	180	35/36/43	**NN882927**
2 **Sgor Gaoith**	**1118**	36	52	36/43	**NN902989**
3 Meall Dubhag	998		230	35/36/43	NN880955
4 Carn Ban Mor.	1052		123	35/36/43	NN893971
5 Sgoran Dubh Mor	1111		59	36	NH905002
6 Meall Buidhe	976		289	35/36	NH891001
7 Geal-charn	920		481	35/36	NH884014
WESTERN CAIRNGORMS					
8 **Beinn Bhrotain**	**1157**	19	28	43	**NN954922**
9 Carn Cloich-mhuilinn	942		395	43	NN968907
10 **Monadh Mor**	**1113**	40	57	43	**NN938942**
11 Tom Dubh.	918		494	36/43	NN921952
12 **The Devil's Point**	**1004**	130	207	36/43	**NN976951**
13 **Cairn Toul**	**1291**	4	4	36/43	**NN963972**
14 Stob Coire an t-Saighdeir	1213		14	36/43	NN962963
15 **Sgor an Lochain Uaine**.	**1258**	5	6	36/43	**NN954976**
16 **Braeriach**	**1296**	3	3	36/43	**NN953999**
17 Carn na Criche.	1265		5	36/43	NN939982
18 Sron na Lairige.	1184		16	36	NH964006
BEN MACDUI - CAIRN GORM					
19 **Carn a'Mhaim**	**1037**	95	151	36/43	**NN994951**
20 **Ben Macdui**	**1309**	2	2	36/43	**NN989989**
21 Sron Riach	1110c		62	36/43	NN999977
22 Carn Etchachan	1120		49	36	NJ003009
23 **Cairn Gorm**	**1244**	6	7	36	**NJ005040**
24 Creag an Leth-choin	1053		121	36	NH968033
25 Cairn Lochan	1215		12	36	NH985025
26 Stob Coire an t-Sneachda	1176		23	36	NH996029
27 Cnap Coire na Spreidhe	1150		33	36	NJ013049

SECTION 8 (continued)

Name	Height (metres)	No. in order of height Mtn.	No. in order of height Top	O.S. Map Sheet	Map Ref.
LAIRIG AN LAOIGH HILLS					
28 **Derry Cairngorm**.	**1155**	**20**	**29**	**36/43**	**NO017980**
29 Sgurr an Lochan Uaine	983		266	36/43	NO025991
30 Creagan a'Choire Etchachan. . .	1108		64	36/43	NO011996
31 **Beinn Mheadhoin**.	**1182**	**13**	**18**	**36**	**NJ024016**
32 Stob Coire Etchachan	1082		92	36	NJ024005
33 Stacan Dubha	1014		186	36	NJ012014
34 **Bynack More**	**1090**	**54**	**82**	**36**	**NJ041063**
35 A'Choinneach.	1016		184	36	NJ032049
36 Bynack Beg.	970		305	36	NJ035068
37 **Beinn Bhreac**	**931**	**249**	**431**	**43/36**	**NO058971**
38 West Top.	927		448	43/36	NO052972
39 **Beinn a'Chaorainn**	**1083**	**58**	**88**	**36**	**NJ045013**
40 Beinn a'Chaorainn Bheag	1017		182	36	NJ058017
EASTERN CAIRNGORMS					
Beinn a'Bhuird -					
41 **Beinn a'Bhuird - North Top**. . . .	**1197**	**11**	**15**	**36**	**NJ092006**
42 South Top	1179		20	43/36	NO093986
43 Cnap a'Chleirich	1174		25	36	NJ107010
44 Stob an t-Sluichd	1107		66	36	NJ112027
Ben Avon -					
45 **Leabaidh an Daimh Bhuidhe** . .	**1171**	**17**	**26**	**36**	**NJ131018**
46 East Meur Gorm Craig	935		420	36	NJ159042
47 West Meur Gorm Craig.	1023		173	36	NJ153036
48 Carn Eas	1089		84	43/36	NO122992
49 Creag an Dail Mhor.	972		304	43/36	NO131982

Cairn Toul (centre) and Sgor an Lochain Uaine (right) from Ben Macdui

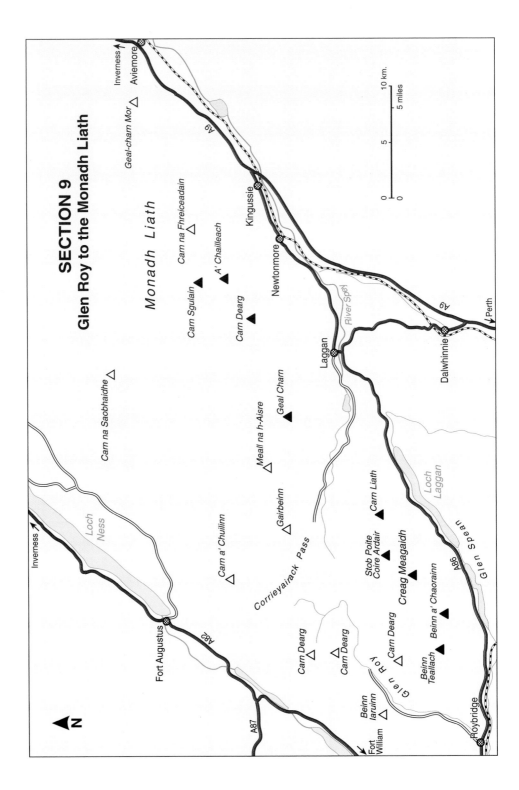

SECTION 9
Glen Roy to the Monadh Liath

SECTION 9

Glen Roy to the Monadh Liath

Name	Height (metres)	No. in order of height Mtn.	Top	O.S. Map Sheet	Map Ref.
LOCH LAGGAN HILLS					
1 **Beinn Teallach**...............	915	282	506	34/41	**NN361859**
2 **Beinn a'Chaorainn**	1049*	80	127	34/41	**NN386851**
3 South Top	1049*		128	34/41	NN386845
4 North Top..................	1043		143	34/41	NN383857
5 **Creag Meagaidh**	1128	30	44	34/42	**NN418875**
6 An Cearcallach..............	993		241	34/42	NN422853
7 Meall Coire Choille-rais	1028		164	34/42	NN432862
8 Puist Coire Ardair	1071		102	34/42	NN437872
9 Sron a'Choire	1001		220	34/42	NN448878
10 **Stob Poite Coire Ardair**	1054	76	119	34/42	**NN428888**
11 Sron Coire a'Chriochairein	993		244	34/42	NN447899
12 **Carn Liath**	1006	127	203	34	**NN472903**
13 Meall an t-Snaim	969		308	34	NN459904
14 Stob Coire Dubh	916		505	34	NN496916
MONADH LIATH					
15 **Geal Charn**..................	926	260	456	35	**NH561987**
16 **Carn Dearg**..................	945	225	385	35	**NH635023**
17 South-east Top	923		467	35	NH637017
18 Carn Ban....................	942		394	35	NH632031
19 Carn Ballach................	920		477	35	NH643045
20 **Carn Sgulain**	920	271	479	35	**NH683058**
21 **A'Chailleach**	930	251	435	35	**NH681041**

* Observation on the ground suggests that the central peak is the highest point

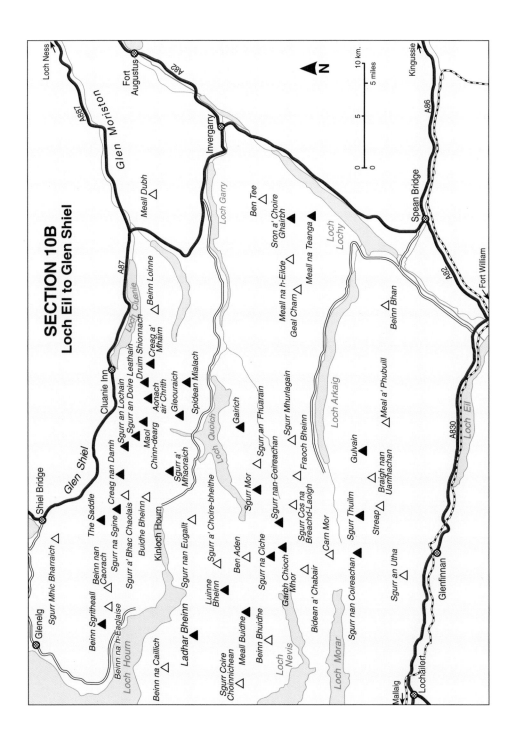

SECTION 10B
Loch Eil to Glen Shiel

SECTION 10

Loch Eil to Glen Shiel

Name	Height (metres)	No. in order of height Mtn.	No. in order of height Top	O.S. Map Sheet	Map Ref.
LOCH LOCHY HILLS					
1 Meall na Teanga	918	275	488	34	NN220924
2 Sron a'Choire Ghairbh.	937	239	417	34	NN222945
GLEN FINNAN					
3 Sgurr nan Coireachan.	956	206	352	40	NM902880
4 Sgurr Thuilm.	963	193	326	40	NM939879
5 Gulvain	987	161	258	41	NN002875
6 South Top	962		328	40	NM996864
GLEN DESSARRY - GLEN KINGIE					
7 Sgurr na Ciche.	1040	92	148	33/40	NM902966
8 Garbh Chioch Mhor	1013	116	187	33/40	NM909961
9 Garbh Chioch Bheag	968		310	33/40	NM918959
10 Sgurr nan Coireachan.	953	213	365	33/40	NM933958
11 Sgurr Mor	1003	132	210	33/40	NM965980
12 Gairich	919	272	482	33	NN025995
KNOYDART					
13 Meall Buidhe.	946	222	382	33/40	NM849989
14 South-east Top	942		396	33/40	NM852987
15 Luinne Bheinn	939	234	405	33	NG869007
16 East Top	937		416	33	NG872007
17 Ladhar Bheinn.	1020	111	177	33	NG823039
18 Stob a'Choire Odhair.	960c		336	33	NG830043
LOCH QUOICH					
19 Sgurr a'Mhaoraich	1027	104	167	33	NG983065
20 Sgurr a'Mhaoraich Beag	948		372	33	NG977067
21 Gleouraich.	1035	97	154	33	NH039053
22 Craig Coire na Fiar Bhealaich. .	1006		204	33	NH047051
23 Spidean Mialach.	996	146	236	33	NH066043
SGRITHEALL					
24 Beinn Sgritheall	974	183	296	33	NG835126
25 North-west Top	928		440	33	NG834131

Garbh Chioch Mhor (left) and Sgurr na Ciche (centre) from Sgurr nan Coireachan

SECTION 10 (continued)

Name	Height (metres)	No. in order of height Mtn.	No. in order of height Top	O.S. Map Sheet	Map Ref.
SOUTH GLEN SHIEL					
26 The Saddle..................	1010	121	194	33	NG936131
27 Sgurr Leac nan Each	919		483	33	NG917133
28 Spidean Dhomhuill Bhric	939		408	33	NG922129
29 Sgurr na Forcan	963		324	33	NG940130
30 Sgurr na Sgine	946	223	383	33	NG946113
31 North-west Top	942		398	33	NG943115
32 Creag nan Damh.............	918	274	485	33	NG913111
33 Sgurr an Lochain.............	1004	131	209	33	NH005104
34 Sgurr an Doire Leathain	1010	122	195	33	NH015199
35 Maol Chinn-dearg............	981	168	270	33	NH032087
36 Aonach air Chrith............	1021	109	174	33	NH050083
37 Druim Shionnach............	987	160	257	33	NH074084
38 West Top...................	938		411	33	NH062082
39 Creag a'Mhaim	947	218	375	33	NH087077

Ladhar Bheinn from Sgurr nan Eugallt

Spidean Mialach and Gleouraich from the South Glen Shiel ridge

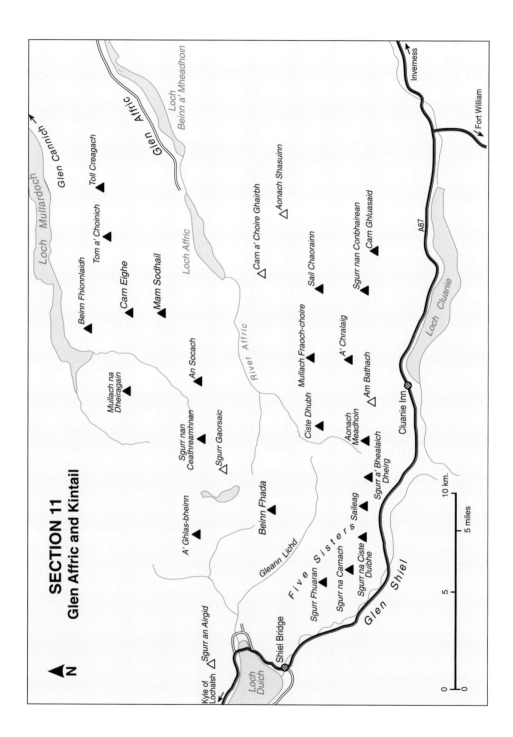

SECTION 11
Glen Affric and Kintail

SECTION 11
Glen Affric and Kintail

Name	Height (metres)	No. in order of height Mtn.	Top	O.S. Map Sheet	Map Ref.
THE FIVE SISTERS to CISTE DHUBH					
1 Sgurr Fhuaran	1067	70	110	33	NG978166
2 Sgurr nan Saighead	929		438	33	NG974177
3 Sgurr na Carnach	1002	134	213	33	NG977158
4 Sgurr na Ciste Duibhe	1027	105	168	33	NG984149
5 Sgurr nan Spainteach	990		250	33	NG991150
6 Saileag	956	205	350	33	NH017148
7 Sgurr a'Bhealaich Dheirg	1036	96	152	33	NH035143
8 Aonach Meadhoin	1001	135	214	33	NH049137
9 Sgurr an Fhuarail	987		259	33	NH054139
10 Ciste Dhubh	979	173	279	33	NH062166
A'CHRALAIG - CONBHAIREAN GROUP					
11 A'Chralaig	1120	33	48	33	NH094148
12 Stob Coire na Cralaig	1008		199	33	NH091163
13 A'Chioch	947		374	34	NH108152
14 Mullach Fraoch-choire	1102	49	74	33	NH095171
15 Carn Ghluasaid	957	203	347	34	NH145125
16 Sgurr nan Conbhairean	1109	44	63	34	NH129138
17 Drochaid an Tuill Easaich	1001		216	34	NH120134
18 Creag a'Chaorainn	998		229	34	NH137131
19 Sail Chaorainn	1002	133	212	34	NH133154
20 Carn na Coire Mheadhoin	1001		215	34	NH134158
21 Tigh Mor na Seilge	929		439	34	NH140166
BEN ATTOW					
22 Beinn Fhada	1032	100	157	33	NH018192
23 Meall an Fhuarain Mhoir	954		359	33	NG999196
24 Sgurr a' Dubh Doire	962		329	33	NH034185
25 A'Ghlas-bheinn	918	273	484	25/33	NH008230

SECTION 11 (continued)

Name	Height (metres)	No. in order of height Mtn.	Top	O.S. Map Sheet	Map Ref.
GLEN AFFRIC					
26 Sgurr nan Ceathreamhnan.....	1151	22	31	25/33	NH057228
27 West Top..................	1143		37	25/33	NH053228
28 Stuc Bheag	1075		99	25/33	NH053237
29 Stuc Mor..................	1041		146	25/33	NH053242
30 Stuc Fraoch Choire	918		493	25/33	NH052253
31 Stob Coire na Cloiche	915		509	25/33	NH075227
32 Mullach na Dheiragain	982	167	269	25/33	NH080259
33 Carn na Con Dhu...........	967		314	25/33	NH072241
34 Mullach Sithidh	974		301	25/33	NH082264
35 An Socach	921	269	475	25/33	NH088230
36 Mam Sodhail................	1181	14	19	25	NH120253
37 Creag Coire nan Each	1055		117	25	NH113232
38 An Tudair..................	1074		100	25	NH127239
39 Mullach Cadha Rainich.......	996		235	25	NH139246
40 Sgurr na Lapaich	1036		153	25	NH154243
41 Carn Eighe.................	1183	12	17	25	NH123262
42 Stob Coire Lochan	917		500	25	NH119272
43 Stob a'Choire Dhomhain......	1147		36	25	NH131264
44 Stob Coire Dhomhnuill	1137		38	25	NH138262
45 Sron Garbh.................	1131		40	25	NH145263
46 Beinn Fhionnlaidh	1005	128	205	25	NH115282
47 Tom a'Choinich..............	1112	41	58	25	NH164273
48 Tom a' Choinich Beag	1032		158	25	NH157273
49 An Leth-chreag	1051		124	25	NH153269
50 Toll Creagach................	1054	77	120	25	NH194282
51 West Top..................	951		369	25	NH177275

Sgurr na Lapaich, Glen Affric

The Five Sisters of Kintail from Loch Duich

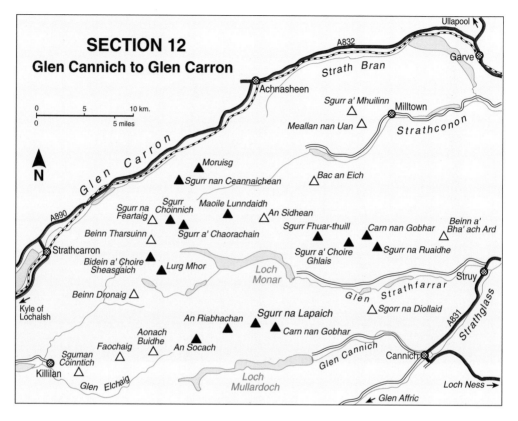

SECTION 12

Glen Cannich to Glen Carron

Name	Height (metres)	No. in order of height Mtn.	No. in order of height Top	O.S. Map Sheet	Map Ref.
SGURR NA LAPAICH GROUP					
1 **An Socach**	**1069**	**67**	**104**	**25**	**NH100332**
2 **An Riabhachan**	**1129**	**29**	**43**	**25**	**NH133344**
3 South-west Top	1086		86	25	NH123336
4 West Top.	1040		147	25	NH117337
5 **Sgurr na Lapaich**.	**1150**	**24**	**34**	**25**	**NH160351**
6 Sgurr nan Clachan Geala	1095		79	25	NH161342
7 **Carn nan Gobhar**	**992**	**152**	**245**	**25**	**NH181343**
8 Creag Dubh	945		386	25	NH199350
EAST of ACHNASHELLACH					
9 **Bidein a' Choire Sheasgaich** . . .	**945**	**224**	**384**	**25**	**NH049412**
10 **Lurg Mhor**	**986**	**163**	**261**	**25**	**NH065404**
11 Meall Mor.	974		299	25	NH072405

Lurg Mhor

SECTION 12 (continued)

Name	Height (metres)	Mtn.	Top	O.S. Map Sheet	Map Ref.
		No. in order of height			
12 Sgurr Choinnich	999	139	224	25	NH076446
13 Sgurr a'Chaorachain	1053	78	122	25	NH087447
14 Bidean an Eoin Deirg	1046		136	25	NH103443
15 Maoile Lunndaidh	1007	125	201	25	NH135458
16 Carn nam Fiaclan.	996		234	25	NH123454
17 Sgurr nan Ceannaichean	915	284	508	25	NH087480
18 Moruisg	928	255	446	25	NH101499
STRATHFARRAR HILLS					
19 Sgurr Fhuar-thuill	1049	82	130	25	NH235437
20 Creag Ghorm a' Bhealaich	1030		159	25	NH244435
21 Sgurr na Fearstaig	1015		185	25	NH228437
22 Sgurr a'Choire Ghlais	1083	60	91	25	NH259430
23 Carn nan Gobhar	992	153	246	25	NH273439
24 Sgurr na Ruaidhe	993	151	243	25	NH288426

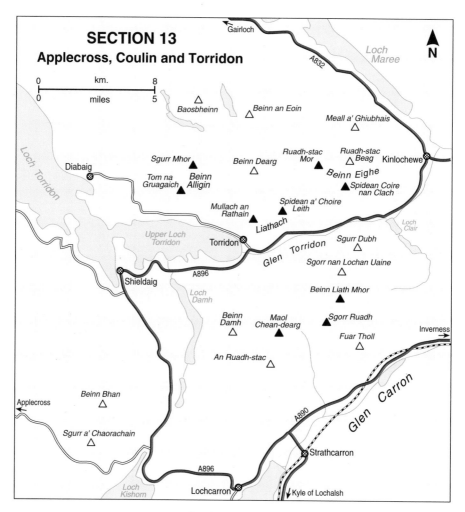

SECTION 13

Coulin and Torridon

	Name	Height (metres)	No. in order of height Mtn.	Top	O.S. Map Sheet	Map Ref.
	COULIN FOREST					
1	**Maol Chean-dearg**	933	247	429	25	**NG924499**
2	**Sgorr Ruadh**	962	195	330	25	**NG959505**
3	**Beinn Liath Mhor**	926	258	453	25	**NG964519**
	TORRIDON Beinn Alligin -					
4	**Tom na Gruagaich**	922	268	470	19/24	**NG859601**

Spidean a' Choire Leith from Stuc a' Choire Dhuibh Bhig

SECTION 13 (continued)

	Name	Height (metres)	No. in order of height Mtn.	Top	O.S. Map Sheet	Map Ref.
5	**Sgurr Mhor**	**986**	**162**	**260**	**19/24**	**NG865613**
	Liathach -					
6	**Mullach an Rathain**	**1023**	**108**	**172**	**25**	**NG912577**
7	Meall Dearg (Northern Pinnacles)	955		355	25	NG913579
8	Am Fasarinen..............	927		447	25	NG923574
9	**Spidean a'Choire Leith**	**1055**	**75**	**118**	**25**	**NG929579**
10	Stob a'Coire Liath Mhor	983		267	25	NG932581
11	Stuc a'Choire Dhuibh Bhig	915		510	25	NG942582
	Beinn Eighe -					
12	**Ruadh-stac Mor**..............	**1010**	**120**	**193**	**25**	**NG951611**
13	**Spidean Coire nan Clach**......	**993**	**150**	**242**	**25**	**NG966597**
14	Sail Mhor	980		277	25	NG938605
15	Coinneach Mhor	976		288	25	NG944600
16	Sgurr Ban	970		307	25	NG974600
17	Sgurr nan Fhir Duibhe	963		325	25	NG981600

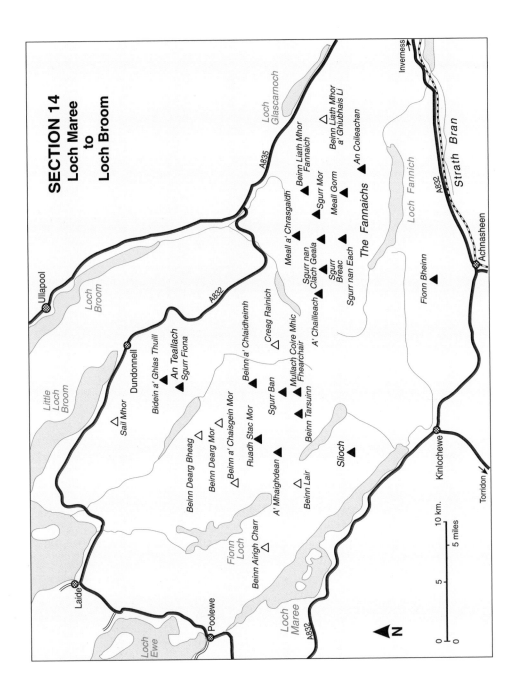

SECTION 14
Loch Maree
to
Loch Broom

SECTION 14

Loch Maree to Loch Broom

Name	Height (metres)	No. in order of height Mtn.	Top	O.S. Map Sheet	Map Ref.
LETTEREWE and FISHERFIELD					
1 Slioch - North Top	981	170	273	19	NH004690
2 Sgurr an Tuill Bhain	934		425	19	NH018688
3 A'Mhaighdean.	967	189	313	19	NH007749
4 Ruadh Stac Mor	918	276	489	19	NH018756
5 Beinn Tarsuinn	937	238	415	19	NH039728
6 Mullach Coire Mhic Fhearchair	1018	115	181	19	NH052735
7 East Top	981		272	19	NH056734
8 Sgurr Dubh.	918		491	19	NH061729
9 Sgurr Ban.	989	157	254	19	NH055745
10 Beinn a' Chlaidheimh	916	280	501	19	NH061775
THE FANNAICHS					
11 Fionn Bheinn.	933	246	428	20	NH147621
12 A'Chailleach	997	144	232	19	NH136714
13 Toman Coinich.	935		422	20	NH148713
14 Sgurr Breac	999	138	223	20	NH158711
15 Sgurr nan Each	923	267	469	20	NH184697
16 Sgurr nan Clach Geala	1093	53	81	20	NH184715
17 Meall a'Chrasgaidh	934	243	424	20	NH184733
18 Sgurr Mor	1110	43	61	20	NH203718
19 Carn na Criche.	961		331	20	NH196725
20 Meall nam Peithirean	974		300	20	NH207708
21 Beinn Liath Mhor Fannaich . . .	954	209	358	20	NH219724
22 Meall Gorm.	949	215	370	20	NH221696
23 South-east Top	922		472	20	NH232692
24 An Coileachan.	923	266	465	20	NH241680
AN TEALLACH					
25 Sgurr Fiona	1060	73	115	19	NH064837
26 Sail Liath.	954		360	19	NH071824
27 Stob Cadha Gobhlach	960		337	19	NH068825
28 Corrag Bhuidhe	1047		132	19	NH064834
29 Lord Berkeley's Seat	1030c		160	19	NH064835
30 Sgurr Creag an Eich.	1017		183	19	NH055838
31 Bidein a'Ghlas Thuill.	1062	72	112	19	NH068843
32 Glas Mheall Liath	960		335	19	NH077840
33 Glas Mheall Mor	979		280	19	NH076853

Mullach Coire Mhic Fhearchair (left) and Beinn Tarsuinn (centre) from the east ridge of Beinn Dearg Mor

An Teallach

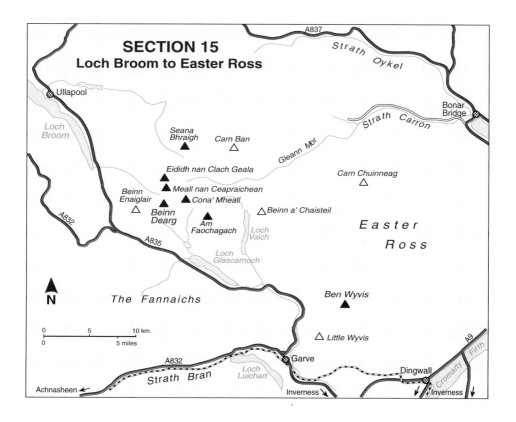

SECTION 15

Loch Broom to Easter Ross

Name	Height (metres)	No. in order of height Mtn.	Top	O.S. Map Sheet	Map Ref.
BEN WYVIS					
1 **Glas Leathad Mor**	**1046**	**85**	**135**	**20**	**NH463683**
2 An Cabar	946		379	20	NH450665
3 Tom a'Choinnich	953		366	20	NH463700
4 Glas Leathad Beag	928		442	20	NH492706
BEINN DEARG GROUP					
5 **Beinn Dearg**	**1084**	**57**	**87**	**20**	**NH259811**
6 **Cona' Mheall**	**978**	**176**	**283**	**20**	**NH274816**
7 **Meall nan Ceapraichean**	**977**	**177**	**286**	**20**	**NH257825**
8 Ceann Garbh	968		309	20	NH259830
9 **Eididh nan Clach Geala**	**927**	**257**	**451**	**20**	**NH257842**
10 **Seana Bhraigh**	**926**	**262**	**458**	**20**	**NH281878**
11 **Am Faochagach**	**953**	**210**	**361**	**20**	**NH303793**

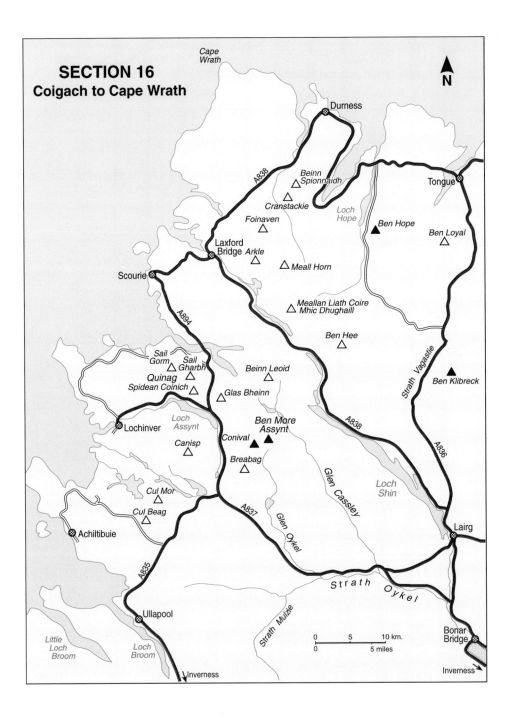

SECTION 16
Coigach to Cape Wrath

Ben Hope across Loch Eriboll from Beinn Spionnaidh

SECTION 16

Coigach to Cape Wrath

Name	Height (metres)	No. in order of height Mtn.	Top	O.S. Map Sheet	Map Ref.
ASSYNT					
1 Conival...................	987	158	255	15	NC303199
2 Ben More Assynt	998	141	227	15	NC318201
3 South Top.................	960		334	15	NC324192
KLIBRECK and HOPE					
4 Ben Klibreck - Meall nan Con .	962	194	327	16	NC585299
5 Ben Hope..................	927	256	449	9	NC477501

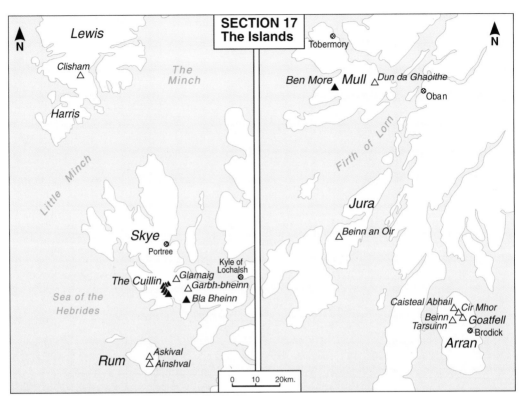

Sgurr Alasdair (left) and Sgurr Dearg (right) from Sgurr a' Ghreadaidh

SECTION 17

The Islands

Name	Height (metres)	No. in order of height Mtn.	Top	O.S. Map Sheet	Map Ref.
MULL					
1 **Ben More**	**966**	**189**	**316**	**48**	**NM525330**
SKYE					
2 **Sgurr nan Eag**	**924**	**265**	**464**	**32**	**NG457195**
3 **Sgurr Dubh Mor**	**944**	**228**	**389**	**32**	**NG457205**
4 Sgurr Dubh an Da Bheinn	938		412	32	NG455204
5 **Sgurr Alasdair**	**992**	**154**	**247**	**32**	**NG450207**
6 Sgurr Sgumain	947		378	32	NG448206
7 Sgurr Thearlaich	978		285	32	NG451208
8 **Sgurr Mhic Choinnich**	**948**	**217**	**373**	**32**	**NG450210**
9 **Sgurr Dearg-Inaccessible Pinnacle**	**986**	**164**	**263**	**32**	**NG444215**
10 **Sgurr na Banachdich**	**965**	**190**	**319**	**32**	**NG440224**
11 Central Top	942		397	32	NG441223
12 Sgurr Thormaid	926		459	32	NG441226
13 **Sgurr a'Ghreadaidh**	**973**	**185**	**303**	**32**	**NG445232**
14 South Top	970		306	32	NG445230
15 **Sgurr a'Mhadaidh**	**918**	**277**	**490**	**32**	**NG446235**
16 **Bruach na Frithe**	**958**	**200**	**342**	**32**	**NG461252**
17 Sgurr a'Fionn Choire	935		421	32	NG464252
18 **Am Basteir**	**934**	**242**	**423**	**32**	**NG465253**
19 Bhasteir Tooth	916		503	32	NG464252
20 **Sgurr nan Gillean**	**964**	**191**	**320**	**32**	**NG471252**
21 Knight's Peak	914		511	32	NG471254
22 **Bla Bheinn**	**928**	**252**	**441**	**32**	**NG529217**
23 South Top	926		455	32	NG528215

TABLE 2. The Munros & Tops in Order of Height

Name	Height (metres)	No. in order of height Mtn.	Top	O.S. Map Sheet	Section Ref.
Ben Nevis	1344	1	1	41	4 - 18
Ben Macdui	1309	2	2	36/43	8 - 20
Braeriach	1296	3	3	36/43	8 - 16
Cairn Toul	1291	4	4	36/43	8 - 13
Carn na Criche	1265		5	36/43	8 - 17
Sgor an Lochain Uaine	1258	5	6	36/43	8 - 15
Cairn Gorm	1244	6	7	36	8 - 23
Aonach Beag (Glen Nevis)	1234	7	8	41	4 - 23
Aonach Mor	1221	8	9	41	4 - 26
Carn Dearg (North-west of Ben Nevis)	1221		10	41	4 - 20
Carn Mor Dearg	1220	9	11	41	4 - 21
Cairn Lochan	1215		12	36	8 - 25
Ben Lawers	1214	10	13	51	2 - 27
Stob Coire an t-Saighdeir	1213		14	36/43	8 - 14
Beinn a'Bhuird - North Top	1197	11	15	36	8 - 41
Sron na Lairige	1184		16	36	8 - 18
Carn Eighe	1183	12	17	25	11 - 41
Beinn Mheadhoin	1182	13	18	36	8 - 31
Mam Sodhail	1181	14	19	25	11 - 36
Beinn a'Bhuird - South Top	1179		20	43/36	8 - 42
Carn Dearg Meadhonach	1179		21	41	4 - 22
Stob Choire Claurigh	1177	15	22	41	4 - 36
Stob Coire an t-Sneachda	1176		23	36	8 - 26
Ben More	1174	16	24	51	1 - 22
Cnap a'Chleirich	1174		25	36	8 - 43
Ben Avon - Leabaidh an Daimh Bhuidhe	1171	17	26	36	8 - 45
Stob Binnein	1165	18	27	51	1 - 19
Beinn Bhrotain	1157	19	28	43	8 - 8
Derry Cairngorm	1155	20	29	36/43	8 - 28
Lochnagar - Cac Carn Beag	1155	21	30	44	7 - 25
Sgurr nan Ceathreamhnan	1151	22	31	25/33	11 - 26
Bidean nam Bian	1150	23	32	41	3 - 33
Cnap Coire na Spreidhe	1150		33	36	8 - 27
Sgurr na Lapaich (Mullardoch)	1150	24	34	25	12 - 5
Ben Alder	1148	25	35	42	4 - 51
Stob a'Choire Dhomhain	1147		36	25	11 - 43
Sgurr nan Ceathreamhnan - West Top	1143		37	25/33	11 - 27
Stob Coire Dhomhnuill	1137		38	25	11 - 44
Geal - Charn (Alder District)	1132	26	39	42	4 - 58
Sron Garbh	1131		40	25	11 - 45
Binnein Mor	1130	27	41	41	4 - 13

Name	Height (metres)	No. in order of height Mtn.	Top	O.S. Map Sheet	Section Ref.
Ben Lui	1130	28	42	50	1 - 9
An Riabhachan	1129	29	43	25	12 - 2
Creag Meagaidh	1128	30	44	34/42	9 - 5
Ben Cruachan	1126	31	45	50	3 - 1
Stob Coire na Ceannain	1123		46	41	4 - 38
Beinn a'Ghlo - Carn nan Gabhar	1121	32	47	43	6 - 7
A'Chralaig	1120	33	48	33	11 - 11
Carn Etchachan	1120		49	36	8 - 22
An Stuc	1118	34	50	51	2 - 29
Meall Garbh (Ben Lawers)	1118	35	51	51	2 - 30
Sgor Gaoith	1118	36	52	36/43	8 - 2
Aonach Beag (Alder District)	1116	37	53	42	4 - 57
Stob Coire an Laoigh	1116	38	54	41	4 - 31
Stob Coire Easain (Loch Treig)	1115	39	55	41	4 - 41
Stob Coire nan Lochan	1115		56	41	3 - 35
Monadh Mor	1113	40	57	43	8 - 10
Tom a'Choinich	1112	41	58	25	11 - 47
Sgoran Dubh Mor	1111		59	36	8 - 5
Carn a'Choire Bhoidheach	1110	42	60	44	7 - 21
Sgurr Mor (Fannaichs)	1110	43	61	20	14 - 18
Sron Riach	1110c		62	36/43	8 - 21
Sgurr nan Conbhairean	1109	44	63	34	11 - 16
Creagan a'Choire Etchachan	1108		64	36/43	8 - 30
Meall a'Bhuiridh	1108	45	65	41	3 - 25
Stob an t-Sluichd	1107		66	36	8 - 44
Stob Coire nam Beith	1107		67	41	3 - 34
Caisteil	1106		68	41	4 - 33
Stob a'Choire Leith	1105		69	41	4 - 37
Stob a'Choire Mheadhoin	1105	46	70	41	4 - 42
Stob Dearg (Taynuilt Peak)	1104		71	50	3 - 2
Beinn Ghlas	1103	47	72	51	2 - 26
Beinn Eibhinn	1102	48	73	42	4 - 54
Mullach Fraoch-choire	1102	49	74	33	11 - 14
Creise	1100	50	75	41	3 - 22
Stob Coire Bhealaich	1100c		76	41	4 - 24
Clach Leathad	1099		77	50	3 - 23
Sgurr a'Mhaim	1099	51	78	41	4 - 4
Sgurr nan Clachan Geala	1095		79	25	12 - 6
Sgurr Choinnich Mor	1094	52	80	41	4 - 29
Sgurr nan Clach Geala	1093	53	81	20	14 - 16
Bynack More	1090	54	82	36	8 - 34
Stob Ghabhar	1090	55	83	50	3 - 18
Carn Eas	1089		84	43/36	8 - 48

Name	Height (metres)	No. in order of height Mtn.	No. in order of height Top	O.S. Map Sheet	Section Ref.
Beinn a'Chlachair	1087	56	85	42	**4 - 62**
An Riabhachan - South-west Top	1086		86	25	12 - 3
Beinn Dearg (Ullapool)	1084	57	87	20	**15 - 5**
Beinn a'Chaorainn (Glen Derry)	1083	58	88	36	**8 - 39**
Cuidhe Crom	1083		89	44	7 - 27
Schiehallion	1083	59	90	51/52	**2 - 42**
Sgurr a'Choire Ghlais	1083	60	91	25	**12 - 22**
Stob Coire Etchachan	1082		92	36	8 - 32
Beinn a'Chreachain	1081	61	93	50	**2 - 15**
Stob Coire Easain (Grey Corries)	1080		94	41	4 - 32
Stob Coire Cath na Sine	1079		95	41	4 - 35
Beinn Heasgarnich	1078	62	96	51	**2 - 9**
Ben Starav	1078	63	97	50	**3 - 11**
Beinn Dorain	1076	64	98	50	**2 - 11**
Stuc Bheag	1075		99	25/33	11 - 28
An Tudair	1074		100	25	11 - 38
Stob Coire Sgreamhach	1072	65	101	41	**3 - 36**
Puist Coire Ardair	1071		102	34/42	9 - 8
Braigh Coire Chruinn-bhalgain	1070	66	103	43	**6 - 6**
An Socach (Lapaichs)	1069	67	104	25	**12 - 1**
Meall Corranaich	1069	68	105	51	**2 - 24**
Creag a'Ghlas-uillt	1068		106	44	7 - 22
Glas Maol	1068	69	107	43	**7 - 3**
Stob an Cul Choire	1068		108	41	4 - 27
Stob Coire an Lochain (Stob Binnein)	1068		109	51	1 - 20
Sgurr Fhuaran	1067	70	110	33	**11 - 1**
Cairn of Claise	1064	71	111	43	**7 - 6**
An Teallach - Bidein a'Ghlas Thuill	1062	72	112	19	**14 - 31**
Binnein Mor - South Top	1062		113	41	4 - 14
Airgiod Bheinn	1061		114	43	6 - 8
An Teallach - Sgurr Fiona	1060	73	115	19	**14 - 25**
Na Gruagaichean	1056	74	116	41	**4 - 11**
Creag Coire nan Each	1055		117	25	11 - 37
Liathach - Spidean a'Choire Leith	1055	75	118	25	**13 - 9**
Stob Poite Coire Ardair	1054	76	119	34/42	**9 - 10**
Toll Creagach	1054	77	120	25	**11 - 50**
Creag an Leth-choin	1053		121	36	8 - 24
Sgurr a'Chaorachain (Monar)	1053	78	122	25	**12 - 13**
Carn Ban Mor	1052		123	35/36/43	8 - 4
An Leth-chreag	1051		124	25	11 - 49
Eagle's Rock	1051		125	44	7 - 23
Glas Tulaichean	1051	79	126	43	**6 - 9**
Beinn a'Chaorainn (Laggan)	1049	80	127	34/41	**9 - 2**

Name	Height (metres)	No. in order of height Mtn.	Top	O.S. Map Sheet	Section Ref.
Beinn a'Chaorainn - South Top (Laggan) . .	1049		128	34/41	9 - 3
Geal Charn -Mullach Coire an Iubhair . .	**1049**	**81**	**129**	**42**	**4 - 63**
Sgurr Fhuar-thuill	**1049**	**82**	**130**	**25**	**12 - 19**
Carn an t-Sagairt Mor	**1047**	**83**	**131**	**44**	**7 - 20**
Corrag Bhuidhe	1047		132	19	14 - 28
Creag an Fhithich	1047		133	51	2 - 28
Creag Mhor	**1047**	**84**	**134**	**50**	**2 - 7**
Ben Wyvis - Glas Leathad Mor	**1046**	**85**	**135**	**20**	**15 - 1**
Bidean an Eoin Deirg	1046		136	25	12 - 14
Chno Dearg	**1046**	**86**	**137**	**41**	**4 - 44**
Cruach Ardrain	**1046**	**87**	**138**	**51/56**	**1 - 17**
Beinn Iutharn Mhor	**1045**	**88**	**139**	**43**	**6 - 11**
Carn an t-Sagairt Beag	1044		140	44	7 - 24
Meall nan Tarmachan	**1044**	**89**	**141**	**51**	**2 - 19**
Stob Coir'an Albannaich	**1044**	**90**	**142**	**50**	**3 - 16**
Beinn a'Chaorainn - North Top (Laggan) .	1043		143	34/41	9 - 4
Carn Mairg	**1041**	**91**	**144**	**51**	**2 - 38**
Na Gruagaichean - North-west Top	1041		145	41	4 - 12
Stuc Mor	1041		146	25/33	11 - 29
An Riabhachan - West Top	1040		147	25	12 - 4
Sgurr na Ciche	**1040**	**92**	**148**	**33/40**	**10 - 7**
Meall Ghaordie	**1039**	**93**	**149**	**51**	**2 - 10**
Beinn Achaladair	**1038**	**94**	**150**	**50**	**2 - 13**
Carn a'Mhaim	**1037**	**95**	**151**	**36/43**	**8 - 19**
Sgurr a'Bhealaich Dheirg	**1036**	**96**	**152**	**33**	**11 - 7**
Sgurr na Lapaich (Affric)	1036		153	25	11 - 40
Gleouraich	**1035**	**97**	**154**	**33**	**10 - 21**
Carn Dearg (Alder District)	**1034**	**98**	**155**	**42**	**4 - 60**
Am Bodach (Mamores)	**1032**	**99**	**156**	**41**	**4 - 7**
Beinn Fhada (Kintail)	**1032**	**100**	**157**	**33**	**11 - 22**
Tom a' Choinich Beag	1032		158	25	11 - 48
Creag Ghorm a' Bhealaich	1030		159	25	12 - 20
Lord Berkeley's Seat	1030c		160	19	14 - 29
Ben Oss	**1029**	**101**	**161**	**50**	**1 - 10**
Carn an Righ	**1029**	**102**	**162**	**43**	**6 - 10**
Carn Gorm	**1029**	**103**	**163**	**51**	**2 - 35**
Meall Coire Choille-rais	1028		164	34/42	9 - 7
Sgor Iutharn	1028		165	42	4 - 59
Stob Coire Dheirg	1028		166	50	3 - 14
Sgurr a'Mhaoraich	**1027**	**104**	**167**	**33**	**10 - 19**
Sgurr na Ciste Duibhe	**1027**	**105**	**168**	**33**	**11 - 4**
Meall Garbh (Tarmachans)	1026		169	51	2 - 21
Ben Challum	**1025**	**106**	**170**	**50**	**2 - 1**

Name	Height (metres)	No. in order of height		O.S. Map Sheet	Section Ref.
		Mtn.	Top		
Sgorr Dhearg (Beinn a'Bheithir)........	**1024**	**107**	**171**	**41**	**3 - 31**
Liathach - Mullach an Rathain	**1023**	**108**	**172**	**25**	**13 - 6**
West Meur Gorm Craig................	1023		173	36	8 - 47
Aonach air Chrith....................	**1021**	**109**	**174**	**33**	**10 - 36**
Stob Dearg (Buachaille Etive Mor)......	**1021**	**110**	**175**	**41**	**3 - 43**
Carn Dearg (South-west of Ben Nevis) ...	1020		176	41	4 - 19
Ladhar Bheinn......................	**1020**	**111**	**177**	**33**	**10 - 17**
Beinn Bheoil	**1019**	**112**	**178**	**42**	**4 - 52**
Carn an Tuirc......................	**1019**	**113**	**179**	**43**	**7 - 8**
Mullach Clach a'Bhlair	**1019**	**114**	**180**	**35/36/43**	**8 - 1**
Mullach Coire Mhic Fhearchair	**1018**	**115**	**181**	**19**	**14 - 6**
Beinn a'Chaorainn Bheag	1017		182	36	8 - 40
Sgurr Creag an Eich..................	1017		183	19	14 - 30
A'Choinneach........................	1016		184	36	8 - 35
Sgurr na Fearstaig	1015		185	25	12 - 21
Stacan Dubha	1014		186	36	8 - 33
Garbh Chioch Mhor.................	**1013**	**116**	**187**	**33/40**	**10 - 8**
Cairn Bannoch.....................	**1012**	**117**	**188**	**44**	**7 - 16**
Meall Liath (Carn Mairg)	1012		189	51	2 - 39
Beinn Ime.	**1011**	**118**	**190**	**56**	**1 - 3**
Beinn Udlamain	**1011**	**119**	**191**	**42**	**5 - 2**
Stob na Doire	1011		192	41	3 - 44
Beinn Eighe - Ruadh-stac Mor	**1010**	**120**	**193**	**25**	**13 - 12**
The Saddle........................	**1010**	**121**	**194**	**33**	**10 - 26**
Sgurr an Doire Leathain..............	**1010**	**122**	**195**	**33**	**10 - 34**
Sgurr Eilde Mor....................	**1010**	**123**	**196**	**41**	**4 - 17**
Drochaid Ghlas	1009		197	50	3 - 4
Beinn Dearg (Atholl)	**1008**	**124**	**198**	**43**	**6 - 1**
Stob Coire na Cralaig.................	1008		199	33	11 - 12
Beinn na Socaich	1007		200	41	4 - 34
Maoile Lunndaidh	**1007**	**125**	**201**	**25**	**12 - 15**
An Sgarsoch.......................	**1006**	**126**	**202**	**43**	**6 - 4**
Carn Liath (Creag Meagaidh)	**1006**	**127**	**203**	**34**	**9 - 12**
Craig Coire na Fiar Bhealaich..........	1006		204	33	10 - 22
Beinn Fhionnlaidh (Affric)	**1005**	**128**	**205**	**25**	**11 - 46**
Beinn an Dothaidh.................	**1004**	**129**	**206**	**50**	**2 - 12**
The Devil's Point	**1004**	**130**	**207**	**36/43**	**8 - 12**
Meall a'Bharr	1004		208	51	2 - 40
Sgurr an Lochain...................	**1004**	**131**	**209**	**33**	**10 - 33**
Sgurr Mor.........................	**1003**	**132**	**210**	**33/40**	**10 - 11**
Beinn Achaladair - South Top..........	1002		211	50	2 - 14
Sail Chaorainn.....................	**1002**	**133**	**212**	**34**	**11 - 19**
Sgurr na Carnach	**1002**	**134**	**213**	**33**	**11 - 3**

Name	Height (metres)	No. in order of height Mtn.	No. in order of height Top	O.S. Map Sheet	Section Ref.
Aonach Meadhoin	**1001**	**135**	214	33	**11 - 8**
Carn na Coire Mheadhoin.	1001		215	34	11 - 20
Drochaid an Tuill Easaich	1001		216	34	11 - 17
Meall Greigh	**1001**	**136**	217	51	**2 - 31**
Sgor an Iubhair.	1001		218	41	4 - 5
Sgorr Dhonuill (Beinn a'Bheithir)	**1001**	**137**	219	41	**3 - 30**
Sron a'Choire	1001		220	34/42	9 - 9
Beinn nan Eachan	1000		221	51	2 - 22
Fafernie.	1000		222	44	7 - 17
Sgurr Breac.	**999**	**138**	223	20	**14 - 14**
Sgurr Choinnich	**999**	**139**	224	25	**12 - 12**
Stob Ban (Mamores)	**999**	**140**	225	41	**4 - 3**
Ben Challum - South Top	998		226	50	2 - 2
Ben More Assynt.	**998**	**141**	227	15	**16 - 2**
Broad Cairn	**998**	**142**	228	44	**7 - 14**
Creag a'Chaorainn.	998		229	34	11 - 18
Meall Dubhag.	998		230	35/36/43	8 - 3
Stob Diamh	**998**	**143**	231	50	**3 - 5**
A'Chailleach (Fannaichs)	**997**	**144**	232	19	**14 - 12**
Glas Bheinn Mhor	**997**	**145**	233	50	**3 - 15**
Carn nam Fiaclan.	996		234	25	12 - 16
Mullach Cadha Rainich.	996		235	25	11 - 39
Spidean Mialach	**996**	**146**	236	33	**10 - 23**
Stob a'Ghlais Choire	996		237	41	3 - 24
An Caisteal.	**995**	**147**	238	50/56	**1 - 13**
Carn an Fhidhleir (Carn Ealar)	**994**	**148**	239	43	**6 - 3**
Sgor na h-Ulaidh.	**994**	**149**	240	41	**3 - 28**
An Cearcallach	993		241	34/42	9 - 6
Beinn Eighe - Spidean Coire nan Clach. .	**993**	**150**	242	25	**13 - 13**
Sgurr na Ruaidhe	**993**	**151**	243	25	**12 - 24**
Sron Coire a'Chriochairein	993		244	34/42	9 - 11
Carn nan Gobhar (Lapaichs)	**992**	**152**	245	25	**12 - 7**
Carn nan Gobhar (Strathfarrar).	**992**	**153**	246	25	**12 - 23**
Sgurr Alasdair.	**992**	**154**	247	32	**17 - 5**
Cairn of Gowal.	991		248	44	7 - 18
Sgairneach Mhor.	**991**	**155**	249	42	**5 - 1**
Sgurr nan Spainteach.	990		250	33	11 - 5
Sron a'Ghearrain	990		251	50	3 - 20
Stob Choire a'Mhail	990		252	41	4 - 6
Beinn Eunaich	**989**	**156**	253	50	**3 - 9**
Sgurr Ban (Letterewe).	**989**	**157**	254	19	**14 - 9**
Conival.	**987**	**158**	255	15	**16 - 1**
Creag Leacach	**987**	**159**	256	43	**7 - 1**

Name	Height (metres)	No. in order of height Mtn.	Top	O.S. Map Sheet	Section Ref.
Druim Shionnach	987	160	257	33	**10 - 37**
Gulvain	987	161	258	41	**10 - 5**
Sgurr an Fhuarail	987		259	33	11 - 9
Sgurr Mhor - Beinn Alligin	986	162	260	19/24	**13 - 5**
Lurg Mhor	986	163	261	25	**12 - 10**
Mam nan Carn	986		262	43	6 - 12
Sgurr Dearg - Inaccessible Pinnacle	986	164	263	32	**17 - 9**
Ben Vorlich (Loch Earn)	985	165	264	57	**1 - 24**
Creag an Dubh-loch	983		265	44	7 - 15
Sgurr an Lochan Uaine (Derry Cairngorm)	983		266	36/43	8 - 29
Stob a'Coire Liath Mhor	983		267	25	13 - 10
An Gearanach	982	166	268	41	**4 - 9**
Mullach na Dheiragain	982	167	269	25/33	**11 - 32**
Maol Chinn-dearg	981	168	270	33	**10 - 35**
Meall nan Aighean	981	169	271	51	**2 - 41**
Mullach Coire Mhic Fhearchair - East Top	981		272	19	14 - 7
Slioch - North Top	981	170	273	19	**14 - 1**
Stob Coire a'Chairn	981	171	274	41	**4 - 8**
Beinn a'Chochuill	980	172	275	50	**3 - 8**
Meikle Pap	980		276	44	7 - 29
Sail Mhor	980		277	25	13 - 14
Stob Garbh (Ben Cruachan)	980		278	50	3 - 6
Ciste Dhubh	979	173	279	33	**11 - 10**
Glas Mheall Mor	979		280	19	14 - 33
Stob Coire Sgriodain	979	174	281	41	**4 - 46**
Beinn Dubhchraig	978	175	282	50	**1 - 11**
Cona' Mheall	978	176	283	20	**15 - 6**
Meall Buidhe (Beinn a'Chreachain)	978		284	50	2 - 16
Sgurr Thearlaich	978		285	32	17 - 7
Meall nan Ceapraichean	977	177	286	20	**15 - 7**
Stob Ban (Grey Corries)	977	178	287	41	**4 - 40**
Coinneach Mhor	976		288	25	13 - 15
Meall Buidhe (Glen Feshie)	976		289	35/36	8 - 6
Meall Garbh (Chno Dearg)	976		290	41	4 - 45
A'Mharconaich	975	179	291	42	**5 - 3**
An Garbhanach	975		292	41	4 - 10
Carn a'Gheoidh	975	180	293	43	**6 - 18**
Carn Liath (Beinn a'Ghlo)	975	181	294	43	**6 - 5**
Stuc a'Chroin	975	182	295	57	**1 - 23**
Beinn Sgritheall	974	183	296	33	**10 - 24**
Ben Lomond	974	184	297	56	**1 - 1**
Meall Coire na Saobhaidhe	974		298	44	7 - 26
Meall Mor	974		299	25	12 - 11

Name	Height (metres)	No. in order of height Mtn.	Top	O.S. Map Sheet	Section Ref.
Meall nam Peithirean.	974		300	20	14 - 20
Mullach Sithidh	974		301	25/33	11 - 34
Little Glas Maol	973		302	43	7 - 5
Sgurr a'Ghreadaidh	**973**	**185**	**303**	**32**	**17 - 13**
Creag an Dail Mhor.	972		304	43/36	8 - 49
Bynack Beg.	970		305	36	8 - 36
Sgurr a'Ghreadaidh - South Top.	970		306	32	17 - 14
Sgurr Ban (Beinn Eighe)	970		307	25	13 - 16
Meall an t-Snaim	969		308	34	9 - 13
Ceann Garbh	968		309	20	15 - 8
Garbh Chioch Bheag	968		310	33/40	10 - 9
Meall Garbh (Carn Mairg).	**968**	**186**	**311**	**51**	**2 - 37**
Stob an Fhuarain	968		312	41	3 - 29
A'Mhaighdean.	**967**	**187**	**313**	**19**	**14 - 3**
Carn na Con Dhu.	967		314	25/33	11 - 33
Sgorr nam Fiannaidh	**967**	**188**	**315**	**41**	**3 - 45**
Ben More (Mull)	**966**	**189**	**316**	**48**	**17 - 1**
Meall na Dige.	966		317	51	1 - 21
Sron an Isean	966		318	50	3 - 7
Sgurr na Banachdich	**965**	**190**	**319**	**32**	**17 - 10**
Sgurr nan Gillean	**964**	**191**	**320**	**32**	**17 - 20**
Carn a'Chlamain	**963**	**192**	**321**	**43**	**6 - 2**
Sgurr a'Bhuic	963		322	41	4 - 25
Sgurr Choinnich Beag	963		323	41	4 - 30
Sgurr na Forcan	963		324	33	10 - 29
Sgurr nan Fhir Duibhe.	963		325	25	13 - 17
Sgurr Thuilm.	**963**	**193**	**326**	**40**	**10 - 4**
Ben Klibreck - Meall nan Con	**962**	**194**	**327**	**16**	**16 - 4**
Gulvain - South Top.	962		328	40	10 - 6
Sgurr a' Dubh Doire	962		329	33	11 - 24
Sgorr Ruadh.	**962**	**195**	**330**	**25**	**13 - 2**
Carn na Criche	961		331	20	14 - 19
Druim Mor	961		332	43	7 - 7
Beinn nan Aighenan.	**960**	**196**	**333**	**50**	**3 - 10**
Ben More Assynt - South Top	960		334	15	16 - 3
Glas Mheall Liath.	960		335	19	14 - 32
Stob a'Choire Odhair.	960c		336	33	10 - 18
Stob Cadha Gobhlach	960		337	19	14 - 27
Stuchd an Lochain	**960**	**197**	**338**	**51**	**2 - 32**
Beinn Fhionnlaidh (Appin).	**959**	**198**	**339**	**50**	**3 - 27**
Meall Glas	**959**	**199**	**340**	**51**	**2 - 3**
Stob Garbh	959		341	51/56	1 - 18
Bruach na Frithe	**958**	**200**	**342**	**32**	**17 - 16**

Name	Height (metres)	No. in order of height Mtn.	Top	O.S. Map Sheet	Section Ref.
Stob Coire na Gaibhre	958		343	41	4 - 39
Stob Coire Sgriodain - South Top	958		344	41	4 - 47
Stob Dubh (Buachaille Etive Beag)	**958**	**201**	**345**	**41**	**3 - 39**
Tolmount	**958**	**202**	**346**	**44**	**7 - 12**
Carn Ghluasaid	**957**	**203**	**347**	**34**	**11 - 15**
Tom Buidhe	**957**	**204**	**348**	**44**	**7 - 11**
Little Pap	956		349	44	7 - 28
Saileag	**956**	**205**	**350**	**33**	**11 - 6**
Sgor Eilde Beag	956		351	41	4 - 15
Sgurr nan Coireachan (Glen Finnan)	**956**	**206**	**352**	**40**	**10 - 3**
Stob na Broige	**956**	**207**	**353**	**41**	**3 - 41**
Stob nan Clach	956		354	50	2 - 8
Meall Dearg (Northern Pinnacles)	955		355	25	13 - 7
Sgor Gaibhre	**955**	**208**	**356**	**42**	**4 - 49**
Sron Coire na h-Iolaire	955		357	42	4 - 53
Beinn Liath Mhor Fannaich	**954**	**209**	**358**	**20**	**14 - 21**
Meall an Fhuarain Mhoir	954		359	33	11 - 23
Sail Liath	954		360	19	14 - 26
Am Faochagach	**953**	**210**	**361**	**20**	**15 - 11**
Beinn Iutharn Bheag	953		362	43	6 - 13
Beinn Mhanach	**953**	**211**	**363**	**50**	**2 - 17**
Meall Dearg (Aonach Eagach)	**953**	**212**	**364**	**41**	**3 - 47**
Sgurr nan Coireachan (Glen Dessarry)	**953**	**213**	**365**	**33/40**	**10 - 10**
Tom a'Choinnich (Ben Wyvis)	953		366	20	15 - 3
Beinn Fhada (Glen Coe)	952		367	41	3 - 37
Meall Chuaich	**951**	**214**	**368**	**42**	**5 - 8**
Toll Creagach - West Top	951		369	25	11 - 51
Meall Gorm	**949**	**215**	**370**	**20**	**14 - 22**
Beinn Bhuidhe	**948**	**216**	**371**	**56/50**	**1 - 7**
Sgurr a'Mhaoraich Beag	948		372	33	10 - 20
Sgurr Mhic Choinnich	**948**	**217**	**373**	**32**	**17 - 8**
A'Chioch	947		374	34	11 - 13
Creag a'Mhaim	**947**	**218**	**375**	**33**	**10 - 39**
Driesh	**947**	**219**	**376**	**44**	**7 - 9**
Sgorr Bhan	947		377	41	3 - 32
Sgurr Sgumain	947		378	32	17 - 6
An Cabar	946		379	20	15 - 2
Beinn Tulaichean	**946**	**220**	**380**	**56**	**1 - 16**
Carn Bhac	**946**	**221**	**381**	**43**	**6 - 14**
Meall Buidhe (Knoydart)	**946**	**222**	**382**	**33/40**	**10 - 13**
Sgurr na Sgine	**946**	**223**	**383**	**33**	**10 - 30**
Bidein a' Choire Sheasgaich	**945**	**224**	**384**	**25**	**12 - 9**
Carn Dearg (Monadh Liath)	**945**	**225**	**385**	**35**	**9 - 16**

Name	Height (metres)	No. in order of height Mtn.	Top	O.S. Map Sheet	Section Ref.
Creag Dubh	945		386	25	12 - 8
Stob a'Choire Odhair	945	226	387	50	**3 - 21**
An Socach (Glen Ey)	944	227	388	43	**6 - 16**
Sgurr Dubh Mor	944	228	389	32	**17 - 3**
Am Bodach (Aonach Eagach)	943		390	41	3 - 48
Ben Vorlich (Arrochar)	943	229	391	56/50	**1 - 5**
Binnein Beag	943	230	392	41	**4 - 16**
Creag Leacach - South-west Top	943		393	43	7 - 2
Carn Ban	942		394	35	9 - 18
Carn Cloich-mhuilinn	942		395	43	8 - 9
Meall Buidhe - South-east Top (Knoydart)	942		396	33/40	10 - 14
Sgurr na Banachdich - Central Top	942		397	32	17 - 11
Sgurr na Sgine - North-west Top	942		398	33	10 - 31
Carn Dearg (Corrour)	941	231	399	42	**4 - 48**
Carn na Caim	941	232	400	42	**5 - 7**
Stob a'Bhruaich Leith	941		401	50	3 - 19
Stob Coire Altruim	941		402	41	3 - 42
Beinn a'Chroin	940	233	403	50/56	**1 - 14**
Stob Coire Leith	940		404	41	3 - 46
Luinne Bheinn	939	234	405	33	**10 - 15**
Mount Keen	939	235	406	44	**7 - 30**
Mullach nan Coirean	939	236	407	41	**4 - 1**
Spidean Dhomhuill Bhric	939		408	33	10 - 28
An Socach - East Top (Glen Ey)	938		409	43	6 - 17
Beinn a'Chroin - West Top	938		410	50/56	1 - 15
Druim Shionnach - West Top	938		411	33	10 - 38
Sgurr Dubh an Da Bheinn	938		412	32	17 - 4
Beinn Cheathaich	937		413	51	2 - 4
Beinn Sgulaird	937	237	414	50	**3 - 26**
Beinn Tarsuinn	937	238	415	19	**14 - 5**
Luinne Bheinn - East Top	937		416	33	10 - 16
Sron a'Choire Ghairbh	937	239	417	34	**10 - 2**
A'Bhuidheanach Bheag	936	240	418	42	**5 - 5**
Beinn na Lap	935	241	419	41	**4 - 43**
East Meur Gorm Craig	935		420	36	8 - 46
Sgurr a'Fionn Choire	935		421	32	17 - 17
Toman Coinich	935		422	20	14 - 13
Am Basteir	934	242	423	32	**17 - 18**
Meall a'Chrasgaidh	934	243	424	20	**14 - 17**
Sgurr an Tuill Bhain	934		425	19	14 - 2
Beinn Chabhair	933	244	426	50/56	**1 - 12**
The Cairnwell	933	245	427	43	**6 - 20**
Fionn Bheinn	933	246	428	20	**14 - 11**

Name	Height (metres)	No. in order of height Mtn.	Top	O.S. Map Sheet	Section Ref.
Maol Chean-dearg	933	247	429	25	**13 - 1**
Meall Buidhe (Glen Lyon)	932	248	430	51	**2 - 34**
Beinn Bhreac	931	249	431	43/36	**8 - 37**
Beinn Fhada - North-east Top (Glen Coe) .	931		432	41	3 - 38
Ben Chonzie	931	250	433	51/52	**1 - 25**
Ben Vorlich - North Top (Arrochar)	931		434	56/50	1 - 6
A'Chailleach (Monadh Liath)	930	251	435	35	**9 - 21**
Meall Cruidh	930		436	50	3 - 13
Sgor Choinnich.	929		437	42	4 - 50
Sgurr nan Saighead	929		438	33	11 - 2
Tigh Mor na Seilge.	929		439	34	11 - 21
Beinn Sgritheall - North-west Top	928		440	33	10 - 25
Bla Bheinn	928	252	441	32	**17 - 22**
Glas Leathad Beag	928		442	20	15 - 4
Glas Mheall Mor	928		443	42	5 - 6
Mayar	928	253	444	44	**7 - 10**
Meall nan Eun	928	254	445	50	**3 - 17**
Moruisg	928	255	446	25	**12 - 18**
Am Fasarinen.	927		447	25	13 - 8
Beinn Bhreac - West Top	927		448	43/36	8 - 38
Ben Hope	927	256	449	9	**16 - 5**
Craig of Gowal.	927		450	44	7 - 19
Eididh nan Clach Geala	927	257	451	20	**15 - 9**
Sron Chona Choirein	927		452	51	2 - 33
Beinn Liath Mhor	926	258	453	25	**13 - 3**
Beinn Narnain	926	259	454	56	**1 - 2**
Bla Bheinn - South Top	926		455	32	17 - 23
Geal Charn (Monadh Liath)	926	260	456	35	**9 - 15**
Meall a'Choire Leith.	926	261	457	51	**2 - 25**
Seana Bhraigh	926	262	458	20	**15 - 10**
Sgurr Thormaid	926		459	32	17 - 12
Stob Coire Raineach	925	263	460	41	**3 - 40**
An Sgorr	924		461	51	2 - 36
Creag Pitridh	924	264	462	42	**4 - 64**
Meall Glas Choire	924		463	42	4 - 56
Sgurr nan Eag	924	265	464	32	**17 - 2**
An Coileachan.	923	266	465	20	**14 - 24**
Beinn a'Chuirn.	923		466	50	2 - 18
Carn Dearg South-east Top (Monadh Liath)	923		467	35	9 - 17
Meall nan Tarmachan - South-east Top . . .	923		468	51	2 - 20
Sgurr nan Each	923	267	469	20	**14 - 15**
Tom na Gruagaich - Beinn Alligin	922	268	470	19/24	**13 - 4**

Name	Height (metres)	No. in order of height Mtn.	Top	O.S. Map Sheet	Section Ref.
Diollaid a'Chairn	922		471	42	4 - 61
Meall Gorm - South-east Top	922		472	20	14 - 23
Meall Odhar	922		473	43	7 - 4
Mullach Coire nan Nead	922		474	42	4 - 55
An Socach (Glen Affric)	**921**	**269**	**475**	**25/33**	**11 - 35**
Sgiath Chuil	**921**	**270**	**476**	**51**	**2 - 5**
Carn Ballach	920		477	35	9 - 19
Carn Bhac - South-west Top	920		478	43	6 - 15
Carn Sgulain	**920**	**271**	**479**	**35**	**9 - 20**
Crow Craigies	920		480	44	7 - 13
Geal-charn (Glen Feshie)	920		481	35/36	8 - 7
Gairich	**919**	**272**	**482**	**33**	**10 - 12**
Sgurr Leac nan Each	919		483	33	10 - 27
A'Ghlas-bheinn	**918**	**273**	**484**	**25/33**	**11 - 25**
Creag nan Damh	**918**	**274**	**485**	**33**	**10 - 32**
Meall a'Churain	918		486	51	2 - 6
Meall Cuanail	918		487	50	3 - 3
Meall na Teanga	**918**	**275**	**488**	**34**	**10 - 1**
Ruadh Stac Mor	**918**	**276**	**489**	**19**	**14 - 4**
Sgurr a'Mhadaidh	**918**	**277**	**490**	**32**	**17 - 15**
Sgurr Dubh	918		491	19	14 - 8
Stob an Duine Ruaidh	918		492	50	3 - 12
Stuc Fraoch Choire	918		493	25/33	11 - 30
Tom Dubh	918		494	36/43	8 - 11
Tom na Sroine	918		495	41	4 - 28
Carn Aosda	**917**	**278**	**496**	**43**	**6 - 21**
Carn Bhinnein	917		497	43	6 -19
Geal-charn (Drumochter)	**917**	**279**	**498**	**42**	**5 - 4**
Mullach nan Coirean - South-east Top	917		499	41	4 - 2
Stob Coire Lochan	917		500	25	11 - 42
Beinn a'Chlaidheimh	**916**	**280**	**501**	**19**	**14 - 10**
Beinn a'Chleibh	**916**	**281**	**502**	**50**	**1 - 8**
Bhasteir Tooth	916		503	32	17 - 19
Creag na Caillich	916		504	51	2 - 23
Stob Coire Dubh	916		505	34	9 - 14
Beinn Teallach	**915**	**282**	**506**	**34/41**	**9 - 1**
Ben Vane	**915**	**283**	**507**	**56**	**1 - 4**
Sgurr nan Ceannaichean	**915**	**284**	**508**	**25**	**12 - 17**
Stob Coire na Cloiche	915		509	25/33	11 - 31
Stuc a'Choire Dhuibh Bhig	915		510	25	13 - 11
Knight's Peak	914		511	32	17 - 21

Index to Munro's Tables

Name	Section Reference	Name	Section Reference
A'Bhuidheanach Bheag	5 - 5	Binnein Beag	4 - 16
A'Chailleach (Monadh Liath)	9 - 21	Binnein Mor	4 - 13/14
A'Chailleach (Fannaichs)	14 - 12	Bla Bheinn	17 - 22/23
Achaladair, Beinn	2 - 13/14	Braeriach	8 - 16
A'Chioch	11 - 13	Braigh Coire Chruinn-bhalgain	6 - 6
A'Choinneach	8 - 35	Broad Cairn	7 - 14
A'Chralaig	11 - 11	Bruach na Frithe	17 - 16
A'Ghlas-bheinn	11 - 25	Buachaille Etive Beag	3 - 39/40
Aighenan, Beinn nan	3 - 10	Buachaille Etive Mor	3 - 41/43
Airgiod Bheinn	6 - 8	Bynack Beg	8 - 36
Alder, Ben	4 - 51	Bynack More	8 - 34
Alligin, Beinn	13 - 4/5	Cac Carn Beag (Lochnagar)	7 - 25
Am Basteir	17 - 18	Cairn Bannoch	7 - 16
Am Bodach (Aonach Eagach)	3 - 48	Cairn Gorm	8 - 23
Am Bodach (Mamores)	4 - 7	Cairn Lochan	8 - 25
Am Faochagach	15 - 11	Cairn of Claise	7 - 6
Am Fasarinen	13 - 8	Cairn of Gowal	7 - 18
A'Mhaighdean	14 - 3	Cairn Toul	8 - 13
A'Mharconaich	5 - 3	Cairnwell, The	6 - 20
An Cabar	15 - 2	Caisteal	4 - 33
An Caisteal	1 - 13	Carn a'Chlamain	6 - 2
An Cearcallach	9 - 6	Carn a'Choire Bhoidheach	7 - 21
An Coileachan	14 - 24	Carn a'Gheoidh	6 - 18
An Garbhanach	4 - 10	Carn a'Mhaim	8 - 19
An Gearanach	4 - 9	Carn an Fhidhleir (Carn Ealar)	6 - 3
An Leth-chreag	11 - 49	Carn an Righ	6 - 10
An Riabhachan	12 - 2/3/4	Carn an t-Sagairt Beag	7 - 24
An Sgarsoch	6 - 4	Carn an t-Sagairt Mor	7 - 20
An Sgorr	2 - 36	Carn an Tuirc	7 - 8
An Socach (Glen Ey)	6 - 16	Carn Aosda	6 - 21
An Socach (Glen Affric)	11 - 35	Carn Ballach	9 - 19
An Socach (Loch Mullardoch)	12 - 1	Carn Ban	9 - 18
An Stuc	2 - 29	Carn Ban Mor	8 - 4
An Teallach	14 - 25/31	Carn Bhac	6 - 14/15
An Tudair	11 - 38	Carn Bhinnein	6 -19
Aonach air Chrith	10 - 36	Carn Cloich-mhuilinn	8 - 9
Aonach Beag (Glen Nevis)	4 - 23	Carn Dearg (NW & SW of Ben Nevis)	4 - 19/20
Aonach Beag (Alder District)	4 - 57	Carn Dearg (Corrour)	4 - 48
Aonach Meadhoin	11 - 8	Carn Dearg (Alder District)	4 - 60
Aonach Mor	4 - 26	Carn Dearg (Monadh Liath)	9 - 16/17
Avon, Ben	8 - 45	Carn Dearg Meadhonach	4 - 22
Ben, Beinn, Bheinn, Beinn a' etc see next word		Carn Eas	8 - 48
Bhasteir Tooth	17 - 19	Carn Eighe	11 - 41
Bheoil, Beinn	4 - 52	Carn Etchachan	8 - 22
Bhreac, Beinn	8 - 37/38	Carn Ghluasaid	11 - 15
Bhrotain, Beinn	8 - 8	Carn Gorm	2 - 35
Bhuidhe, Beinn	1 - 7	Carn Liath (Beinn a'Ghlo)	6 - 5
Bhuird, Beinn a'	8 - 41/42	Carn Liath (Creag Meagaidh)	9 - 12
Bidean an Eoin Deirg	12 - 14	Carn Mairg	2 - 38
Bidean nam Bian	3 - 33	Carn Mor Dearg	4 - 21
Bidein a' Choire Sheasgaich	12 - 9	Carn na Caim	5 - 7
Bidein a'Ghlas Thuill (An Teallach)	14 - 31	Carn na Coire Mheadhoin	11 - 20

Name	Section Reference	Name	Section Reference
Carn na Con Dhu	11 - 33	Dearg, Beinn (Atholl)	6 - 1
Carn na Criche (Braeriach)	8 - 17	Dearg, Beinn (Ullapool)	15 - 5
Carn na Criche (Fannaichs)	14 - 19	Derry Cairngorm	8 - 28
Carn nam Fiaclan	12 - 16	Devil's Point, The	8 - 12
Carn nan Gabhar (Beinn a'Ghlo)	6 - 7	Diollaid a'Chairn	4 - 61
Carn nan Gobhar (Glen Cannich)	12 - 7	Dorain, Beinn	2 - 11
Carn nan Gobhar (Strathfarrar)	12 - 23	Dothaidh, Beinn an	2 - 12
Carn Sgulain	9 - 20	Driesh	7 - 9
Ceann Garbh	15 - 8	Drochaid an Tuill Easaich	11 - 17
Chabhair, Beinn	1 - 12	Drochaid Ghlas	3 - 4
Challum, Ben	2 - 1/2	Druim Mor	7 - 7
Chaorainn, Beinn a' (Laggan)	9 - 2/3/4	Druim Shionnach	10 - 37/38
Chaorainn, Beinn a' (Glen Derry)	8 - 39	Dubhchraig, Beinn	1 - 11
Chaorainn Bheag, Beinn a'	8 - 40	Eachan, Beinn nan	2 - 22
Cheathaich, Beinn	2 - 4	Eagle's Rock	7 - 23
Chlaidheimh, Beinn a'	14 - 10	East Meur Gorm Craig	8 - 46
Chlachair, Beinn a'	4 - 62	Eibhinn, Beinn	4 - 54
Chleibh, Beinn a'	1 - 8	Eididh nan Clach Geala	15 - 9
Chno Dearg	4 - 44	Eighe, Beinn	13 - 12/13
Chochuill, Beinn a'	3 - 8	Eunaich, Beinn	3 - 9
Chonzie, Ben	1 - 25	Fafernie	7 - 17
Chreachain, Beinn a'	2 - 15	Fhada, Beinn (Glen Coe)	3 - 37/38
Chroin, Beinn a'	1 - 14/15	Fhada, Beinn (Kintail)	11 - 22
Chuirn, Beinn a'	2 - 18	Fhionnlaidh, Beinn (Creran)	3 - 27
Ciste Dhubh	11 - 10	Fhionnlaidh, Beinn (Affric)	11 - 46
Clach Leathad	3 - 23	Fionn Bheinn	14 - 11
Cnap a'Chleirich	8 - 43	Gairich	10 - 12
Cnap Coire na Spreidhe	8 - 27	Garbh Chioch Bheag	10 - 9
Coinneach Mhor	13 - 15	Garbh Chioch Mhor	10 - 8
Cona'Mheall	15 - 6	Geal - Charn (Alder District)	4 - 58
Conival	16 - 1	Geal Charn -Mullach Coire an Iubhair	4 - 63
Corrag Bhuidhe	14 - 28	Geal-charn (Drumochter)	5 - 4
Craig Coire na Fiar Bhealaich	10 - 22	Geal-charn (Glen Feshie)	8 - 7
Craig of Gowal	7 - 19	Geal Charn (Monadh Liath)	9 - 15
Creag a'Chaorainn	11 - 18	Ghlas, Beinn	2 - 26
Creag a'Ghlas-uillt	7 - 22	Ghlo, Beinn a'	6 - 7
Creag a'Mhaim	10 - 39	Glas Bheinn Mhor	3 - 15
Creagan a'Choire Etchachan	8 - 30	Glas Leathad Beag	15 - 4
Creag an Dail Mhor	8 - 49	Glas Leathad Mor (Ben Wyvis)	15 - 1
Creag an Dubh-loch	7 - 15	Glas Maol	7 - 3
Creag an Fhithich	2 - 28	Glas Mheall Liath	14 - 32
Creag an Leth-choin	8 - 24	Glas Mheall Mor (Drumochter)	5 - 6
Creag Coire nan Each	11 - 37	Glas Mheall Mor (An Teallach)	14 - 33
Creag Dubh	12 - 8	Glas Tulaichean	6 - 9
Creag Ghorm a' Bhealaich	12 - 20	Gleouraich	10 - 21
Creag Leacach	7 - 1/2	Gulvain	10 - 5/6
Creag Meagaidh	9 - 5	Heasgarnich, Beinn	2 - 9
Creag Mhor	2 - 7	Hope, Ben	16 - 5
Creag na Caillich	2 - 23	Ime, Beinn	1 - 3
Creag nan Damh	10 - 32	Inaccessible Pinnacle	17 - 9
Creag Pitridh	4 - 64	Iutharn Bheag, Beinn	6 - 13
Creise	3 - 22	Iutharn Mhor, Beinn	6 - 11
Crow Craigies	7 - 13	Klibreck, Ben	16 - 4
Cruachan, Ben	3 - 1	Knight's Peak	17 - 21
Cruach Ardrain	1 - 17	Ladhar Bheinn	10 - 17
Cuidhe Crom	7 - 27	Lap, Beinn na	4 - 43

Name	Section Reference	Name	Section Reference
Lawers, Ben	2 - 27	Meall nan Eun	3 - 17
Leabaidh an Daimh Bhuidhe (Avon)	8 - 45	Meall nan Tarmachan	2 - 19/20
Liathach	13 - 6/9	Meall na Teanga	10 - 1
Liath Mhor, Beinn	13 - 3	Meall Odhar	7 - 4
Liath Mhor Fannaich, Beinn	14 - 21	Meikle Pap	7 - 29
Little Glas Maol	7 - 5	Mhanach, Beinn	2 - 17
Little Pap	7 - 28	Mheadhoin, Beinn	8 - 31
Lochnagar	7 - 25	Monadh Mor	8 - 10
Lomond, Ben	1 - 1	More, Ben (Perthshire)	1 - 22
Lord Berkeley's Seat	14 - 29	More, Ben (Mull)	17 - 1
Lui, Ben	1 - 9	More Assynt, Ben	16 - 2/3
Luinne Bheinn	10 - 15/16	Moruisg	12 - 18
Lurg Mhor	12 - 10	Mount Keen	7 - 30
Macdui, Ben	8 - 20	Mullach an Rathain (Liathach)	13 - 6
Mam nan Carn	6 - 12	Mullach Cadha Rainich	11 - 39
Mam Sodhail	11 - 36	Mullach Clach a'Bhlair	8 - 1
Maoile Lunndaidh	12 - 15	Mullach Coire Mhic Fhearchair	14 - 6/7
Maol Chean-dearg	13 - 1	Mullach Coire nan Nead	4 - 55
Maol Chinn-dearg	10 - 35	Mullach Fraoch-choire	11 - 14
Mayar	7 - 10	Mullach na Dheiragain	11 - 32
Meall a'Bharr	2 - 40	Mullach nan Coirean	4 - 1/2
Meall a'Bhuiridh	3 - 25	Mullach Sithidh	11 - 34
Meall a'Choire Leith	2 - 25	Na Gruagaichean	4 - 11
Meall a'Chrasgaidh	14 - 17	Narnain, Beinn	1 - 2
Meall a'Churain	2 - 6	Nevis, Ben	4 - 18
Meall an Fhuarain Mhoir	11 - 23	Northern Pinnacles (Liathach)	13 - 7
Meall an t-Snaim	9 - 13	Oss, Ben	1 - 10
Meall Buidhe (Beinn a'Chreachain)	2 - 16	Puist Coire Ardair	9 - 8
Meall Buidhe (Glen Lyon)	2 - 34	Ruadh-stac Mor (Beinn Eighe)	13 - 12
Meall Buidhe (Glen Feshie)	8 - 6	Ruadh Stac Mor (Fisherfield)	14 - 4
Meall Buidhe (Knoydart)	10 - 13/14	Saddle, The	10 - 26
Meall Chuaich	5 - 8	Sail Chaorainn	11 - 19
Meall Coire Choille-rais	9 - 7	Saileag	11 - 6
Meall Coire na Saobhaidhe	7 - 26	Sail Liath	14 - 26
Meall Corranaich	2 - 24	Sail Mhor	13 - 14
Meall Cruidh	3 - 13	Schiehallion	2 - 42
Meall Cuanail	3 - 3	Seana Bhraigh	15 - 10
Meall Dearg (Aonach Eagach)	3 - 47	Sgairneach Mhor	5 - 1
Meall Dearg (Liathach)	13 - 7	Sgiath Chuil	2 - 5
Meall Dubhag	8 - 3	Sgoran Dubh Mor	8 - 5
Meall Garbh (Tarmachans)	2 - 21	Sgor an Iubhair	4 - 5
Meall Garbh (Ben Lawers)	2 - 30	Sgor an Lochain Uaine (Cairn Toul)	8 - 15
Meall Garbh (Carn Mairg)	2 - 37	Sgor Choinnich	4 - 50
Meall Garbh (Chno Dearg)	4 - 45	Sgor Eilde Beag	4 - 15
Meall Ghaordie	2 - 10	Sgor Gaibhre	4 - 49
Meall Glas	2 - 3	Sgor Gaoith	8 - 2
Meall Glas Choire	4 - 56	Sgor Iutharn	4 - 59
Meall Gorm	14 - 22/23	Sgor na h-Ulaidh	3 - 28
Meall Greigh	2 - 31	Sgorr Bhan	3 - 32
Meall Liath	2 - 39	Sgorr Dhearg (Beinn a'Bheithir)	3 - 31
Meall Mor	12 - 11	Sgorr Dhonuill (Beinn a'Bheithir)	3 - 30
Meall nan Aighean	2 - 41	Sgorr nam Fiannaidh	3 - 45
Meall na Dige	1 - 21	Sgorr Ruadh	13 - 2
Meall nam Peithirean	14 - 20	Sgritheall, Beinn	10 - 24/25
Meall nan Ceapraichean	15 - 7	Sgulaird, Beinn	3 - 26
Meall nan Con (Ben Klibreck)	16 - 4	Sgurr a'Bhealaich Dheirg	11 - 7

Name	Section Reference	Name	Section Reference
Sgurr a'Bhuic	4 - 25	Sgurr nan Saighead	11 - 2
Sgurr a'Chaorachain (Monar)	12 - 13	Sgurr nan Spainteach	11 - 5
Sgurr a'Choire Ghlais	12 - 22	Sgurr Sgumain	17 - 6
Sgurr a' Dubh Doire	11 - 24	Sgurr Thearlaich	17 - 7
Sgurr a'Fionn Choire	17 - 17	Sgurr Thormaid	17 - 12
Sgurr a'Ghreadaidh	17 - 13/14	Sgurr Thuilm	10 - 4
Sgurr Alasdair	17 - 5	Slioch	14 - 1
Sgurr a'Mhadaidh	17 - 15	Socaich, Beinn na	4 - 34
Sgurr a'Mhaim	4 - 4	Spidean a'Choire Leith (Liathach)	13 - 9
Sgurr a'Mhaoraich	10 - 19	Spidean Coire nan Clach (Beinn Eighe)	13 - 13
Sgurr a'Mhaoraich Beag	10 - 20	Spidean Dhomhuill Bhric	10 - 28
Sgurr an Doire Leathain	10 - 34	Spidean Mialach	10 - 23
Sgurr an Fhuarail	11 - 9	Sron a'Choire	9 - 9
Sgurr an Lochain	10 - 33	Sron a'Choire Ghairbh	10 - 2
Sgurr an Lochan Uaine (Glen Derry)	8 - 29	Sron a'Ghearrain	3 - 20
Sgurr an Tuill Bhain	14 - 2	Sron an Isean	3 - 7
Sgurr Ban (Beinn Eighe)	13 - 16	Sron Chona Choirein	2 - 33
Sgurr Ban (Letterewe)	14 - 9	Sron Coire a'Chriochairein	9 - 11
Sgurr Breac	14 - 14	Sron Coire na h-Iolaire	4 - 53
Sgurr Choinnich	12 - 12	Sron Garbh	11 - 45
Sgurr Choinnich Beag	4 - 30	Sron na Lairige	8 - 18
Sgurr Choinnich Mor	4 - 29	Sron Riach	8 - 21
Sgurr Creag an Eich	14 - 30	Stacan Dubha	8 - 33
Sgurr Dubh	14 - 8	Starav, Ben	3 - 11
Sgurr Dubh an Da Bheinn	17 - 4	Stob a'Bhruaich Leith	3 - 19
Sgurr Dubh Mor	17 - 3	Stob a'Choire Dhomhain	11 - 43
Sgurr Eilde Mor	4 - 17	Stob a'Choire Leith	4 - 37
Sgurr Fhuaran	11 - 1	Stob a'Choire Mheadhoin	4 - 42
Sgurr Fhuar-thuill	12 - 19	Stob a'Choire Odhair (Blackmount)	3 - 21
Sgurr Fiona (An Teallach)	14 - 25	Stob a'Choire Odhair (Ladhar Bheinn)	10 - 18
Sgurr Leac nan Each	10 - 27	Stob a'Coire Liath Mhor	13 - 10
Sgurr Mhic Choinnich	17 - 8	Stob a'Ghlais Choire	3 - 24
Sgurr Mhor (Beinn Alligin)	13 - 5	Stob an Cul Choire	4 - 27
Sgurr Mor (Quoich)	10 - 11	Stob an Duine Ruaidh	3 - 12
Sgurr Mor (Fannaichs)	14 - 18	Stob an Fhuarain	3 - 29
Sgurr na Banachdich	17 - 10/11	Stob an t-Sluichd	8 - 44
Sgurr na Carnach	11 - 3	Stob Ban (Mamores)	4 - 3
Sgurr na Ciche	10 - 7	Stob Ban (Grey Corries)	4 - 40
Sgurr na Ciste Duibhe	11 - 4	Stob Binnein	1 - 19
Sgurr na Fearstaig	12 - 21	Stob Cadha Gobhlach	14 - 27
Sgurr na Forcan	10 - 29	Stob Choire a'Mhail	4 - 6
Sgurr na Lapaich (Affric)	11 - 40	Stob Choire Claurigh	4 - 36
Sgurr na Lapaich (Mullardoch)	12 - 5	Stob Coir'an Albannaich	3 - 16
Sgurr na Ruaidhe	12 - 24	Stob Coire a'Chairn	4 - 8
Sgurr na Sgine	10 - 30/31	Stob Coire Altruim	3 - 42
Sgurr nan Ceannaichean	12 - 17	Stob Coire an Laoigh	4 - 31
Sgurr nan Ceathreamhnan	11 - 26/27	Stob Coire an Lochain (Stob Binnein)	1 - 20
Sgurr nan Clach Geala	14 - 16	Stob Coire an t-Saighdeir	8 - 14
Sgurr nan Clachan Geala	12 - 6	Stob Coire an t-Sneachda	8 - 26
Sgurr nan Coireachan (Glenfinnan)	10 - 3	Stob Coire Bhealaich	4 - 24
Sgurr nan Coireachan (Glen Dessary)	10 - 10	Stob Coire Cath na Sine	4 - 35
Sgurr nan Conbhairean	11 - 16	Stob Coire Dheirg	3 - 14
Sgurr nan Each	14 - 15	Stob Coire Dhomhnuill	11 - 44
Sgurr nan Eag	17 - 2	Stob Coire Dubh	9 - 14
Sgurr nan Fhir Duibhe	13 - 17	Stob Coire Easain (Grey Corries)	4 - 32
Sgurr nan Gillean	17 - 20	Stob Coire Easain (Loch Treig)	4 - 41

Name	Section Reference	Name	Section Reference
Stob Coire Etchachan	8 - 32	Stuc a'Chroin	1 - 23
Stob Coire Leith	3 - 46	Stuc Fraoch Choire	11 - 30
Stob Coire Lochan	11 - 42	Stuchd an Lochain	2 - 32
Stob Coire na Ceannain	4 - 38	Stuc Mor	11 - 29
Stob Coire na Cloiche	11 - 31	Tarsuinn, Beinn	14 - 5
Stob Coire na Cralaig	11 - 12	Teallach, Beinn	9 - 1
Stob Coire na Gaibhre	4 - 39	Tigh Mor na Seilge	11 - 21
Stob Coire nam Beith	3 - 34	Toll Creagach	11 - 50/51
Stob Coire nan Lochan (Glen Coe)	3 - 35	Tolmount	7 - 12
Stob Coire Raineach	3 - 40	Tom a'Choinich (Affric)	11 - 47
Stob Coire Sgreamhach	3 - 36	Tom a' Choinich Beag	11 - 48
Stob Coire Sgriodain	4 - 46/47	Tom a'Choinnich (Ben Wyvis)	15 - 3
Stob Dearg (Taynuilt Peak)	3 - 2	Toman Coinich	14 - 13
Stob Dearg (Buachaille Etive Mor)	3 - 43	Tom Buidhe	7 - 11
Stob Diamh	3 - 5	Tom Dubh	8 - 11
Stob Dubh (Buachaille Etive Beag)	3 - 39	Tom na Gruagaich	13 - 4
Stob Garbh (Cruach Ardrain)	1 - 18	Tom na Sroine	4 - 28
Stob Garbh (Ben Cruachan)	3 - 6	Tulaichean, Beinn	1 - 16
Stob Ghabhar	3 - 18	Udlamain, Beinn	5 - 2
Stob na Broige	3 - 41	Vane, Ben	1 - 4
Stob na Doire	3 - 44	Vorlich, Ben (Arrochar)	1 - 5/6
Stob nan Clach	2 - 8	Vorlich, Ben (Loch Earn)	1 - 24
Stob Poite Coire Ardair	9 - 10	West Meur Gorm Craig	8 - 47
Stuc Bheag	11 - 28	Wyvis, Ben	15 - 1
Stuc a'Choire Dhuibh Bhig	13 - 11		

List of Munroists

The following list shows those who have compleated the Munros as listed in the 1990 or earlier editions of the Tables. Future claims must be based on this edition and should be sent to Dr Chris Huntley, Old Medwyn, Spittal, Carnwath ML11 8LY. Those who are listed below, and who are still sound in body, will be expected to take heed of the changes in this edition as their conscience dictates. The list is updated annually and appears in the SMC Journal. From 1985, the list is compiled in order of notification rather than by date of completion.

*denotes a member or former member of the SMC.
**denotes a member or former member of the Ladies Scottish Climbing Club.

	Name	Munros	Tops	Furths		Name	Munros	Tops	Furths
1	* Rev. A.E. Robertson . . .	1901			41	Mrs. K.M. Watson	1960		
2	* Rev. A.R.G. Burn	1923	1923		42	J.R. Watson	1960		
3	* J.A. Parker	1927		1929	43	* J.C. Donaldson	1961		
4	* J.R. Corbett	1930	1930		44	P.A. Larder	1961		1961
5	* J. Dow	1933	1947	1956	45	P.N.L. Tranter	1961		
6	J. Robertson	1938					1964		
7	* G.G. Elliot	1938			46	* J.C.I. Wedderburn	1962		
8	* A.L. Cram	1939	1939		47	J.M. Burnett	1962		
		1978	1978		48	A.E. Robinson	1962		
9	J. Hirst	1947	1947		49	K.D. Shaw	1962		
10	Mrs. J. Hirst	1947	1947		50	Miss L. Ticehurst	1962	1962	1962
11	* E.W. Hodge	1947			51	* K.M. Andrew	1962	1969	
12	* B. Horsburgh	1947			52	* G.H. Smith	1962		
13	* W.M. Docharty	1948	1948	1949	53	* G.M. Smith	1963	1966	1968
14	W.D. McKinlay	1948					1969	1969	1971
15	J. Campbell	1949			54	* W.L. Wood	1963		
16	* C.V. Dodgson	1951	1951		55	I.A. Robertson	1963		1961
17	H. Hampton	1952					1986		
18	* G.S. Ritchie	1953			56	J. Cosgrove	1963		
19	J.S. Anderson	1953	1953	1958			1974		
20	* G.G. MacPhee	1954	1955		57	* J.N. Ledingham	1963		
21	* P.J.L. Heron	1954		1956	58	A. Farquharson	1963		
22	* J.F. Hamilton	1954		1956	59	* A.R. Thrippleton	1964		
23	* M. Hutchinson	1955	1955	1970	60	J.G. Fleming	1964		
		1992			61	W.D. Fraser	1964		
24	E.I. Lawson	1955	1955		62	* Hamish M Brown	1965	1965	1967
25	W.T. Allan	1956					1969		1969
26	* J. Mallinson	1956					1970		1971
27	* J. Ferrier	1956					1974		1978
28	* G. Peat	1957	1967				1975		1979
29	* J.A. Watt	1957	1957	1958			1979		
30	E. Maxwell	1957	1957	1958	63	* W.T. Taylor	1965	1966	1967
		1966	1966		64	R.M. Milne	1965		
31	C.G. Macdonald	1958			65	H.S.K. Stapley	1965		1965
32	* J.Y. Macdonald	1958			66	R. Hutchinson	1965		
33	A.G. McKenzie	1958		1980	67	G.C. Sime	1966	1966	1969
		1980			68	* W.D. Nicoll	1966		
34	J.C. Grant	1959		1961	69	* D.C.H. Green	1966	1966	1969
35	T.P. Kemp	1959			70	* G. King	1966		
36	Mrs. J. Ferrier	1960			71	* D. Barclay	1966		
37	Mrs. M Linklater-Shirras	1960			72	D. Hawksworth	1967		1969
38	** Miss A.J. Littlejohn . . .	1960	1960	1960	73	A.M. Fraser	1967	1980	1977
39	** Miss A.D. Miller	1960		1961			1978		
40	* T. Nicholson	1960	1961				1986		

	Name	Munros	Tops	Furths
74	A.C. Gardner	1967		1970
75	** Miss M. McCallum ...	1967	1968	
76	Mathew J. Moulton ...	1968	1982	1982
		1971		
		1978		
		1980		
		1982		
77	R. Smith	1968	1968	
78	** Miss L.W. Urquhart ...	1968		
79	** Miss E. MacKay	1968		
80	A.J. Main	1968		
81	* R.D. Walton	1968		
82	W. Shand	1968	1968	1974
83	G.G. Shand	1968	1968	1974
84	R.L. Pearce	1968		
85	Barbara M. Tulloch ...	1968		
86	Helen M. Scrimgeour .	1968		
87	* John Hinde	1968		
88	R.W.G. Wood	1969		
89	I.T. Stephen	1969		
90	R.J. Grant	1969		
91	* W.T. Tauber	1969		
92	R. Hainsworth	1969	1969	
93	K.R. Cox	1969	1969	1983
94	R. Armour	1969	1982	1985
		1979		
95	Mrs. E.R. Innes	1969		
96	W.G. Carter	1969	1970	1971
		1983		
97	B. Finlayson	1970		
98	* G. Chisholm	1970		
99	J.W. Brydie	1970		
100	* M.G. Geddes	1970	1970	
101	R. Gilbert	1971		
102	G. Downs	1971		
		1987		
103	P. Edwards	1971	1980	1980
104	I. Rae	1971		
105	Irvine Butterfield	1971		
106	John Gillies	1971	1988	1983
107	* Andrew Nisbet	1972	1991	1991
		1984		
		1996		
108	B.K.E. Edridge	1972		
		1982		
109	* G.S. Roger	1972		
110	Colin Turner	1973	1973	
111	R. Cook	1973	1973	1973
112	Peter Roberts	1973	1975	
		1986		
		1993		
113	W.G. Barbour	1973		
114	Donald Smith	1973	1982	1982
		1988		
115	K. MacLean	1973		
116	A. Robertson	1973		
117	J. Dawson	1973		
118	Diane Standring	1973		
119	** Janet Clark	1973		1983
120	John Mills	1973		
121	Don Smithies	1973		
122	W.C.T. Sarson	1973	1973	
123	A.L. Mackenzie	1973		
124	Archibald Grant	1973		
125	A.R. Dunn	1974		
126	A.E. Lawson	1974	1974	1976
127	D.J. Farrant	1974		
128	R. Hardie	1974		
129	* J.W. Simpson	1974		
130	J. Sloane	1974		
131	Lily MacKenzie	1975		
132	R. Millar	1975		
133	* F.R. Wylie	1975		
134	Colin Marsden	1976	1976	
135	D. Hunter	1976		
136	R.L.St.C. Murray	1976	1980	1980
137	I.C. Spence	1974		1976
138	Ruth Payne	1976		
139	W. Douglas	1976		
140	M. Keates	1976		
141	E. Pilling	1976		
142	Richard Morgan	1976	1976	1977
		1985	1985	1986
143	A.E. Law	1976	1983	
144	D. Tooke	1976		
145	R. Graham	1976		
146	* Campbell R. Steven ...	1976		
147	R. Davie	1976		
148	* D. Whalley	1976	1982	1989
		1982	1989	
		1986		
		1991		
		1995		
149	T. MacDonald	1976		
150	D. Henderson	1976		
151	Murdo E. MacDonald .	1977		
152	Erlend Flett	1977		
153	A.N. Darbyshire	1977		1990
154	Jock Murray	1977		
155	Edward F. Emley	1977		1980
156	R.D. Leitch	1977		
157	* W.M.S. Myles	1977		
158	M.H. MacKinnon	1977		
159	Denise Marsden	1977	1977	
160	W.A. Donaldson	1977		
161	A.F. des Moulins	1977		1988
		1981		
		1988		
162	Duncan C. Gray	1978		
163	Iain G. Gray	1978		
164	Nigel Hawkins	1978		
165	* J.L. Morning	1978		
166	T. Moore	1978		
167	J. Allan	1978		

	Name	Munros	Tops	Furths			Name	Munros	Tops	Furths
168	S. Robertson	1978				219	* R. Hillcoat	1980		
169	A.S. Bowie	1978				220	Peter Edward	1980		
170	J.E. Smith	1978				221	Raymond Hutcheson	1980		
171	F. Wiley	1978				222	Ronald Crawford	1980		
172	I.C. Murray	1978				223	Carole M. Davie	1980		
173	I.C. Munro	1978	1978			224	Stanley Grant	1980		
174	** Mrs. Pat Bell	1978	1978			225	Alan L. Brook	1980	1980	1978
175	A.G. MacLean	1978	1979	1978		226	M.W. McCue	1980	1980	1980
176	S. Craven	1978				227	* Donald Mill	1980		
177	A.F. Craven	1978				228	Alan Gately	1980		
178	D.A. Shanks	1978				229	Stan Bradshaw	1980	1980	1980
179	R.C. Munro	1978	1978			230	John Howorth	1980	1980	1980
180	J. Stewart	1978				231	C.R. Knowles	1980	1980	
181	Mrs. A.L. Cram	1978	1978			232	* Trevor Ransley	1980		
182	W. Steele	1978				233	** Sheila Cormack	1980	1980	1985
183	A. Stevens	1978				234	Anne McGeachie	1980		
184	S. Beck	1978				235	George McGeachie	1980		
185	Susan MacKenzie	1978				236	R.W.J. Webster	1981		
186	C.E. Barton	1979	1987	1988		237	* Haswell Oldham	1969	1972	1966
187	Sue Robertson	1979				238	Connie Thompson	1980		
188	D.A. Peet	1979				239	Frank Tildesley	1980		
189	David Lane	1979				240	Mike Lidwell	1980	1980	
190	A.L. Bartlet	1979		1979		241	Roger Clarke	1980		
191	P. Cooper	1979	1979	1976		242	Rona M. Craig	1981		
192	Carole Smithies	1979				243	Fiona M. Wilkie	1981		
193	Pamela Brown	1979				244	* Roger O'Donovan	1981		
194	P.D. Brown	1979				245	David A. Williams	1981		
195	Leonard Jamieson	1979 1989	1987	1986		246	John M. Dunn	1981		
						247	K.J. Hay	1981	1982	1982
196	M.R. Don	1979				248	W.Lindsay Wyllie	1981 1996		
197	John Rogers	1979								
198	S.R. Palmer	1979 1986	1980	1980		249	Andrew Martin	1981		
						250	Leonard Moss	1981 1994		
199	Dewi Jones	1979								
200	F. Telfer	1979				251	Christopher Townsend	1981 1996	1996	
201	M. Tildesley	1979								
202	H. Thomson	1979				252	Elizabeth Devenay	1981		
203	D. Foster	1979				253	William T. Devenay	1981		
204	Christopher Bond	1980	1986	1986		254	* James Renny	1981 1996	1994	
205	Tom Rix	1980 1987		1983						
						255	W.D. Duncan	1981		
206	I.H. Chuter	1980				256	H.F. Barron	1981	1988	1997
207	* Ivan Waller	1980	1981	1982		257	John Colls	1981		
208	Brian Batty	1980				258	I.R.W. Park	1981		
209	Patricia Batty	1980 1995				259	* Derek A. Bearhop	1981 1988 1994	1988	
210	Archie Mitchell	1973								
211	Fergus McIntosh	1979	1980	1980		260	Geraldine Guestsmith	1981 1984 1987 1990 1992 1995	1984 1987 1992	1986 1987
212	W.Ross Napier	1980								
213	Ronald Leask	1980	1980							
214	Sue Jardine	1980								
215	D. Alastair Baird	1980 1990	1981	1982						
216	Jeremy Fenton	1980 1995	1984	1982		261	Robert I. Scott	1981		
217	J.R.M. Lubbock	1976	1982			262	Roger Robb	1981		
218	P.D. Binnie	1977				263	James Boyd	1981		
						264	Don Vass	1981		

#	Name	Munros	Tops	Furths
265	G.H. Maynard	1981		
266	Norman McDonald	1965		1966
267	Martin Hudson	1981	1981	1982
268	Patience Barton	1982		
		1988		
269	Winnie Reid	1982		
270	David Reid	1982		
271	E.D. Clements	1969		1982
272	Robert Durran	1982		
273	A.M. Snodgrass	1982		
274	Edward MacGregor	1982		
275	David C. Phillips	1982	1982	
276	Gerry Knight	1982	1982	1983
277	Ewan C. Douglas	1982		1988
278	Donald Ross	1982		
279	Jim Wyllie	1982		
		1988		
		1995		
280	Chris Andrews	1995		
281	Christine Dale	1982		
282	Michael Dale	1982		
283	Simon Dale	1982		
284	THE UNKNOWN MUNROIST†			
285	J.L. Campbell	1982		
286	Donald McCall	1982		
287	Catherine MacMillan	1982		
288	Jim Braid	1982	1982	
289	D.L. Sands	1982		
290	Kenneth J. MacIver	1982		
291	Donald MacLeod Duthie	1982		
292	** Kathy Murgatroyd	1982		1985
293	W.G. Park	1982		
294	D.M. Inglis	1982		
295	Angus Mitchell	1982		1990
296	John E. Ramsay	1983		1982
297	Duncan MacNiven	1983		
298	Ian Bryce	1983		
299	L. Skuodas	1983		
300	* Derek G. Pyper	1983		
301	R.D. Whittal	1983		
302	Alan C. Sloan	1983	1983	1983
303	Neil C. Cromar	1983		
304	E. Martin	1983		
305	Tom Proudfoot	1973		
306	* Gilbert Little	1974	1974	
307	Donald K. Walker	1980		
308	Dan Doherty	1986		
309	John Ward	1983		
310	Lena M. Carter	1983		
311	G.F. Burton	1983		
312	David Sibbald	1983		
313	Alastair MacNee	1983		
314	Robert Carson	1983	1983	
315	Robert Paton	1983	1983	
		1993		
316	* James H. Clark	1983		1983
317	* Grahame Nicoll	1984	1993	
		1997		
318	* J. Michael Taylor	1984		
319	K.P. Whyte	1984	1987	1987
320	John Wild	1984		
321	Alister Sword	1984	1988	1991
322	David Trainer	1981		
323	* H.W.F. Taylor	1976		
324	G.P. Deasy	1979		
325	* Neil Mather	1980		
326	Chris P. Jackson	1981		
327	R. Stewart Logan	1981	1981	1981
		1984	1984	1985
		1987	1987	1987
		1989	1989	
		1990	1990	
		1992	1992	
		1994	1994	
		1996	1996	
328	A.G. Hayley	1981	1981	1981
		1986	1986	
		1989		
329	Donald Lamont	1981	1981	
		1989		
		1995		
330	Hugh Lyons	1982	1983	1965
331	James Gallacher	1982		
332	Stephen Bates	1983		
333	Jack Winters	1983		
334	Garry McCreath	1984	1986	
		1992		
335	Graeme Carracher	1984		
336	Stephen T. Ramsden	1984		1989
		1993		
		1996		
337	Robert Rae	1984		
		1992		
338	Margaret Rae	1984		
		1992		
339	** Pamela Cain	1977		
340	Eric L. Furness	1984		
341	J.F. Fedo	1984		
342	Alice Simons	1984		
343	Tim Simons	1984		
344	Iain K. MacLeod	1984		
345	John Burdin	1984		
346	John L. Brown	1980		1990
		1985		
		1990		
347	Howard Ashton	1984		
348	Ken David	1984		
349	David C. Culshaw	1984		
350	Ian D. Clark	1984		
351	George Keeping	1984		
352	John Havard	1984	1991	1991
353	Robert H. Morton	1984		
354	George J. Borland	1984	1984	
		1989		
355	Ian Milne	1984		
356	Janet A. Davies	1984		

† There is an explanation for this entry in the 1983 edition of the SMC Journal

	Name	Munros	Tops	Furths		Name	Munros	Tops	Furths
357	John D. Davies	1984			407	David S. Simpson	1985		
358	Michael B. Slater	1984	1987	1987	408	Ken Falconer	1985		
		1988			409	J. Brewster	1985		
		1990					1995		
359	Alf Barnard	1984			410	Alan MacIntyre	1985	1985	
360	Charles Alexander	1984			411	William S. Lockyer . . .	1985		
361	K.W. Deas	1984		1991	412	Len Cerajowski	1985		
362	John F. Robinson	1982			413	Lorna Liddell	1985		
363	David Binns	1982			414	Brenda Jones	1985		
364	Brian Dick	1984			415	Ray Peel	1985		
		1992			416	David MacFadzean . . .	1985		
365	* Nigel M. Suess	1984	1988	1986	417	Paul Morgan	1985		
366	D. Ashton	1984			418	Barbara Morgan	1985		
367	Gillian Mather	1984			419	Gareth Morgan	1985		
368	W.M. Morrison	1984			420	Caroline Morgan	1985		
369	J.M. Souness	1984			421	* Alex G. Cousins	1985		
370	A.R. Sutherland	1984			422	George Wostenholme .	1985	1985	
371	Helen Donnelly	1984			423	Catherine McVean	1985		
372	* Donald J. Bennet	1984			424	Kenneth McVean	1985		
373	J.N.S. Neill	1984			425	Eleanor Christie	1985		
374	** Pat Ransley	1984			426	James MacKay	1985		
375	Robert H. MacDonald .	1984		1989	427	James Macrae	1985		
		1987			428	Graham R. Wyllie	1985		
		1990			429	Brian D. Souness	1985		
		1992			430	Ian R.F. Ross	1985		
		1995			431	Mark McCann	1985		1990
376	Simon Stewart	1984			432	Arthur C. Dickie	1985		
377	Neil Stewart	1984			433	* Brian Shackleton	1985		
378	William A. Bain	1984			434	David Matthews	1985	1985	
379	John G. Wallace	1984			435	Margaret K. Foster . . .	1985	1985	1986
380	Tom Stewart	1984			436	James D. Foster	1985	1985	1986
381	J.T. Robertson	1984			437	Bill Barlow	1985		
382	Roger Stonebridge	1985			438	Dorothy Batchelor	1985		
383	* Martin Moran	1985			439	Leslie A. Knight	1985		
384	J.M. Gear	1985			440	William S. Milne	1980	1981	
		1996			441	Brian G. Coull	1981		
385	John Peacegood	1980			442	Fraser R. Simpson	1983		
386	William MacKenzie . . .	1982			443	Peter Keillar	1985		
387	Richard Fuller	1984	1984	1985	444	Alexander Petrie	1982		
388	Steven Fuller	1984	1984	1985	445	Alan Ingram	1986		1989
389	Jane O'Donovan	1985			446	Alan Wilson	1985		
390	May Grant	1985			447	Beryl Leatherland	1985	1986	
391	Brenda D. Griffin	1985	1989		448	Tom Leatherland	1985	1986	
392	Mervyn Griffin	1985	1989		449	Sheila Murray	1985		
393	Jennifer M. Irving	1985			450	Gordon M. McAndrew	1986		
394	Joe Stewart	1985			451	Craig Caldwell	1984		
395	Ron Payne	1985					1985		
396	Alan Douglas	1985			452	Ann Bowker	1986	1986	1983
397	Isobel M. Hughes	1985			453	Walter M. Stephen	1986	1989	1988
398	Ian S. Hughes	1985			454	John G. Crummett	1986	1986	1981
399	Ian T. Stalker	1985			455	Laurence A. Rudkin . .	1986	1991	1989
400	Roger Chapman	1985			456	Dave Atkins	1986		
401	John Limbach	1985	1986		457	James A. Bloomer	1986		1986
402	Allan MacLeod	1985	1985		458	Fiona Cameron	1986		
403	Sandra Gordon	1985			459	Alan J. Henderson	1986		
404	Douglas Gordon	1985			460	C.W. Pringle	1986	1986	
405	Donald D. MacAusland	1985			461	Ian V. Douglas	1986	1986	
406	Peter R. Mills	1985			462	Roger Booth	1986		

	Name	Munros	Tops	Furths		Name	Munros	Tops	Furths
463	* William R. Morrison	1986	1986		515	Dawn Strickland	1987		1987
		1992			516	M.R. Lees	1987		
464	J.G. Cooney	1986	1986	1986	517	W.A.B. Kerr	1986		1986
465	Jim Barton	1986		1978	518	John Wyllie	1980		1991
466	James Byers	1986		1989	519	Ashley Cooper	1986	1986	1986
467	Ronald E. Dow	1986			520	Chris W. Lilley	1987		
468	Trixie Robertson	1986			521	Robert T. Walker	1987		
469	Nick Kempe	1986			522	David Smith	1985		
470	Graeme Cornwallis ...	1986			523	Jacqueline Brodie	1986	1986	
471	Francis H. Scott	1986	1986	1986	524	Nigel F. Toothill	1986	1986	
472	Stephen E. Powell	1986	1986	1986	525	John B. McKay	1986		1986
473	Kathleen Slocum	1986			526	R.J. Buchan	1987		
474	Stephen Scobie	1986			527	Ian C. McCallum	1987		
475	Ronald Torano	1986			528	William Harrower	1987		
476	Margaret MacLennan .	1986			529	J.A. Baird	1987		
477	Mark Kirby	1986			530	Julian Lines	1987		
478	Jack R.F. Burt	1986			531	Coll Findlay	1987		
479	James S. Bell	1986			532	Sandy Donald	1987		1988
480	Andrew Finnimore ...	1986	1986	1986	533	Leon D. Firth	1987		1987
481	Stephen Poulton	1986			534	Peter Warburton	1987		
482	Shirley Poulton	1986			535	John Town	1987		
483	Peter Ilieve	1986	1991	1991	536	John Crombie	1987		
484	Jeremy Wray	1986			537	J.A. Scott	1986		
485	* Graeme Morrison	1986			538	William Harkins	1987		1989
486	Peter Bellarby	1987	1987	1987	539	Diana J. Harkins	1987		1989
487	Robert Ward	1987			540	Jim Teesdale	1974		
488	Ian Leighton	1978		1978	541	Jim Chalmers	1985		1983
		1984			542	Margaret Cadenhead .	1986		
489	Mike West	1987			543	Charles Cadenhead ...	1986		
490	Neville Kale	1987			544	Janet Sutcliffe	1987	1990	1981
491	Jane Kale	1987			545	Geoff Eccles	1987		1987
492	Andrew Kale	1987			546	George R. Craig	1987		1987
493	David Kale	1987			547	Andrew Mackin	1987		
494	Terry Butterworth	1987			548	Kenneth Layhe	1987		1981
495	David S. Adam	1987			549	Elizabeth Layhe	1987		1981
496	** Edna Stewart	1987			550	Jim Montgomery	1987	1987	
497	* J. Stanley Stewart	1987			551	Keith Relzin	1987		
498	Douglas Wylie	1987		1989	552	John Cameron	1987		
499	Vaughan Hammond ..	1987			553	Uinseann MacEoin ...	1987		
500	Graham S. Wilson	1987	1987		554	Edward A. Dick	1987		
501	Iain Crosbie	1987	1987		555	Robin Howie	1982	1984	1987
502	Ian R. Young	1987	1987				1984	1987	
503	Robert A. Grant	1976					1987	1992	
		1986					1990		
504	John Speakman	1980					1992		
505	Bobby Grenfell	1980					1995		
506	Crystal Brown	1980			556	Malcolm Lamont	1986		
507	Stewart Brown	1980			557	Georgie McCrae	1987		
508	David Alexander	1986			558	James V. Mathieson ...	1986		
509	Alex M. Drummond ..	1987			559	James Tarvet	1987		
510	D.H.W. Taylor	1987		1989	560	Thomas H. MacEwan .	1986		
511	M.C. Davenport	1981			561	Michael A. Taylor	1987		
512	Timothy C. Outten ...	1986			562	Jill Evans	1987		
513	Raymond G. Porter ...	1987			563	William S. Gray	1988		
514	David H. Purser	1986	1987	1991	564	Brian Covell	1987		
		1991			565	Alexander Baxter	1988		
		1995			566	Fiona Torbet	1987		

Name	Munros	Tops	Furths		Name	Munros	Tops	Furths
567	Ian A. Wallace	1987			622	Robert Wilson	1988		1995
568	Charles L. Scott	1987			623	Maurice Watson	1988		1991
569	G. Collinson	1988					1994		
570	Jack Veitch	1988			624	John C.S. Vaughan	1988		
571	Douglas Rennie	1988					1993		
572	Douglas M. Fraser	1988			625	Katherine Jamieson ...	1988		1987
573	Tommy Hepburn	1988	1988		626	Peter H. Nall	1988		
574	F.G. North	1988			627	Neil D. Robertson	1988		
575	John Blair-Fish	1988			628	* John M. Burley	1988		
576	Donald Shiach	1988			629	Kay Simpson	1988		
577	James R. Brocklehurst .	1988			630	C. Clinch	1988	1988	1988
578	G.D. Moylan	1988			631	W.A. Simpson	1988		
579	Cyril M. Smith	1988			632	John Adams	1988		
580	John Green	1988	1989	1989	633	John Harrison	1986		
581	Keith Skeens	1988			634	Bill Miller	1987		1991
582	Dave Cording	1988			635	Maggie Miller	1987		
583	Alec M. Synge	1988	1988		636	John Allen	1988		1996
584	David R. Bird	1988			637	Roger D.L. Guthrie ...	1989		
585	** Helen Steven	1988			638	Frank W. Garforth	1989		
586	Marcus H. Ward	1988			639	** Ann Wakeling	1989		
587	Harry Robinson	1988			640	Matthew Bramley	1989		1990
588	David W. Eadington ..	1988			641	William Nimmo Smith	1989		
589	T.E. Edwards	1988			642	Allan R. Neil	1989	1989	
590	H. Gordon Adshead ..	1987	1988	1987	643	David E. Purchase	1989		1989
591	Fraser Hamilton	1988		1988	644	Jack Ashcroft	1989		
592	David F Geddes	1988	1989	1991	645	Darrell Pickles	1989		
593	W. Brian Carlyle	1988			646	* Iain H. Ogilvie	1989		
594	Andrew C.B. Dempster	1988			647	William R. Mowbray ..	1989		
595	Stewart Lang	1988	1988		648	James Binnie	1989	1989	1990
596	Brian R. Johnson	1988			649	James Brown	1989		
597	Andrew Kerr	1988			650	Paul Riley	1989		
598	John Gibson	1988			651	Innes Mitchell	1989		1990
599	James Taylor	1988			652	Leslie B. Aird	1989		
		1994			653	Irene D. Aird	1989		
600	Hugh R. Shercliff	1987			654	W. Douglas Allan	1989		1990
601	Christopher Allan	1988			655	David McGill	1989		
602	Irvin John Cushnie ...	1988	1988	1991	656	N. Keith Rutter	1989		
603	Kay Turner	1988		1989	657	Kenneth Brown	1989		
604	Nev Wiseman	1988			658	Douglas A. Anderson .	1989		
605	Mal Newlyn	1988			659	David A. Smith	1989		
606	Ian Holland	1988			660	Paul Gillies	1989		
607	Mark Elsegood	1988			661	* Matthew G.D. Shaw ..	1989	1989	1989
608	Alasdair MacLennan ..	1988			662	John Barker	1989		1991
609	Seonaid Wood	1988			663	Ruth Barker	1989		1991
610	Dairena Gaffney	1988			664	Elsie Middlemiss	1989		
611	* Roger D. Everett	1988			665	John Coop	1989		
612	Ian M. Williams	1986			666	See Footnote†			
	....	1988			667	Jim F. Stuart	1989	1989	
613	* Andrew Tibbs	1988			668	Ian Henderson	1989		1989
614	George Bruce	1987			669	Anne M. Marker	1989		
615	** Jadwiga Kowalska	1987			670	Willis B. Marker	1989		
616	** Anne Murray	1987			671	Mike Paterson	1989		
617	Roger Owen	1988			672	Brian McKay	1986		
618	Hamish H. Johnston ..	1988			673	Robert Dale	1988	1989	
619	A. Kinghorn	1988			674	C. Andrew Scott	1988		
620	Norrie Muir	1988			675	Geoff Skeaping	1988		
621	Alistair Milner	1988			676	James G. Bell	1988	1988	1990

† There is an explanation for this entry in the 1983 edition of the SMC Journal

	Name	Munros	Tops	Furths		Name	Munros	Tops	Furths
677	Anne Bennet	1989			734	Bertha Rostron	1990		
678	Stuart Benn	1989	1989	1990	735	James W. Rostron	1990		
679	Peter Williams	1989			736	Neil Clough	1990		
680	Garth Broomfield	1989			737	Graham North	1990		
681	George Graham	1989			738	William Paterson	1990		
682	Iain M. Brown	1989		1989	739	Ian J.B. Murray	1990		
683	S.J. Henderson	1989			740	Dan A. Carmichael	1990		
684	Nigel K. Saxton	1989			741	Andrew R. Kilbride	1990		
685	Derek G. Sime	1989	1989	1990	742	Kenneth Pierce	1990		1990
686	David McAvoy	1989			743	Ian Turner	1990		
687	Graham Tutton	1989			744	W. John Webb	1990		
688	Anne H. Lindsay	1989			745	John Barrett	1990		1990
689	Ian A. Jones	1989		1990	746	James C. Waterton	1990		
690	* David J. Broadhead	1989			747	Leonard J. Thomson	1990		
691	Roderick L.G. Brodie	1989			748	Raymond Horner	1990		
692	Chris R. Peart	1989			749	Marion Faulds	1990		
693	Arnold T. Morrison	1989			750	David A. Henderson	1990		
694	Donald F. Maclean	1989			751	Gerry Bowes	1990	1990	1987
695	John C.M. Blair	1989			752	Philip Massey	1990	1990	1987
696	J. Michael Barron	1989			753	Andrew Brown	1990		
697	Michael Thomson	1989			754	Charles R. Haigh	1988		
698	John M. Uytman	1989	1989		755	J. Stanley Roberts	1988		
699	Cherie Chapman	1989	1989		756	W.G.C. Lamb	1988		
700	Terry McDonagh	1989	1990		757	J.W. Quine	1990		
701	Archie Given	1989			758	John Norrie	1990		
702	Ellen Sanderson	1989			759	Alistair M. Beeley	1990	1990	1990
703	J. Kenneth Oakley	1989			760	David M. Clark	1990		
704	Peter Lomax Yates	1989	1989		761	Chris B. Cormack	1990	1990	
705	John S. Alexander	1989			762	Tommy Kilpatrick	1988	1989	
706	Michael W. Kelly	1989	1989		763	Brian D. Curle	1990	1991	1991
707	Robert F. Gibson	1989			764	Andrew S. Templeton	1990	1991	
708	Michael Milmoe	1989	1989		765	Andrew Grundy	1990		
709	James W. Stewart	1989	1989		766	John Leftley	1990		
710	Robert L. Cameron	1989			767	Dee Lacy	1990		
711	Alex A. Hanton	1989			768	Tony Rogers	1990		
712	Richard G. Ross	1989			769	Tony Taylor	1990	1990	
713	Peter Kemp	1989			770	Alexander Laing	1990		
714	George McCall	1989			771	John Russell	1990		
715	William Russell	1989			772	Robert D. Worth	1990		
716	* Neil Bielby	1989	1989		773	George G. Sim	1990	1990	
717	H.H. Tsai	1989			774	Andrew Murdoch	1990		
718	Edgar Emmerson	1989	1990		775	Peter Malone	1990	1995	
719	Chris Smith	1989			776	D. Nairne Gray	1990		
720	Stewart Love	1989			777	Hugh Symonds	1990		
721	Jack Greenway	1990			778	J.E.R. Ullock	1990		
722	Dave Duff	1990			779	James Haddow	1990		
723	V.R. Davey	1990			780	Eddie Sutherland	1990 1996	1996	1991
724	John R. Davis	1990							
725	Eric Campbell Knox	1990			781	Norma Sutherland	1990 1996		1991
726	Robert MacCallum	1990							
727	Kenneth Critchley	1990			782	Guy Semple	1990		
728	William R. Maltman	1989	1991		783	Frances A. Wilson	1990		
729	Bill Lackenby	1990			784	Peter Wilson	1990		
730	Peter Ellis	1990		1990	785	John W. Richardson	1990	1990	
731	Paul Russell	1990			786	Jonathan de Ferranti	1990		
732	* B.E.H. Maden	1990	1991		787	Neil Williams	1990		
733	Duncan L. Murray	1990			788	Klaus Schwartz	1990	1990	

	Name	Munros	Tops	Furths
789	Malcolm J.J. Arney ...	1990		
790	James D. Gentles	1990		
791	Bethan Steele	1990	1990	1992
792	David Steele	1990	1990	1992
793	Andrew M. McCosh ..	1990		
794	Iain A.J. Coker	1990		1973
795	Dennis Alexander	1990		
796	David Stallard	1990		
797	Alexander MacCalman	1990		
798	Margaret Graham	1990		
799	Fraser Brown	1988		
800	Harold R.E. Clarke ...	1987	1990	
801	Bertram W. Logie	1990	1990	
802	Neil G. Spalding	1990		
803	Andrew J. Matheson ..	1990		
804	Hugh Ormiston	1986	1989	
805	Colin G. Powell	1989		
806	Ben Thompson	1989	1989	1991
807	D.C. Hunter Scott	1990		
808	John Barnard	1990		1990
809	David Jones	1990		
810	Martin Wilson	1990		
811	W. Shaw Murray	1987		
812	Stuart Clements	1990		
813	Katharine Weyman ...	1990		
814	Dennis J.W. Usher	1990		
815	Andrew R. Beckett ...	1990		
816	Rob H. Woodall	1990	1995	1990
817	John Patrick	1990		
818	Peter A. Dawes	1987	1987	
819	Fergus Macbeth	1987		
820	** Molly Johnstone	1990		
821	Alasdair M. Dutton ...	1990		
822	Rory N. Dutton	1990		
823	Jack Sugden	1990		
824	Harry E.M. Dott	1990		
825	Bernard Smith	1990		
826	Ian Young	1990		
827	Pete Craven	1990		
828	Gordon Colthart	1990		
829	Connie McCreath	1990		
830	J. Peter S. Gray	1990		
831	William Mackenzie ...	1982		
832	Les Rothnie	1990	1990	
833	Jonathan D. Groves ...	1990		1992
834	Harry A. Minns	1967		1967
835	Alfred Slack	1950		
836	Margaret Guy	1990		
837	Allan Boath	1990		
838	Bruce G. Lindsay	1990		
839	Gordon F. Lindsay	1990		
840	Ian S. Robertson	1990	1990	
841	Richard James Revill ..	1989		
842	Allan Downie	1990		
843	Angela Soper	1991		
844	Michael A. Underwood	1990		
845	Marjorie Powrie	1990		
846	Arthur C. Custance ...	1988		
847	John Philip Hansford .	1989 1992	1991	1992
848	Hew B. Fraser	1990		
849	John M. Knight	1990		
850	A.J. Muston	1990		
851	H.G. Sillitoe	1988		
852	Nick Picozzi	1990		
853	Robert F. McKay	1991		
854	Douglas McHardy	1990		
855	Alan W. Patrick	1990		
856	Ivan Young	1983	1989	1989
857	Peter Norman Hughill	1990		1990
858	Iain M. Gilbert	1991		
859	Ivan McA.G. Smith ...	1991	1991	1993
860	Peter Sellers	1991	1991	1981
861	Sylvia Sellers	1991	1991	1981
862	Tom Anderson	1991		1991
863	Iain D. Shepherd	1991		
864	Kenneth Fraser	1984		
865	Tibbie Fraser	1984		
866	David A. Kydd	1991		
867	Alan Gott	1989	1991	1992
868	Alastair Grant	1991	1991	
869	Stephen J. Hagan	1991		
870	John Wainwright	1991		
871	Robert Gordon Buchan	1991		
872	William Knowles	1991		
873	Wolf Gruellich	1991		
874	J.S. Huddart	1991		
875	Mark Sinclair	1991		
876	Elsa Yates	1991 1996		1991
877	Robert W. Yates	1991 1996		1991
878	Pat Eady	1991		
879	Ken Parnham	1991		
880	David Rhodes	1991		1990
881	Geoffrey D. Carter	1991	1993	
882	Irene Cook	1991		1991
883	Ken G. Telfer	1991		
884	Mark Wrightam	1991		
885	Gibson McGeachie ...	1991		
886	Lynne McGeachie	1991		
887	George D. Ferguson ..	1991		
888	John Hetherington	1985		
889	Adrienne Simcock	1991		
890	Peter Simcock	1991		
891	Lynn M. Youngs	1990		
892	Jamie F. Stone	1991		
893	Patricia A. Horner	1991		
894	Douglas Marr	1991		
895	Anthony J. Sanford ...	1991		
896	Linda Moxey-Sanford .	1991		
897	Derek Blackburn	1991		
898	Jack Escritt	1991	1991	
899	John Nelson	1991		

Name	Munros	Tops	Furths		Name	Munros	Tops	Furths
900 Ann Landers	1991				957 George Herraghty	1991		
901 Pedro Landers	1991				958 Dave Foy	1991		
902 Robin W. Dempsey	1991				959 Mike Dixon	1991		
903 * Christopher M. Huntley	1991				960 Stephen Dunn	1991		
904 Martin J.B. Lowe	1991				961 Ron A. Henderson	1991		
905 Richard P. Wood	1991	1991			962 Bob Connell	1991	1991	1994
906 Mike Futty	1991				963 Howard A. Sowerby	1991	1991	1994
907 Alun Gwyn Thomas	1991				964 Thomas Cull	1991		
908 Elizabeth M. Thomas	1991				965 Ian Cumming	1991		
909 Ian R. Mitchell	1991				966 J.R. Anderson	1991		
910 Eric Drew	1991	1992	1993		967 Andy Sargeant	1991		
911 Derek R. Snowdon	1991		1992		968 Derek Finlay	1991		
912 Alan Chow	1991				969 Jack Harrison	1991		
913 Cameron McNeish	1991				970 Robert Alexander	1991		
914 William F. Buchanan	1991				971 Brian Gardiner	1991		
915 Marian P. Elmes	1991				972 William Redford	1991		
916 John Neave	1991				973 James Entwistle	1991		
917 John Baxter	1991				974 G.A.C. Binnie	1986		
918 Peter Lockett	1991				975 Alan R. Munro	1991	1991	
919 Michael Gairey	1991				976 Denis E. O'N. Johnson	1989		
920 Colin A. Simpson	1991				977 Dave Myles	1986		
921 Gordon Keir	1991				978 Stan Stewart	1986		
922 Irene I. Clark	1991				979 Alan D. Armstrong	1991		
923 Peter Jack	1989				980 Brian J. MacDonald	1991		
924 J. Alan Fyfe	1991				981 Ian Dargie	1991		
925 Peter Newley	1991				982 John A. Stark	1991		
926 ** Heather King	1991				983 John Inglis	1988		
927 Dorothy Spencer	1991	1991			984 Andrew McD. Craig	1990		
928 Graham J. Gainey	1991				985 John Pownall	1991		
929 Goff Cantley	1984				986 Elizabeth S. Heath	1990		
930 Judy Cantley	1984				987 William Watson	1991		
931 James G. Benson	1991				988 Alan M. Henry	1991		
932 Gerald Orchard	1990	1991	1991		989 W.A. Simpson	1988		
933 Alan J.L. Rodger	1990				990 Brian Gardiner	1991		
934 Peter Collin	1991				991 R. Keith Bootle	1991		
935 Dave Crawford	1990				992 Patrick M. Leahy	1991	1991	1995
936 Bob Sharp	1991				993 Stuart F. Ingham	1991		
937 Peter N. Jones	1991				994 Stuart Irvine	1991		
938 John Whyte Thomson	1991				995 Graham H. Howie	1988		
939 Frank Morris	1984				996 Donald C. McCallum	1991		
940 Pamela Harper	1987				997 Lindsay D. Munro	1991		
941 Wal Clark	1990				998 Roderick C. Munro	1991		
942 Tony Heath	1991				999 Robert B. Robertson	1988	1991	1993
943 Bruce Hassell	1989	1989	1990		1000 Angus K. Robertson	1989		
944 John Starbuck	1991	1991			1001 R. Bramley	1991		
945 Jennie Boulter	1990				1002 Derrick Harman	1991		
946 Peter Boulter	1990				1003 Charlie Ramsay	1991		
947 Anne R. Robson	1991				1004 Teresa Lingard	1990		
948 Ben Bate	1984				1005 Tom M. Millar	1991		
949 Doug Allan	1984				1006 Allan Bantick	1991		
950 Cliff White	1984				1007 Paul Cassell	1989		
951 Andy Harrison	1991				1008 Nigel Orr	1991		
952 Iain Smith	1991				1009 Cedric Y. Harben	1991		
953 David N. Gothard	1991				1010 David Lowther	1991		
954 Robert B. Gunn	1991	1991			1011 Mary McIlroy	1991		
955 Joyce C. Stephens	1991	1991			1012 John Barrowman	1990		
956 Neil Heaton	1991				1013 A.G.F. Aitken	1992		

	Name	Munros	Tops	Furths
1014	Anthony Wragg	1991		
1015	W.D. Borthwick	1991		
1016	Clifford Simpson	1992		
1017	Janet Hartley	1991		
1018	Roger Hill-Cottingham	1991		
1019	James I.R. Tees	1992		
1020	Jane Wainwright	1992		
1021	Haydn Thomas	1992		1992
1022	T. Kenneth Taylor	1989		
1023	W. Alan Fortune	1992		
1024	Martin Douglas Kydd	1992		
1025	Peter Douglas Buck	1992		
1026	William Platts	1992		
1027	Gordon Taylor	1992		
1028	Barbara Redford	1992		
1029	Andrew Naylor	1992		
1030	James G. Halkett	1992		
1031	* Iain A. MacLeod	1992		
1032	Eric Ivison	1992		
1033	Fred Goodyear	1992		
1034	Cyril Henderson	1986		
1035	Paul M. Child	1992		
1036	Mick Biggin	1992		
1037	Elda Morrison	1992		
1038	Alexander J. Sim	1992		
1039	Iain K. Mitchell	1992		
1040	James Gordon	1992		
1041	Dave Park	1992		
1042	Rod Harrison	1992	1992	
1043	Mark Douglas	1992	1992	
1044	Peter Bailey	1992		1995
1045	Steve Fallon	1992	1993	
		1994		
		1995		
1046	David Todd	1992		
1047	G. Watters	1992		1992
1048	John C.B. Kelly	1992	1992	1992
1049	Richard Gatehouse	1992		
1050	Frank A. Mellor	1992	1992	
1051	Jennifer Mellor	1992	1992	
1052	David C. Sievewright	1992		
1053	Matthew Glover	1991		
1054	David Hoyle	1992		
1055	Roger Coates Smith	1992		
1056	Simon Bolam	1992		
1057	William A. McKenzie	1992		
1058	A.G. Brooks	1991	1991	
1059	Alexander R.B. Taylor	1992		
1060	Paul K. Williamson	1985		
1061	Bill Faimaner	1992		
1062	Susan M. Miller	1992		
1063	John B. Jones	1992		
1064	John Nuttal	1992		
1065	Veronica Gray	1992		
1066	John Peel	1992		
1067	Frank Malloy	1992		
1068	John B. Mitchell	1992		
1069	Alistair J. Montgomery	1992		
1070	* Dave Dawson	1992		
1071	Hedly Horsler	1992		
1072	Valerie Horsler	1992		
1073	Ian B. Pyper	1992		
1074	M.J. Poznanski	1992		
1075	Sandy Wood	1992		
1076	A.W. Ridler	1992		
1077	David Murray	1992		
1078	Patricia J. Brodie	1992		
1079	Patrick J. Temporal	1992	1992	
1080	Jeffrey C. Stone	1992		
1081	Jim Wright	1992		
1082	John B. McKeown	1992		
1083	James W. Marshall	1992		
1084**	Meryl Marshall	1992		
1085	C.D. Evans	1992	1992	
1086	James Anthony Fenner	1992		
1087	Tim Pickles	1992		1996
1088	James Dignall	1992	1992	
1089	Penny Barron	1992		
1090	Christina B. Morton	1992		
1091	John C. Chappell	1992		
1092	Alan Fielding	1992		
1093	Terry Barclay	1992	1992	
1094	Calum N. White	1992	1992	
1095	Brendan J. Hamill	1992		
1096	Margaret Barnett	1992		
1097	Christopher Barclay	1992		
1098	Christopher J. Angwin	1992		
1099	Nancy Thomson	1992		
1100	Christopher Bantoft	1992		
1101	David I. Harris	1992		
1102	Richard Wiles	1992		1992
1103	Mark Rigby	1992		
1104	Peter Reynolds	1992		
1105	Duncan Hunter	1992		
1106	Pamela L. Clark	1992		
1107	Margaret Hall	1992		
1108	George S. Deas	1992		1994
1109	Graham Benny	1992		
1110	Christopher G. Butcher	1992		
1111	Brian Ewing	1992		
1112	Denis A. Oidgeon	1992		
1113	Kenneth Oliver	1989	1991	
		1996		
1114	Colin H. McNab	1992		
1115	Raymond Shaw	1992		
1116	Nettie Geddes	1992		
1117	Jim Cunningham	1992		
1118	Margaret Riley	1992		
1119	Ronald H. MacGregor	1992		1995
1120	Andy Murphy	1992		
1121	W.H. Smith	1992		
1122	Callum Sword	1992		
1123	Marjorie Langmuir	1992		
1124	Geraldine Newlyn	1992		

	Name	Munros	Tops	Furths		Name	Munros	Tops	Furths
1125	John Hendry	1992			1182	Chris J. Upson	1993		
1126	Margaret Hendry	1992			1183	Mike Fry	1993		
1127	Herbert S. Clarke	1992			1184	John B. Matthews	1993		
1128	Marion K.W. Clarke	1992			1185	John Johnson	1993		
1129	Betty Hamer	1992			1186	Peter Lincoln	1993		1993
1130	John Hamer	1992			1187	Bill J. Bowers	1993		
1131	Susan Howard	1989			1188**	Karin Froebel	1993		
1132	Paul Howard	1990			1189	J.S. Burrows	1993		
1133	Wattie Ramage	1992			1190	Donald Rich	1993		
1134	Allan Kernohan	1992			1191	David Slater	1993		
1135	James C. Ashby	1992		1996	1192	David Unsworth	1993	1995	1994
1136	Ian Dickson	1992					1996		
1137	Mike Weedon	1989			1193	Linda Aitken	1993		
1138	Terence M. O'Brien	1992	1992	1992	1194	William Aitken	1993		
1139	Gordon McI. Bruce	1992			1195	Mary Hepburn	1993		
1140	Norman F. Hazelton	1992			1196	Alan H. Holmes	1993	1993	1993
1141	Rory Gibson	1992			1197	George W. Morl	1993	1993	1993
1142	Andrew Johnston	1992			1198	John Martin	1993		
1143	Stephen P. Evans	1993	1997		1199	Roy D. Williamson	1993		
1144	Christopher Dyos	1993			1200	Margaret L. Brooker	1993		
1145 *	W.H. Jones	1993		1993	1201	David Baker	1993	1993	1993
1146	G. Dobrzynski	1993		1981	1202	Kenneth Brown	1993		
1147	Robert Robertson	1993			1203	Jean M. Gayton	1993	1993	
1148	Colin Wilson	1993			1204	Robert J. Tait	1993	1993	
1149	David Thatcher	1993			1205	Carole Baillie	1993		
1150	David I. Nixon	1993			1206	Michael Baillie	1993		
1151	David Waterson	1993			1207	David Jaap	1993		
1152	R.M. Kerry	1993			1208	William Sinclair	1993	1993	
1153	Alan Keegan	1993			1209	Carl Morris	1993		
1154	Mike J. Westmorland	1993			1210	Jack Berryman	1993		
1155	Rita Norrie	1993			1211	Charlie Sutherland	1993		
1156	John T. MacLeod	1993			1212	David Haworth	1993		
1157	David Douglas	1993			1213	Andy Whitehead	1992		
1158	C. Knowles	1993			1214	Dorothy Wilson	1993		1988
1159	Margaret Russell	1993			1215	Maurice E. Twentyman	1993		
1160	Peter Collins	1993		1994	1216	Ian Donnelly	1993		
1161	Eric Cook	1993		1993	1217	Joyce Cosby	1993		
1162	Sandra Stead	1993			1218	Brian Cosby	1993		
1163	Mike Heckford	1993			1219	Valerie Moffat	1993	1993	1993
1164	Brian D. Panton	1993			1220	Andrew Moffat	1993	1993	1993
1165	Charles M. Mackay	1993			1221	John F. Wilson	1993		
1166	Iona Bowden	1993			1222	Gilmour Strang	1992	1992	
1167	Roy Bowden	1993			1223	Chris Lee	1993		
1168	Stephen Crabbe	1992			1224	Iain S. MacDuffie	1993		
1169	Garth B. Fenton	1993			1225	Jeff J. Burgum	1993	1993	1993
1170	Elaine S. Fenton	1993			1226	W.P. Maxwell	1993		
1171	Harry Kirkwood	1993			1227	Martin C. Powell	1993		
1172	Jeanette Barr	1993			1228	Heather Ogorman	1993		
1173	Bernhard Lapp	1993			1229	John Holder	1993		
1174	Ian Collie	1993			1230	Iain King	1993		
1175	W.R. Shipway	1993			1231	James A.D. Convery	1993		
1176	Peter Drummond	1993			1232	Levan Bryn	1992		
1177	Peter McPhail	1993	1993	1993	1233	Arthur W. Ager	1993		
1178	Christine E. Tulloch	1993			1234	Dave Stanford	1993		
1179	David I. Hill	1993			1235	Winifred Graham	1992		
1180	Dave Peck	1993			1236	Robert L. Plumb	1993		
1181	Theodore Cadoux	1993			1237	Heather Coakes	1993		

	Name	Munros	Tops	Furths		Name	Munros	Tops	Furths
1238	R.J. Anderson	1993			1295	William Beattie	1994		
1239	Roger C. Henshaw	1993			1296	Alex D. Grant	1994		
1240	Michael Atkins	1993			1297	David W. Duncan	1994		
1241	John G. Carrie	1993			1298	Graham T. Illing	1994		
1242	James L.W. Baxter	1993			1299	Michael McLaggan	1994		
1243	Richard T. Griffiths	1993			1300	W. Harvey Condliffe	1994		
1244	Duncan Foster	1993			1301	Keith Moody	1994		
1245	Norman Carrington	1993			1302	Roberta Taylor	1994		
1246	Janey Brogan	1993			1303	Charles M. Taylor	1994		
1247	David Brogan	1993			1304	Eiona Conacher	1994		
1248	S.G. Singleton	1993			1305	John G. Aird	1994		
1249	Morag Wylie	1993			1306	Barbara V. Watson	1994		
1250	Gordon Hopper	1993			1307	Celia Goodman	1994		
1251	Innes Sutherland	1993			1308	Audrey M. Litterick	1994		
1252	Frank Martin	1993			1309	Charles Leggat	1994		
1253	Christine M. May	1993			1310	Fiona Wallace	1994		
1254	Timothy J. May	1993			1311	Terry A. Fuller	1994	1994	1994
1255	Una S. Woods	1993			1312	Paul Krebs	1992		
1256	Keith Yates	1993			1313	Michael J. Smyth	1994		
1257	David A. Cryle	1993		1993	1314	Neil S. Dunford	1994		
1258	Michael Hanlin	1993			1315	J.H. Calvert	1994		
1259	Ian Gray	1993			1316	N.S. Hunnisett	1994		
1260	Brian Cowie	1993			1317	Leigh Sayers	1994		
1261	L. Hunter	1993			1318	Catherine S. Gray	1994		
1262	* Tom W. Boyd	1993			1319	Robert P. Gray	1994		
1263	Michael J. Donaldson	1993			1320	Robert W. Gray	1994		
1264	Iain B. McIntosh	1992			1321	Ian Forder	1994		
1265	Dorothy McLean	1993			1322	Ken A. Butcher	1994		1994
1266	Joan Wilson	1993			1323	Frankie S. Cumming	1994		
1267	Dave Kennedy	1993			1324	Ian McVittie	1994		
1268	Brian Welsh	1993			1325	Charles G. Elliott	1994		
1269	Aida Sutton	1992			1326	Ben S. Cooper	1994		
1270	Alan Sutton	1992			1327	Ian J. Brownell	1994		
1271	Tony M. Deall	1994			1328	Raymond Hay	1994		
1272	Bill R. Johncocks	1994			1329	Gillian M. Green	1994	1994	
1273	G. Fraser Ritchie	1993			1330	John E. Green	1994	1994	
1274	Peter Swindells	1994			1331	John Mackay	1994	1994	
1275	David Smith	1994			1332	Fraser MacGillivray	1994		
1276	Alan Findlay	1993			1333	Kenneth W.C. Stewart	1994		
1277	John M. Barrett	1993			1334	Alex K. Kirk	1994		
1278	Allan P. Lees	1993			1335	J.P. Fish	1994		
1279	Nigel P. Morters	1994			1336	F. David Smith	1994		1996
1280	Adrian M. Lodge	1994			1337	G.W. Hollins	1994		
1281	Carol Lodge	1994			1338	Christine C. Macleod	1994		
1282	Lorraine Nicholson	1994			1339	Rhoda McKinnon	1994		
1283	Harry Blenkinsop	1994		1995	1340	Andrew Balsillie	1993	1994	
1284	John D. Taylor	1994	1994	1996	1341	David Bonham	1994		
1285	Kevin Borman	1994		1996	1342	Irene Crawshaw	1994		
1286	David Williams	1994		1994	1343	Grahame Crawshaw	1994		
1287	Robert J. Shapperd	1994		1995	1344	Pat Craven	1994		
1288	David Fisher	1994			1345	Brian Norman	1994		
1289	Steve Simpson	1994			1346	Gerry Callaghan	1994		
1290	Anne Lochead	1994			1347	George Middleton	1994		
1291	Keith Work	1994			1348	Alistair Patten	1994		1994
1292	Julian P. Ridal	1994		1995	1349	Carol Harper	1994		
1293	Alistair Maitland	1994			1350	Keith Harper	1994		
1294	J. Sebastian Grose	1994	1994		1351	Margaret Beattie	1994		

	Name	Munros	Tops	Furths		Name	Munros	Tops	Furths
1352	Carole Strang	1994			1409	J. B. Murphy	1995		
1353	Martin Horn	1994			1410	David M. Mollison	1995		
1354	Murray Smith	1994			1411	Derek R. L. Borthwick	1995		
1355	Carole George	1994			1412	Bill Patullo	1995		
1356	Iain McManus	1994	1994	1994	1413	Peter Goodwin	1995		
1357	Iain A.B. Wallace	1994			1414	Dominic Goodwin	1995		
1358	Ken Naismith	1994			1415	Anne Hill	1995		
1359	Lyn S. Wilson	1994			1416	Martin E. Hill	1995		
1360	Jeremiah J. Scott	1994			1417	Gillian M. Shirreffs	1995		
1361	Graham Wanless	1994			1418	Richard C. Shirreffs	1995		
1362	Clare Parnell	1994			1419	Donald W. W. Smith	1995		
1363	Simon Halliwell	1994			1420	Brian N. Barron	1995		
1364	A. Haveron	1978			1421	John M.D. Anderson	1995		
1365	J. Coull	1984			1422	Stephen A. Glasper	1995	1995	1995
1366	J. Mitchell	1987			1423	Johan de Jong	1995		1995
1367	R. Shafren	1989			1424	Stuart F. Davidson	1995		
1368	J. Smith	1989			1425	David Harrison-Hall	1995		
1369	K. Higgins	1992			1426	Carlene A. Hamilton	1995		
1370	N. Kenworthy	1993			1427	John D. Hamilton	1995		
1371	A. Julian Spencer	1994			1428	Nigel Murray	1995		
1372	W. Lofthouse	1994			1429	Bill E. Parry	1995		
1373	M. Lofthouse	1994			1430	John W. Haughton	1995		
1374	J. Weir Brown	1994			1431**	Linda J McColl	1995		1995
1375	Stephen Sharp	1994			1432	Karl Nelson	1995	1995	1996
1376	Richard Burt	1994			1433	Elizabeth Skeoch	1995		
1377	John D. Shiel	1994			1434	Irvine J. Skeoch	1995		
1378	John M. Griffin	1994			1435	Judy Middleton	1995		
1379**	Ruth Hannah	1994			1436	Alastair I.F. Barrie	1995		
1380	C.P. Herdman	1994			1437	George Kincaid	1995		
1381	Moira Broadhead	1994			1438	Archie L. Gilbert	1995		
1382	Martin J. Darling	1993			1439	Martin Uppadine	1982		
1383	A.Stuart Duncan	1994			1440	Paul Birrell	1995		
1384	John G. Proud	1994			1441	Jim Bryce	1995	1995	
1385	Allan J. Gordon	1994			1442	Isobel Gordon	1995		
1386	Colin Scales	1986			1443	Ruth Love	1995		
1387	Ian H. Anderson	1994			1444	Simon Love	1995		
1388	Lorna McLaren	1995	1995		1445	Pauline A. Rooker	1995		1995
1389	John King	1994			1446	John A. Rooker	1995		1995
1390	George Galloway	1995	1995		1447	Steve Singleton	1995		
1391	John B. Boyling	1994			1448	Jonathan Whitehead	1995	1995	
1392	Hugh Insley	1995			1449 *	Arthur J. Bennet	1995		
1393	Ron Fosberry	1995			1450	Charlie Lodge	1995		
1394	George C. Gilchrist	1995			1451	Malcolm Lomas	1995		
1395	A.L. McLaren	1995			1452	Eddie B. Dealtry	1995	1995	1994
1396	Gordon Birnie	1995			1453	Patricia Manning	1995		
1397	Douglas R. MacLeod	1995			1454	Thomas W. Wright	1995		
1398	George Page	1995	1995		1455	Jessie R. Milne	1995		
1399	Ron Johnson	1995	1995		1456	William A. Milne	1995		
1400	Kate Potter	1995			1457	Michael Pratt	1995		
1401	Alan Bellis	1995			1458	Patrick Callan	1995		
1402	Graham W. Beckett	1995			1459	Bill Brennan	1995		
1403	Patrick J. P. Nelson	1995			1460	Bryon D. Evans	1995		
1404	Gordon Berry	1991	1991	1995	1461	Michael D. Gillespie	1995		
1405	Harry Hartley	1990	1990	1995	1462	John Coleman	1995		
1406	Charles D. M. Black	1995			1463	David H. Wolfson	1995		
1407	Jacqueline Cummings	1995			1464	Erik Bigland	1995		
1408	Barry M. Rose	1995			1465	Lyn Tett	1995		

Name	Munros	Tops	Furths	Name	Munros	Tops	Furths
1466 Ron Spark	1995	1995		1523 David Hughes	1995		
1467 John C. Brannan	1995			1524 A.N. Bartlett	1996		
1468 George Cruickshank	1995			1525 Keith Barker	1995	1995	
1469 Maureen Daniel	1995	1995		1526 John Farrow	1995	1995	
1470 Richard L. Daniel	1995	1995		1527 A.H. Blandy	1994		
1471 Iain Harkins	1995			1528 James White	1995		
1472 Bill Cluckie	1995			1529 Richard R. Cooper	1994		
1473 L. Linley	1995			1530 K. Malcolm Smith	1995		
1474 Jim S. Bramwell	1995			1531 Douglas Wood	1995		
1475 Duncan W. Borthwick	1995			1532 Margaret Varley	1995	1995	
1476 Vonnie Scott	1995			1533 Graeme Morrison	1995		
1477 David Claymore	1995	1995		1534 Steven Morrison	1995		
1478 Graham Jackson	1995	1995		1535 Keith W.D. Macrosson	1995		
1479 Stephen Hartley	1994	1994		1536 Craig Allardice	1996		
1480 Ian D. Lauriston	1995			1537 Danny Rafferty	1995		
1481 Murray Kelso	1995			1538 D. Hillman	1996		
1482 Victoria M.L. Doran	1995			1539 * Andrew M. James	1996		
1483 Iain Roberts	1993			1540 Willie Black	1996		
1484 Linda Sillery	1995	1995		1541 Mary Macrae	1995		
1485 Neil D. Ross	1995			1542 Alex Macrae	1995	1995	
1486 Graeme Ralph	1995			1543 W. Angus Wallace	1996		
1487 Richard W. Foster	1995			1544 Pat McIntosh	1995		
1488 R.J. Metcalfe	1995			1545 Calum McIntosh	1995		
1489 John Lloyd	1995			1546 Tod Bainbridge	1996		
1490 Kathleen Mowbray	1995			1547 John McPartlin	1996		
1491 Jim Macdonald	1995			1548 Elizabeth B. Smith	1996		
1492 John P. Ross	1995			1549 Eleanor Symon	1996		
1493 William D. Nimmo	1995			1550 Scot Symon	1996		
1494 Judy Vallery	1995			1551 Danny Barr	1996		
1495 Tom Vallery	1995			1552 Colin Firth	1996		
1496 James Martin	1994			1553 Bill Buriton	1996		
1497 Nancy Marsh	1995			1554 Adrian Belton	1996		
1498 Barrie Marsh	1995			1555 John Clark	1996		
1499 Liz Campbell	1995			1556 Ian Dickson	1996		
1500 A. Smith	1995			1557 Andrew Moignard	1996		
1501 Roy Firth	1995			1558 Andy Heald	1996		
1502 Malcolm Gray	1990	1994		1559 Graham G. Hemsley	1996		
1503 Malcolm M. MacRae	1995			1560 Kenneth J. Campbell	1996		
1504 Fraser Gold	1995			1561 Robin L. Calder	1996		
1505 Gordon Logan	1995			1562 Jock Mackinnon	1996		
1506 Peter Budd	1995			1563 Murray Reid	1996		
1507 Graham M. Hamilton	1995			1564 David Spencer	1996	1994	
1508 Elizabeth Sudlow	1995			1565 Ruaridh Pringle	1996		
1509 Michael Sudlow	1995			1566 David Appleyard	1996	1996	
1510 Findlay L. Swinton	1995			1567 Peter J. Mansell	1996	1996	
1511 Mary Copping	1995			1568 Richard Bryan	1996		
1512 Neil H. Martin	1995			1569 Janice Butcher	1996		
1513 Joan S. Lamb	1995	1995		1570 David Butcher	1996		
1514 Richard Love	1995			1571 Robert D. Veitch	1996		
1515 Steven Copping	1995			1572 David Eccles	1996		
1516 Hazel Batty	1995			1573 James Garvie	1996		
1517 Lynn Batty	1995			1574 John Samuel	1996		
1518 R. Martin Adams	1991			1575 Thomas Mason	1996		
1519 G.D. Pirie	1995			1576 Ken Ross	1996		
1520 Colin Sinclair	1995			1577 Alan Gibson	1996		
1521 Elizabeth S. Campbell	1995			1578 Harry Morton	1996		
1522 Alastair Campbell	1995			1579 Richard Wheeler	1996		

Name	Munros	Tops	Furths	Name	Munros	Tops	Furths
1580 Ron W. Elder	1996			1637 Nancy McCombie	1996		
1581 David Broadmeadow	1996			1638 John Stevenson	1995		
1582 William Lawrence	1996			1639 Graham Sage	1996		
1583 Fred C. Alexander	1996			1640 Geoff Scott	1994		
1584 Edward H. Noble	1996			1641 W. Michael Gollan	1994		
1585 Hamish Stewart	1996			1642 Matthew Runciman	1996		
1586 Iain F.D. Gilmour	1996			1643 Ian MacPherson	1996		
1587 John M. Moore	1996			1644 Gerald McPartlin	1996		1996
1588 Iain S. Dickinson	1996			1645 David Gemmell	1996		
1589 Ethel S. Thomson	1996			1646 Anne Stokes	1996		
1590 David L. MacGregor	1996			1647 Euan Nicol	1996		
1591 Michael B. Howard	1996			1648 Andrew Wright	1996		1996
1592 David Graham	1996			1649 Gordon Maclachlan	1996		
1593 Bill Grierson	1996			1650 John J. Fleming	1996		
1594 Jim Dixon	1996			1651 Ron Lyall	1996		
1595 Lynda Woods	1996			1652 Barry K. Smith	1996		
1596 Jonathan Woods	1996			1653 Peter Standing	1996		
1597 Sue Jardine	1996			1654 Ken Coote	1996		
1598 Allan Bantick	1996			1655 Roger Cumming	1996		
1599 Del Evans	1996			1656 Ian Rowe	1996		
1600 Muriel Parry	1996			1657 Des Slavin	1996		
1601 Doris Matheson	1995			1658 John M. Dougherty	1996		
1602 Alex Matheson	1995			1659 David Ritchie	1996		
1603 Kevin A. Tait	1996			1660 John Kirkham	1996		
1604 Susan M. White	1996			1661 Mary Duncan	1995		
1605 Barry J. Hodgson	1996			1662 Jeanette Fenner	1996	1996	
1606 A. Neil K. Brown	1996			1663 W. Weiglhofer	1995		
1607 David Harvey	1996	1996		1664 Ian H. Hill	1996		
1608 Eric Simpson	1996			1665 Kenneth Robertson	1996		
1609 Robert J. Ferguson	1996	1996		1666 David Ollerton	1996		
1610 Elizabeth Harwood	1996			1667 Andrew Ollerton	1996		
1611 Alex Smith	1996			1668 Leslie Barrie	1996		
1612 Steve Mann	1996			1669 Jim Lawson	1996		
1613 Gillian Nisbet	1996		1997	1670 Richard D. Humble	1996		
1614 Susan J. Park	1996	1996		1671 Graham Daniels	1992	1992	
1615 Andy Ritchie	1996			1672 Flora Hunt	1996		
1616 John Calder	1996			1673 Tim Hall	1996		
1617 Ron Neville	1996			1674 Sam Johnston	1996		
1618 Molly E. Grant	1996			1675 Paul Caban	1996		1997
1619 Andrew J.H. Grant	1996			1676 Edward J. Haggarty	1996	1996	
1620 Euan Pyper	1996			1677 John Patterson	1996		
1621 Mhairi Ross	1996			1678 Tom Gailey	1996	1996	1996
1622 Jim Ross	1996			1679 Elliot S. Sloan	1996		
1623 Mike Dales	1996			1680 Elizabeth Carnduff	1996		
1624 Chris Bull	1996			1681 Peter Hastie	1996		
1625 Thomas Paton	1996			1682 David F. Beaumont	1996		
1626 Cameron J. Johnston	1996	1996		1683 John G. Robin	1996		
1627 Alastair Bruce	1996			1684 Jonathan Bellarby	1996		
1628 Roy Bell	1996			1685 James Bellarby	1996		
1629 Steve Frearson	1996			1686 Graham Clark	1996		
1630 J.M. Thomson	1996			1687 Rob Black	1997		
1631 Robert J. Barton	1996			1688 Jennifer M. Thomson	1996		
1632 Andrew R. Dickson	1996			1689 Keith Taylor	1995		
1633 Shona Malcolm	1996			1690 Gordon A. Winton	1996		
1634 Bruce Malcolm	1996			1691 George W. Graham	1996		
1635 Eric Young	1996			1692 Stuart H. Clarke	1996		
1636 James A. Bennett	1996			1693 Graeme Findlay	1996		

Name	Munros	Tops	Furths	Name	Munros	Tops	Furths
1694 Graeme Reid	1996	1996	1996	1720 Alec Hickton	1997		
1695 G.W. Roy Goodwin	1996			1721 Jim Young	1997		
1696 Brenda Lawson	1996			1722 John Newman	1997		
1697 S.L. Grice	1997			1723 Karin Marshall	1997		
1698 Alison Curle	1996			1724 Raymond Marshall	1997		
1699 Keith R. Stratton	1996			1725 Craig Weldon	1997		
1700 Nick J. Wild	1997			1726 Peter Gillman	1997		
1701 Simon C. Jefferies	1996			1727 John Arkell	1997		
1702 John Ferguson	1995			1728 John S. Greener	1997		1997
1703 Gill Lyons	1995			1729 Dennis R. Pickett	1997		
1704 Brian Tomlinson	1996			1730 Keith Anderson	1997	1997	
1705 Dave Delaet	1997			1731 Ian Munro	1997		
1706 John H. Scholtens	1997	1997		1732 Ian Barnett	1997		
1707 Keith Grant	1997			1733 Jean Hunter	1997		
1708 Albert C. McAdam	1995			1734 Andrew Reston	1997		
1709 Matthew Clarke	1997			1735 Joseph Small	1997		
1710 Malcolm Clarke	1997			1736 Lesley Leiper	1997		
1711 Stewart Newman	1997			1737 Malcolm Leiper	1997		
1712 Richard Davison	1997			1738 John Pulford	1997		1990
1713 Derek Thomas	1997			1739 John Maundrell	1996		
1714 Richard Glover	1997			1740 John Kerry	1997		
1715 Sue Hunter	1997			1741 Lorna Macgregor	1997		
1716 J. Gordon Cameron	1997			1742 Mark Swindon	1997		1997
1717 Gordon J. Dykes	1997			1743 * William S. McKerrow	1997		
1718 Paul N. Craven	1997			1744 Alex Cuthbertson	1997		
1719 Lesley Hickton	1997			1745 Mark T. Wight	1997		

The Furths

The following list comprises those summits which are generally recognised as being the 3000ft peaks of the British Isles **furth** of Scotland. The exact number of summits is open to debate but all of the controversial tops would normally be traversed as part of an ascent of the principal peaks. A complete ascent of this list (in addition to completion of the Munros!) is an achievement recognised by the Clerk of the List and is incorporated into the list of Munroists published in this volume.

Name	Height (metres)	Map Reference
England		
Scafell Pike	978	NY215072
Scafell	964	NY206064
Helvellyn	950	NY342151
Ill Crag	935	NY223073
Broad Crag	934	NY218075
Skiddaw	931	NY260290
Wales		
Snowdon	1085	SH609543
Crib y Ddysgl	1065	SH610551
Carnedd Llewelyn	1064	SH683644
Carnedd Dafydd	1044	SH663630
Glyder Fawr	999	SH642579
Glyder Fach	994	SH656582
Pen yr Ole Wen	978	SH655619
Foel Grach	976	SH688658
Yr Elen	962	SH674651
Y Garn	947	SH630595
Foel-fras	942	SH696681
Garnedd Uchaf	926	SH687669
Elidir Fawr	924	SH612613
Crib Goch	923	SH624551
Tryfan	915	SH664593
Ireland		
Carrauntoohill	1039	V 803844
Beenkeragh	1010	V 801852
Caher	1001	V 792839
Cnoc na Peiste	988	V 835841
Caher West Top	975	V 790840
Maolan Bui	973	V 832838
Knockoughter*	959	V 800847
Cnoc an Chuillin	958	V 823833
Brandon Mountain	952	Q 460116
The Big Gun	939	V 840848
Cruach Mhor	932	V 840848
Lugnaquillia	925	T 032917
Galtymore	919	R 878238

*There is some uncertainty as to the correct name for this summit.

PART 2

Corbett's Tables

Scottish Mountains of 2500 feet and under 3000 feet in height with a re-ascent of 500 feet on all sides

Compiled by
J. Rooke Corbett

Later Revisions by
James C. Donaldson
Hamish M. Brown
Derek A. Bearhop

Introduction

John Rooke Corbett was a district valuer based in Bristol and a keen member of the Scottish Mountaineering Club in the years between the two World Wars. He was a distinguished student at Cambridge University and an original member of the Rucksack Club. Corbett was a regular attender at SMC meets, a committee member and joint-editor of the second edition of the *Northern Highlands* guidebook. He completed the Munros and Tops in 1930, only the second person to do so and, more remarkably, he climbed all of Scotland's 2000-foot hills.

Out of this extensive experience and knowledge came Corbett's eponymous tables in which he listed all those hills of between 2500 feet (762m) and 3000 feet (914.4m) in height with a drop of at least 500 feet (152.4m) between each listed hill and any adjacent higher one. In this way the definition of the Corbetts is more clearly expressed than is the case with the Munros, and the fairly large height drop between Corbetts produces summits which tend to be quite distinct, unlike the Munros which do not have rigid separation criteria. After his death, Corbett's list was passed to the SMC by his sister and it was decided to publish it as a record of interest and assistance to hillwalkers generally.

As has been the case with the Munros, the list of Corbetts has changed over the years as a result of changes in hill heights measured by the Ordnance Survey. The geographical sections in this edition have been reorganised to make them the same as the sections in Munros Tables. This produces the anomaly of a Section 0 for the Southern Uplands which does not feature in Munros Tables, but contains several Corbetts. Similarly, Section 10 of Munros Tables would contain a disproportionate number of Corbetts and has been sub-divided for the purposes of clarity into a Section 10A and a Section 10B.

Height alone is no measure of quality and there are in the ranks of the Corbetts many peaks of great character, interest and beauty that are the equal of all but a few of the Munros. Visiting the Corbetts will take the hillwalker into a number of unfamiliar or remote areas of the country which a fixation with the Munros would deny. These hills should not be looked upon as lesser cousins but enjoyed in their own right as part of the wealth of diversity of the Scottish landscape.

Changes made since the 1990 Revision

Removed from Tables :

Section No.   9   Corrieyairack Hill. Height now exceeded by that of Gairbeinn, formerly of equal status.

17   Beinn Talaidh. Latest published height is under 2500 feet.

Added to Tables in this edition :

Section No.   10B   Buidhe Bheinn. Height now shown as being identical to that of Sgurr a' Bhac Chaolais with which it shares equal status.

Total number of Corbetts in this Edition :   221 - 2 +1 = **220**

Cul Beag from Stac Pollaidh

The summit of The Cobbler, Ben Lomond beyond

TABLE 3. The Corbetts by District

SECTION 0
Galloway and the Borders

Name	Height (metres)	O.S. Map Sheet	Map Reference
1. Merrick	843	77	NX427855
2. Shalloch on Minnoch	775	77	NX407905
3. Corserine	814	77	NX497870
4. Cairnsmore of Carsphairn	797	77	NX594979
5. Hart Fell	808	78	NT113135
6. White Coomb	821	79	NT163150
7. Broad Law	840	72	NT146235

SECTION 1
Loch Lomond to Loch Tay

Map on page 12

Name	Height (metres)	O.S. Map Sheet	Map Reference
1. Beinn Bheula	779	56	NS154983
2. Ben Donich	847	56	NN218043
3. The Brack	787	56	NN245030
4. The Cobbler	884	56	NN259058
5. Beinn Luibhean	858	56	NN242079
6. Beinn an Lochain	901	56	NN218079
7. Stob Coire Creagach	817	56/50	NN230109
8. Meall an Fhudair	764	56/50	NN271192
9. Beinn Chuirn	880	50	NN280292
10. Beinn a'Choin	770	56/50	NN354130
11. Stob a'Choin	869	56	NN416159
12. Stob Fear-tomhais	771	57	NN474163
13. Benvane	821	57	NN535137
14. Ben Ledi	879	57	NN562097
15. Meall an t-Seallaidh	852	51	NN542234
16. Creag Mac Ranaich	809	51	NN545255
17. Beinn Each	813	57	NN601158
18. Meall na Fearna	809	57	NN650186
19. Creag Uchdag	879	51	NN708323
20. Creagan na Beinne	888	51	NN744368
21. Auchnafree Hill	789	52	NN808308

SECTION 2
The River Tay to Rannoch Moor
Map on page 14

	Name	Height (metres)	O.S. Map Sheet	Map Reference
1.	Beinn Odhar	901	50	NN337339
2.	Beinn Chaorach	818	50	NN358328
3.	Cam Chreag	885	50	NN375346
4.	Beinn a'Chaisteil.	886	50	NN347364
5.	Beinn nam Fuaran	806	50	NN361381
6.	Beinn nan Imirean	849	51	NN419309
7.	Meall nan Subh.	806	51	NN460397
8.	Beinn nan Oighreag	909	51	NN542412
9.	Meall nam Maigheach	779	51	NN585436
10.	Meall Buidhe.	910	51	NN427449
11.	Sron a'Choire Chnapanaich.	837	51	NN456453
12.	Cam Chreag	862	51	NN536491
13.	Beinn Dearg	830	51	NN609497
14.	Meall Tairneachan	787	52	NN807543
15.	Farragon Hill.	783	52	NN840552

SECTION 3
Northwest Argyll and Appin
Map on page 18

	Name	Height (metres)	O.S. Map Sheet	Map Reference
1.	Beinn a'Bhuiridh.	897	50	NN093283
2.	Beinn Mhic-Mhonaidh	796	50	NN208350
3.	Beinn Udlaidh.	840	50	NN280333
4.	Beinn Bhreac-liath	802	50	NN302339
5.	Creach Bheinn.	810	50	NN023422
6.	Beinn Trilleachan	840c	50	NN086439
7.	Stob Dubh, Beinn Ceitlein	883	50	NN166488
8.	Beinn Mhic Chasgaig	864	41	NN221502
9.	Fraochaidh	879	41	NN029517
10.	Meall Lighiche	772	41	NN094528
11.	Beinn Maol Chaluim	907	41	NN135525
12.	Garbh Bheinn	867	41	NN169601
13.	Beinn a'Chrulaiste	857	41	NN246567

Stob Dubh from the head of Loch Etive

SECTION 4
Loch Leven to Loch Ericht
Map on page 18

	Name	Height (metres)	O.S. Map Sheet	Map Reference
1.	Mam na Gualainn................	796	41	NN115625
2.	Glas Bheinn.....................	792	41	NN259641
3.	Leum Uilleim	909	41	NN330641
4.	Meall na Meoig of Ben Pharlagain	868	42	NN448642
5.	Sgurr Innse	809	41	NN290748
6.	Cruach Innse.....................	857	41	NN280763
7.	The Fara.........................	911	42	NN598843

SECTION 5

The Southern Grampians: Loch Rannoch to Glen Garry

Map on page 26

	Name	Height (metres)	O.S. Map Sheet	Map Reference
1.	Stob an Aonaich Mhoir	855	42	NN537694
2.	Beinn Mholach	841	42	NN587655
3.	Beinn a'Chuallaich	892	42	NN684618
4.	Meall na Leitreach	775	42	NN639703
5.	The Sow of Atholl.	803	42	NN624741
6.	An Dun	827	42	NN716805

SECTION 6

The Southern Grampians: Glen Garry to Glen Shee

Map on page 28

	Name	Height (metres)	O.S. Map Sheet	Map Reference
1.	Ben Vrackie	841	43	NN950632
2.	Ben Vuirich	903	43	NN997700
3.	Ben Gulabin	806	43	NO101722
4.	Beinn Mheadhonach.	901	43	NN880758
5.	Maol Creag an Loch	875	42	NN735807
6.	Leathad an Taobhain	912	43	NN822858
7.	Beinn Bhreac.	912	43	NN868820
8.	Morrone.	859	43	NO132886
9.	Meallach Mhor	769	35	NN776909
10.	Carn Dearg Mor	857	35/43	NN823911

SECTION 7

Glen Shee to Cairn o'Mount

Map on page 30

	Name	Height (metres)	O.S. Map Sheet	Map Reference
1.	Monamenach	807	43	NO176707
2.	Creag nan Gabhar	834	43	NO154841
3.	Conachcraig	865	44	NO279865
4.	Ben Tirran	896	44	NO373746
5.	Mount Battock	778	44	NO549844

Ben Rinnes and Corryhabbie Hill from the northern slopes of Ben Avon

SECTION 8
The Cairngorms and Northeast Grampians
Map on page 32

	Name	Height (metres)	O.S. Map Sheet	Map Reference
1.	Sgor Mor	813	43	NO006914
2.	Carn na Drochaide	818	36/43	NO127938
3.	Carn Liath	862	36/43	NO165977
4.	Culardoch	900	36/43	NO194988
5.	Brown Cow Hill	829	36	NJ221044
6.	Morven	872	37	NJ377040
7.	Creag Mhor	895	36	NJ057048
8.	Meall a'Bhuachaille	810	36	NH990115
9.	Geal Charn	821	36	NJ090127
10.	Carn Ealasaid	792	36	NJ228117
11.	Carn Mor	804	37	NJ265183
12.	Corryhabbie Hill	781	37	NJ281288
13.	Ben Rinnes	840	28	NJ255355

SECTION 9

Glen Roy to the Monadh Liath

Map on page 36

	Name	Height (metres)	O.S. Map Sheet	Map Reference
1.	Beinn Iaruinn	800	34	NN296900
2.	Carn Dearg (East of Glen Roy)	834	34	NN345887
3.	Carn Dearg (South of Gleann Eachach)	768	34	NN357948
4.	Carn Dearg (North of Gleann Eachach)	817	34	NN349966
5.	Gairbeinn.	896	34	NN460985
6.	Meall na h-Aisre	862	35	NH515000
7.	Carn a'Chuilinn	816	34	NH416033
8.	Carn na Fhreiceadain	878	35	NH725071
9.	Geal-charn Mor.	824	35	NH837123
10.	Carn na Saobhaidhe	811	35	NH600145

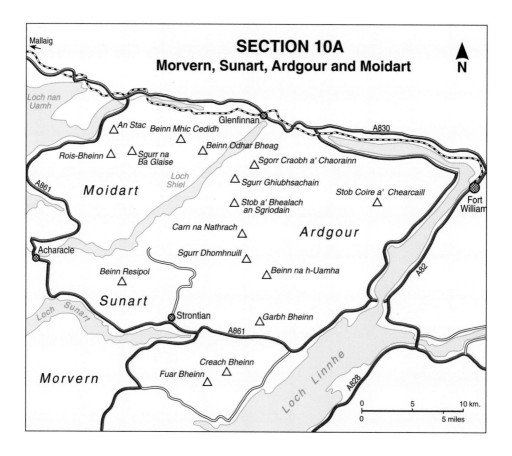

Garbh Bheinn

SECTION 10A
Morvern, Sunart, Ardgour and Moidart

	Name	Height (metres)	O.S. Map Sheet	Map Reference
1.	Fuar Bheinn......................	766	49	NM853564
2.	Creach Bheinn.....................	853	49	NM871577
3.	Beinn Resipol	845	40	NM766654
4.	Garbh Bheinn	885	40	NM904621
5.	Beinn na h-Uamha	762	40	NM917664
6.	Sgurr Dhomhnuill	888	40	NM889678
7.	Carn na Nathrach..................	786	40	NM887699
8.	Stob a'Bhealach an Sgriodain	770	40	NM874727
9.	Sgurr Ghiubhsachain	849	40	NM875751
10.	Sgorr Craobh a'Chaorainn..........	775	40	NM895758
11.	Stob Coire a'Chearcaill............	771	41	NN017727
12.	Rois-Bheinn......................	882	40	NM756778
13.	Sgurr na Ba Glaise	874	40	NM770777
14.	An Stac	814	40	NM828788
15.	Beinn Mhic Cedidh................	783	40	NM828788
16.	Beinn Odhar Bheag	882	40	NM846778

SECTION 10B
Loch Eil to Glen Shiel
Map on page 38

Name	Height (metres)	O.S. Map Sheet	Map Reference
1. Sgurr an Utha	796	40	NM885839
2. Streap.	909	40	NM946863
3. Braigh nan Uamhachan	765	40	NM975866
4. Meall a'Phubuill	774	41	NN029854
5. Beinn Bhan	796	34/41	NN140857
6. Carn Mor.	829	33	NM903909
7. Bidean a'Chabair	867	33	NM889931
8. Sgurr Cos na Breachd-laoigh.	835	33	NM948947
9. Fraoch Bheinn.	858	33	NM986940
10. Sgurr Mhurlagain.	880	33	NN012944
11. Geal Charn	804	34	NN156942
12. Meall na h-Eilde	838	34	NN185946
13. Ben Tee	904	34	NN240971
14. Beinn Bhuidhe	855	33	NM821967
15. Ben Aden.	887	33	NM898986
16. Sgurr an Fhuarain.	901	33	NM987979
17. Sgurr Coire Choinnichean	796	33	NG790010
18. Beinn na Caillich.	785	33	NG795067
19. Sgurr a'Choire-bheithe.	913	33	NG895015
20. Sgurr nan Eugallt	894	33	NG930045
21. Beinn na h-Eaglaise	805	33	NG853119
22. Beinn nan Caorach	774	33	NG871121
23. Sgurr Mhic Bharraich.	779	33	NG917173
24. Buidhe Bheinn	885	33	NG956087
25. Sgurr a'Bhac Chaolais	885	33	NG958110
26. Beinn Loinne.	790	34	NH131077
27. Meall Dubh	788	34	NH245078

SECTION 11
Glen Affric and Kintail
Map on page 42

Name	Height (metres)	O.S. Map Sheet	Map Reference
1. Am Bathach.	798	33	NH073143
2. Carn a'Choire Ghairbh.	865	34	NH136188
3. Aonach Shasuinn	888	34	NH173180
4. Sgurr an Airgid.	841	25/33	NG940227
5. Sgurr Gaorsaic	839	25/33	NH036219

Streap (right) and Streap Comhlaidh (left) from Sgurr Thuilm

SECTION 12
Glen Cannich to Glen Carron
Map on page 46

	Name	Height (metres)	O.S. Map Sheet	Map Reference
1.	Sguman Coinntich	879	25	NG977303
2.	Faochaig	868	25	NH022317
3.	Aonach Buidhe	899	25	NH058324
4.	Sgorr na Diollaid	818	25	NH281362
5.	Beinn Dronaig	797	25	NH037382
6.	Beinn Tharsuinn	863	25	NH055433
7.	Sgurr na Feartaig	862	25	NH054453
8.	An Sidhean	814	25	NH170453
9.	Bac an Eich	849	25	NH222489
10.	Beinn a'Bha'ach Ard	862	26	NH360434
11.	Meallan nan Uan	838	25	NH263544
12.	Sgurr a'Mhuilinn	879	25	NH264557

SECTION 13
Applecross, Coulin and Torridon

Map on page 48

Name	Height (metres)	O.S. Map Sheet	Map Reference
1. Sgurr a'Chaorachain.	792	24	NG796417
2. Beinn Bhan	896	24	NG804450
3. An Ruadh-stac	892	25	NG921480
4. Fuar Tholl	907	25	NG975489
5. Beinn Damh	903	24	NG892502
6. Sgorr nan Lochan Uaine	871	25	NG969531
7. Sgurr Dubh	782	25	NG979558
8. Beinn Dearg	914	24	NG895608
9. Ruadh-stac Beag.	896	19	NG973614
10. Meall a'Ghiubhais	887	19	NG976634
11. Baosbheinn	875	19/24	NG870654
12. Beinn an Eoin	855	19	NG905646

SECTION 14
Loch Maree to Loch Broom

Map on page 50

Name	Height (metres)	O.S. Map Sheet	Map Reference
1. Beinn Airigh Charr.	791	19	NG930761
2. Beinn Lair	859	19	NG981732
3. Beinn a'Chaisgein Mor.	856	19	NG982785
4. Beinn Dearg Bheag.	820	19	NH020811
5. Beinn Dearg Mor	910	19	NH032799
6. Creag Rainich	807	19	NH096751
7. Beinn Liath Mhor a'Ghiubhais Li	766	20	NH281713
8. Sail Mhor.	767	19	NH033887

SECTION 15
Loch Broom to Easter Ross

Map on page 53

Name	Height (metres)	O.S. Map Sheet	Map Reference
1. Little Wyvis.	763	20	NH429645
2. Beinn Enaiglair	890	20	NH225805
3. Beinn a'Chaisteil.	787	20	NH370801
4. Carn Chuinneag	838	20	NH483833
5. Carn Ban	842	20	NH338875

Beinn Damh from the south-east

SECTION 16
Coigach to the Pentland Firth
Map on page 54

	Name	Height (metres)	O.S. Map Sheet	Map Reference
1.	Cul Beag	769	15	NC140088
2.	Cul Mor	849	15	NC162119
3.	Canisp	847	15	NC203187
4.	Breabag	815	15	NC287157
5.	Glas Bheinn	776	15	NC254264
6.	Spidean Coinich, Quinag	764	15	NC206277
7.	Sail Gharbh, Quinag	808	15	NC209292
8.	Sail Gorm, Quinag	776	15	NC198304
9.	Beinn Leoid	792	15	NC320294
10.	Ben Hee	873	16	NC426339
11.	Meallan Liath Coire Mhic Dhughaill	801	15	NC357391
12.	Arkle	787	9	NC302461
13.	Meall Horn	777	9	NC352449
14.	Foinaven	914	9	NC315507
15.	Cranstackie	800	9	NC350556
16.	Beinn Spionnaidh	772	9	NC362573
17.	Ben Loyal	764	10	NC578488

Caisteal Abhail from North Goatfell

SECTION 17
The Islands
Map on page 56

Name	Height (metres)	O.S. Map Sheet	Map Reference
ARRAN			
1. Beinn Tarsuinn	826	69	NR959412
2. Cir Mhor	799	69	NR973430
3. Caisteal Abhail	847	69	NR968443
4. Goatfell	874	69	NR991415
JURA			
5. Beinn an Oir	785	61	NM498749
MULL			
6. Dun da Ghaoithe	785	49	NM672362
RUM			
7. Ainshval	781	39	NG378943
8. Askival	812	39	NG393952
SKYE			
9. Garbh-bheinn	808	32	NG531232
10. Glamaig.	775	32	NG513300
HARRIS			
11. Clisham	799	13/14	NB154073

Index of Corbett's Tables

Name	Section Reference		Name	Section Reference	
Ainshval	17	7	Beinn na h-Eaglaise	10B	21
Am Bathach	11	1	Beinn na h-Uamha	10A	5
An Dun	5	6	Beinn nam Fuaran	2	5
An Ruadh-stac	13	3	Beinn nan Caorach	10B	22
An Sidhean	12	8	Beinn nan Imirean	2	6
An Stac	10A	14	Beinn nan Oighreag	2	8
Aonach Buidhe	12	3	Beinn Odhar	2	1
Aonach Shasuinn	11	3	Beinn Odhar Bheag	10A	16
Arkle	16	12	Beinn Resipol	10A	3
Askival	17	8	Beinn Spionnaidh	16	16
Auchnafree Hill	1	21	Beinn Tarsuinn (Arran)	17	1
Bac an Eich	12	9	Beinn Tharsuinn (Monar)	12	6
Baosbheinn	13	11	Beinn Trilleachan	3	6
Beinn a'Bha'ach Ard	12	10	Beinn Udlaidh	3	3
Beinn a'Bhuiridh	3	1	Ben Aden	10B	15
Beinn a'Chaisgein Mor	14	3	Ben Donich	1	2
Beinn a'Chaisteil (Auch)	2	4	Ben Gulabin	6	3
Beinn a'Chaisteil (Loch Vaich)	15	3	Ben Hee	16	10
Beinn a'Choin	1	10	Ben Ledi	1	14
Beinn a'Chrulaiste	3	13	Ben Loyal	16	17
Beinn a'Chuallaich	5	3	Ben Rinnes	8	13
Beinn Airigh Charr	14	1	Ben Tee	10B	13
Beinn an Eoin	13	12	Ben Tirran	7	4
Beinn an Lochain	1	6	Benvane	1	13
Beinn an Oir	17	5	Ben Vrackie	6	1
Beinn Bhan (Arkaig)	10B	5	Ben Vuirich	6	2
Beinn Bhan (Applecross)	13	2	Bidean a'Chabair	10B	7
Beinn Bheula	1	1	Brack, The	1	3
Beinn Bhreac	6	7	Braigh nan Uamhachan	10B	3
Beinn Bhreac-liath	3	4	Breabag	16	4
Beinn Bhuidhe	10B	14	Broad Law	0	7
Beinn Ceitlein, Stob Dubh	3	7	Brown Cow Hill	8	5
Beinn Chaorach	2	2	Buidhe Bheinn	10B	24
Beinn Chuirn	1	9	Cairnsmore of Carsphairn	0	4
Beinn Damh	13	5	Caisteal Abhail	17	3
Beinn Dearg (Glen Lyon)	2	13	Cam Chreag (Auch)	2	3
Beinn Dearg (Torridon)	13	8	Cam Chreag (Glen Lyon)	2	12
Beinn Dearg Bheag	14	4	Canisp	16	3
Beinn Dearg Mor	14	5	Carn a'Choire Ghairbh	11	2
Beinn Dronaig	12	5	Carn a'Chuilinn	9	7
Beinn Each	1	17	Carn Ban	15	5
Beinn Enaiglair	15	2	Carn Chuinneag	15	4
Beinn Iaruinn	9	1	Carn Dearg (E of Glen Roy)	9	2
Beinn Lair	14	2	Carn Dearg (S of Gleann Eachach)	9	3
Beinn Leoid	16	9	Carn Dearg (N of Gleann Eachach)	9	4
Beinn Liath Mhor a'Ghiubhais Li	14	7	Carn Dearg Mor	6	10
Beinn Loinne	10B	26	Carn Ealasaid	8	10
Beinn Luibhean	1	5	Carn Liath	8	3
Beinn Maol Chaluim	3	11	Carn Mor (Glenlivet)	8	11
Beinn Mheadhonach	6	4	Carn Mor (Glen Dessarry)	10B	6
Beinn Mhic Cedidh	10A	15	Carn na Drochaide	8	2
Beinn Mhic Chasgaig	3	8	Carn na Fhreiceadain	9	8
Beinn Mhic-Mhonaidh	3	2	Carn na Nathrach	10A	7
Beinn Mholach	5	2	Carn na Saobhaidhe	9	10
Beinn na Caillich	10B	18	Cir Mhor	17	2

Name	Section	Reference	Name	Section	Reference
Clisham	17	11	Meall na Fearna	1	18
Cobbler, The	1	4	Meall na h-Aisre	9	6
Conachcraig	7	3	Meall na h-Eilde	10B	12
Corryhabbie Hill	8	12	Meall na Leitreach	5	4
Corserine	0	3	Meall na Meoig of Ben Pharlagain	4	4
Cranstackie	16	15	Meall nam Maigheach	2	9
Creach Bheinn (Loch Creran)	3	5	Meall nan Subh	2	7
Creach Bheinn (Morvern)	10A	2	Meall Tairneachan	2	14
Creagan na Beinne	1	20	Merrick	0	1
Creag Mac Ranaich	1	16	Monamenach	7	1
Creag Mhor	8	7	Morrone	6	8
Creag nan Gabhar	7	2	Morven	8	6
Creag Rainich	14	6	Mount Battock	7	5
Creag Uchdag	1	19	Paps of Jura	17	5
Cruach Innse	4	6	Quinag	16	6-8
Culardoch	8	4	Rois-Bheinn	10A	12
Cul Beag	16	1	Ruadh-stac Beag	13	9
Cul Mor	16	2	Sail Gharbh, Quinag	16	7
Dun da Ghaoithe	17	6	Sail Gorm, Quinag	16	8
Faochaig	12	2	Sail Mhor	14	8
Fara, The	4	7	Sgor Mor	8	1
Farragon Hill	2	15	Sgorr nan Lochan Uaine	13	6
Foinaven	16	14	Sgorr Craobh a'Chaorainn	10A	10
Fraochaidh	3	9	Sgorr na Diollaid	12	4
Fraoch Bheinn	10B	9	Sguman Coinntich	12	1
Fuar Bheinn	10A	1	Sgurr a'Bhac Chaolais	10B	25
Fuar Tholl	13	4	Sgurr a'Chaorachain	13	1
Gairbeinn	9	5	Sgurr a'Choire-bheithe	10B	19
Garbh Bheinn (Loch Leven)	3	12	Sgurr a'Mhuilinn	12	12
Garbh Bheinn (Ardgour)	10A	4	Sgurr an Airgid	11	4
Garbh-bheinn (Red Cuillin)	17	9	Sgurr an Fhuarain	10B	16
Geal Charn (Dorback)	8	9	Sgurr an Utha	10B	1
Geal Charn (Arkaig)	10B	11	Sgurr Coire Choinnichean	10B	17
Geal-charn Mor	9	9	Sgurr Cos na Breachd-laoigh	10B	8
Glamaig	17	10	Sgurr Dhomhnuill	10A	6
Glas Bheinn (Kinlochleven)	4	2	Sgurr Dubh	13	7
Glas Bheinn (Assynt)	16	5	Sgurr Gaorsaic	11	5
Goatfell	17	4	Sgurr Ghiubhsachain	10A	9
Hart Fell	0	5	Sgurr Innse	4	5
Leathad an Taobhain	6	6	Sgurr Mhic Bharraich	10B	23
Leum Uilleim	4	3	Sgurr Mhurlagain	10B	10
Little Wyvis	15	1	Sgurr na Ba Glaise	10A	13
Mam na Gualainn	4	1	Sgurr na Feartaig	12	7
Maol Creag an Loch	6	5	Sgurr nan Eugallt	10B	20
Meall a'Bhuachaille	8	8	Shalloch on Minnoch	0	2
Meallach Mhor	6	9	Sow of Atholl, The	5	5
Meall a'Ghiubhais	13	10	Spidean Coinich, Quinag	16	6
Meall an Fhudair	1	8	Sron a'Choire Chnapanaich	2	11
Meallan Liath Coire Mhic Dhughaill	16	11	Stob a'Bhealach an Sgriodain	10A	8
Meallan nan Uan	12	11	Stob a'Choin	1	11
Meall an t-Seallaidh	1	15	Stob an Aonaich Mhoir	5	1
Meall a'Phubuill	10B	4	Stob Coire a'Chearcaill	10A	11
Meall Buidhe	2	10	Stob Coire Creagach	1	7
Meall Dubh	10B	27	Stob Dubh, Beinn Ceitlein	3	7
Meall Horn	16	13	Stob Fear-tomhais	1	12
Meall Lighiche	3	10	Streap	10B	2
			White Coomb	0	6

PART 3

Donald's Tables

All Hills in the Scottish Lowlands
2000 feet in height and above

Compiled by
Percy Donald

Later Revisions by
James C. Donaldson
Hamish M. Brown
Derek A. Bearhop

Introduction

Ben Ever in the Ochil Hills

Percy Donald's list of hills over 2000 feet in the Scottish Lowlands has been published in this volume for many years. Percy Donald visited every elevation over the 2000 foot threshold while compiling his list and developed a complex formula to distinguish between those points which he classified as 'Hills' and those which he considered to be 'Tops'. With the growing interest in hillwalking in general, and with larger numbers of enthusiasts completing the more well-documented lists of peaks, there has been an increase in the level of interest in Donald's Tables in recent years. It has been suggested that the list should be metricated (perhaps by reducing the threshold to 600 metres) or that the definition should be more precise (relating to a specific measure of reascent from neighbouring peaks). It is felt, however, that Percy Donald has left us a clear, albeit antiquated, definition of his categorisation which produces a list of historical interest which is still relevant to today's hillwalker. The following tables therefore adhere to the traditional definitions.

The exact geographic compass of Donald's Tables was never made clear but the inclusion of the Ochil Hills suggests that his definition of 'Lowland' was a geological one; namely, all of the country south of the Highland Boundary Fault.

If this definition is strictly applied, it becomes clear that Donald overlooked a small group of hills lying to the south of Glen Artney which rise above the 2000-foot level. This group (containing 2 Hills and a further 2 Tops) is added to the tables in this volume. There may be some interesting developments in future if the literal definition is maintained, as there is currently a debate in geological circles as to whether the southern course of the Highland Boundary Fault passes through the island of Arran. In another break with previous practice, those summits in the Cheviot Hills which are entirely within England are not included in this edition.

Previous editions of these Tables have included an Appendix of 'elevations not meriting inclusion as tops, but enclosed by an isolated 610m (2000-feet) contour'. The elevations in the former Appendix have been assessed against Donald's criteria and either incorporated into the main tables or dropped altogether. The source material for this edition is the latest Ordnance Survey 1:25,000 maps which, in combination with the accuracy of satellite mapping techniques, produces a multitude of isolated contours, often representing mere undulations in the terrain. It will be appreciated that the presence of a 10-metre contour on a map does not always represent a 10-metre rise on the ground; just the presence of ground at that altitude. The Appendix is therefore discontinued in this edition.

Hills and Tops were determined by Percy Donald in accordance with the following rules:

'Tops' are all elevations with a drop of 100 feet (30.48m) on all sides and elevations of sufficient topographical merit with a drop of between 100 feet and 50 feet (15.24m) on all sides.

Grouping of Tops into 'Hills', except where inapplicable on topographical grounds, is on the basis that Tops are no more than 17 units from the main top of the 'Hill' to which they belong; where a unit is either one twelfth of a mile measured along the connecting ridge or one 50-foot contour between the lower Top and its connecting col.

This sounds terribly convoluted but the actual result of applying these rules is that, with but few exceptions, a 24-metre drop determines a 'Top' and the 17 unit rule a 'Hill'.

Ordnance Survey sheet numbers and map references are used throughout. The Bartholomew map sheets referred to in previous editions are not at a large enough scale to contain the level of detail necessary to identify many of the elevations referred to in the tables. Spellings are also taken from Ordnance Survey sources.

TABLE 4. The Donalds by District

SECTION 1
Glen Artney Hills

Name	Height (metres)	Hill No.	Top No.	O.S. Map Sheet	Map Reference
1 **Uamh Bheag**	664	57	80	57	**NN691118**
2 Meall Clachach.	621		127	57	NN688125
3 Beinn Odhar.	626		117	57	NN714127
4 **Beinn nan Eun**.	631	74	110	57	**NN723131**

SECTION 2
Ochil Hills

Name	Height (metres)	Hill No.	Top No.	O.S. Map Sheet	Map Reference
1 **Blairdenon Hill**.	631	75	111	58	**NN865018**
2 Ben Ever	622		125	58	NN893001
3 **Ben Cleuch**.	721	25	36	58	**NN902006**
4 The Law	638		104	58	NN910996
5 Andrew Gannel Hill	670		74	58	NN918006
6 **King's Seat Hill**.	648	66	92	58	**NS933999**
7 **Tarmangie Hill**	645	69	95	58	**NN942014**
8 Whitewisp Hill.	643		99	58	NN955014
9 **Innerdownie**	610	89	140	58	**NN966031**

SECTION 3
Moorfoot Hills

Name	Height (metres)	Hill No.	Top No.	O.S. Map Sheet	Map Reference
1 **Windlestraw Law**	659	61	85	73	NT371431
2 Windlestraw Law SW Top	657		86	73	NT362420
3 **Whitehope Law**.	623	82	124	73	NT330445
4 **Bowbeat Hill**	626	77	118	73	NT292469
5 **Blackhope Scar**	651	64	90	73	NT315483
6 **Dundreich**	623	81	123	73	NT274491

SECTION 4

Culter Hills and Tinto

	Name	Height (metres)	Hill No.	Top No.	O.S. Map Sheet	Map Reference
1	Coomb Dod	635		108	72	NT046238
2	**Hillshaw Head**	652	63	89	72	**NT048246**
3	**Gathersnow Hill**	688	43	58	72	**NT058257**
4	Coomb Hill.................	640		102	72	NT069263
5	**Hudderstone**	626	78	119	72	**NT022271**
6	**Culter Fell**	748	14	19	72	**NT052290**
7	**Chapelgill Hill**	696	36	51	72	**NT066303**
8	Cardon Hill	675		70	72	NT065314
9	**Tinto**	711	29	43	58	**NS953343**

SECTION 5

Manor Hills

	Name	Height (metres)	Hill No.	Top No.	O.S. Map Sheet	Map Reference
1	**Talla Cleuch Head**............	690	41	56	72	**NT133218**
2	Clockmore	641		101	72	NT183228
3	**Broad Law**	840	2	2	72	**NT146235**
4	**Cramalt Craig**	831	3	3	72	**NT168247**
5	**Greenside Law**	643	70	97	72	**NT198256**
6	Hunt Law.................	639		103	72	NT150264
7	Fifescar Knowe	811		7	72	NT175270
8	**Dollar Law**.................	817	5	5	72	**NT178278**
9	Notman Law	734		28	72	NT185260
10	Taberon Law................	636		107	72	NT146288
11	**Middle Hill**	716	27	40	72	**NT159294**
12	**Drumelzier Law**	668	53	75	72	**NT149312**
13	**Pykestone Hill**...............	737	19	25	72	**NT173312**
14	The Scrape	719		38	72	NT176324
15	Deer Law	629		113	73	NT222255
16	Conscleuch Head............	624		120	73	NT220262
17	**Black Law**	698	31	46	73	**NT222279**
18	Black Cleuch Hill (Blackhouse Heights)	675		69	73	NT222290
19	**Dun Rig**	744	17	22	73	**NT253315**
20	**Glenrath Heights**	732	20	29	73	**NT241322**
21	**Stob Law**	676	50	68	73	**NT230332**
22	**Birkscairn Hill**................	661	59	82	73	**NT274331**

Looking towards Saddle Yoke from Hart Fell in the Moffat Hills

SECTION 6

Moffat Hills

	Name	Height (metres)	Hill No.	Top No.	O.S. Map Sheet	Map Reference
1	Nether Coomb Craig.........	724		34	78	NT129109
2	**Swatte Fell**.................	**729**	**22**	**31**	**78**	**NT120115**
3	Falcon Craig................	724		33	78	NT122127
4	Saddle Yoke	735		27	78	NT144123
5	**Under Saddle Yoke**..........	**745**	**16**	**21**	**78**	**NT142126**
6	**Hart Fell**....................	**808**	**7**	**8**	**78**	**NT113135**
7	**Whitehope Heights**..........	**637**	**73**	**106**	**78**	**NT095139**
8	**Cape Law**...................	**722**	**24**	**35**	**78**	**NT131150**
9	Din Law	667		77	78	NT124156
10	Great Hill	774		16	78	NT145163
11	**Garelet Dod**.................	**698**	**32**	**47**	**78**	**NT126172**
12	**Erie Hill**...................	**690**	**40**	**55**	**78**	**NT124187**
13	Carlavin Hill	736		26	78	NT142188
14	Laird's Cleuch Rig..........	684		61	78	NT125196
15	Carrifan Gans...............	757		18	79	NT159138
16	**White Coomb**	**821**	**4**	**4**	**79**	**NT163150**
17	Firthhope Rig..............	800		10	79	NT153154
18	**Lochcraig Head**.............	**800**	**9**	**11**	**79**	**NT166177**
19	**Molls Cleuch Dod**...........	**785**	**12**	**14**	**79**	**NT151179**
20	Nickies Knowe..............	760		17	79	NT164191
21	Garelet Hill................	680		63	72	NT124201

SECTION 7

Ettrick Hills

	Name	Height (metres)	Hill No.	Top No.	O.S. Map Sheet	Map Reference
1	Loch Fell...............	688	44	59	79	NT170047
2	West Knowe.............	672		73	79	NT163052
3	Wind Fell..............	665	56	79	79	NT178061
4	Hopetoun Craig..........	632		109	79	NT187067
5	Ettrick Pen...........	692	38	53	79	NT199076
6	Croft Head............	637	72	105	79	NT153056
7	Capel Fell............	678	46	64	79	NT163069
8	Smidhope Hill..........	644		96	79	NT168076
9	White Shank...........	622		126	79	NT169082
10	Bodesbeck Law.........	665	55	78	79	NT169104
11	Mid Rig..............	616		133	79	NT180123
12	Bell Craig............	623	79	121	79	NT186128
13	Andrewhinney Hill	677	47	65	79	NT197138
14	Trowgrain Middle........	628		116	79	NT206150
15	Herman Law	614	87	134	79	NT214157

SECTION 8

Lowther Hills

	Name	Height (metres)	Hill No.	Top No.	O.S. Map Sheet	Map Reference
1	Queensberry	697	34	49	78	NX989997
2	Earncraig Hill	611	88	138	78	NS973013
3	Gana Hill.............	668	54	76	78	NS954010
4	Wedder Law............	672	52	72	78	NS938025
5	Glenleith Fell	612		136	78	NS922023
6	Scaw'd Law	663	58	81	78	NS922035
7	Ballencleuch Law	689	42	57	78	NS935049
8	Rodger Law	688		60	71/78	NS945058
9	Comb Law	645	67	93	71/78	NS943073
10	Cold Moss	628		115	71/78	NS898094
11	East Mount Lowther.......	631	76	112	71/78	NS878100
12	Lowther Hill	725	23	32	71/78	NS890107
13	Green Lowther	732	21	30	71/78	NS900120
14	Dun Law	677	48	66	71/78	NS916136
15	Louise Wood Law	618	86	132	71/78	NS932152

Kirriereoch Hill and Merrick from Rowantree Toll

SECTION 9

Carsphairn Hills

	Name	Height (metres)	Hill No.	Top No.	O.S. Map Sheet	Map Reference
1	**Cairnsmore of Carsphairn**	**797**	**10**	**12**	77	**NX594979**
2	Beninner	710		44	77	NX605971
3	**Moorbrock Hill**	**650**	**65**	**91**	77	**NX620983**
4	Keoch Rig	611		139	77	NX617999
5	**Windy Standard**	**698**	**33**	**48**	77	**NS620014**
6	**Alhang**	**642**	**71**	**100**	77	**NS642010**
7	Alwhat	628		114	77	NS646020
8	Meikledodd Hill	643		98	77	NS661027
9	**Blacklorg Hill**	**681**	**45**	**62**	77	**NS653042**
10	**Blackcraig Hill**	**700**	**30**	**45**	71/77	**NS647064**

SECTION 10
Galloway Hills

Name	Height (metres)	Hill No.	Top No.	O.S. Map Sheet	Map Reference
1 Knee of Cairnsmore..........	656		87	83	NX509656
2 **Cairnsmore of Fleet**	**711**	**28**	**42**	**83**	**NX501670**
3 Meikle Mulltaggart	612		137	83	NX512678
4 **Larg Hill**.................	**676**	**49**	**67**	**77**	**NX424757**
5 **Lamachan Hill**..............	**717**	**26**	**39**	**77**	**NX435769**
6 **Curleywee**	**674**	**51**	**71**	**77**	**NX454769**
7 **Millfore**	**656**	**62**	**88**	**77**	**NX478754**
8 Benyellary..................	719		37	77	NX414839
9 **Merrick**....................	**843**	**1**	**1**	**77**	**NX427855**
10 **Kirriereoch Hill**.............	**786**	**11**	**13**	**77**	**NX420870**
11 Tarfessock - South Top	620		129	77	NX413886
12 **Tarfessock**	**697**	**35**	**50**	**77**	**NX409891**
13 **Shalloch on Minnoch**........	**775**	**13**	**15**	**77**	**NX407905**
14 Sh. on Minnoch - North Top...	659		84	77	NX407905
15 **Craignaw**	**645**	**68**	**94**	**77**	**NX459833**
16 **Dungeon Hill**	**620**	**83**	**128**	**77**	**NX460850**
17 **Mullwharchar**	**692**	**39**	**54**	**77**	**NX454866**
18 **Meikle Millyea**	**746**	**15**	**20**	**77**	**NX518829**
19 **Milldown**..................	**738**	**18**	**24**	**77**	**NX511839**
20 Millfire	716		41	77	NX508848
21 **Corserine**	**814**	**6**	**6**	**77**	**NX497870**
22 **Carlin's Cairn**	**807**	**8**	**9**	**77**	**NX497883**
23 **Meaul**	**695**	**37**	**52**	**77**	**NX500909**
24 **Cairnsgarroch**	**659**	**60**	**83**	**77**	**NX515913**
25 Bow......................	613		135	77	NX508928
26 **Coran of Portmark**	**623**	**80**	**122**	**77**	**NX509936**

SECTION 11
Roxburgh and Cheviot Hills

Name	Height (metres)	Hill No.	Top No.	O.S. Map Sheet	Map Reference
1 **Cauldcleuch Head**............	**619**	**84**	**130**	**79**	**NT456006**
2 **Windy Gyle**	**619**	**85**	**131**	**80**	**NT855152**
3 Cairn Hill - West Top*........	743		23	80	NT896193

* This is the highest point on the Scottish-English border although it is not an actual summit. It cannot therefore be classified as a separate 'hill'.

TABLE 5. The Donalds in Order of Height

Name	Height (metres)	Hill No.	Top No.	Ref. in Table 4
Merrick	843	1	1	10-9
Broad Law	840	2	2	5-3
Cramalt Craig	831	3	3	5-4
White Coomb	821	4	4	6-16
Dollar Law	817	5	5	5-8
Corserine	814	6	6	10-21
Fifescar Knowe	811		7	5-7
Hart Fell	808	7	8	6-6
Carlin's Cairn	807	8	9	10-22
Firthhope Rig	800		10	6-17
Lochcraig Head	800	9	11	6-18
Cairnsmore of Carsphairn	797	10	12	9-1
Kirriereoch Hill	786	11	13	10-10
Molls Cleuch Dod	785	12	14	6-19
Shalloch on Minnoch	775	13	15	10-13
Great Hill	774		16	6-10
Nickies Knowe	760		17	6-20
Carrifan Gans	757		18	6-15
Culter Fell	748	14	19	4-6
Meikle Millyea	746	15	20	10-18
Under Saddle Yoke	745	16	21	6-5
Dun Rig	744	17	22	5-19
Cairn Hill - West Top	743		23	11-3
Milldown	738	18	24	10-19
Pykestone Hill	737	19	25	5-13
Carlavin Hill	736		26	6-13
Saddle Yoke	735		27	6-4
Notman Law	734		28	5-9
Glenrath Heights	732	20	29	5-20
Green Lowther	732	21	30	8-13
Swatte Fell	729	22	31	6-2
Lowther Hill	725	23	32	8-12
Falcon Craig	724		33	6-3
Nether Coomb Craig	724		34	6-1
Cape Law	722	24	35	6-8
Ben Cleuch	721	25	36	2-3
Benyellary	719		37	10-8
The Scrape	719		38	5-14
Lamachan Hill	717	26	39	10-5

Name	Height (metres)	Hill No.	Top No.	Ref. in Table 4
Middle Hill	716	27	40	5-11
Millfire	716		41	10-20
Cairnsmore of Fleet	711	28	42	10-2
Tinto	711	29	43	4-9
Beninner	710		44	9-2
Blackcraig Hill	700	30	45	9-10
Black Law	698	31	46	5-17
Garelet Dod	698	32	47	6-11
Windy Standard	698	33	48	9-5
Queensberry	697	34	49	8-1
Tarfessock	697	35	50	10-12
Chapelgill Hill	696	36	51	4-7
Meaul	695	37	52	10-23
Ettrick Pen	692	38	53	7-5
Mullwharchar	692	39	54	10-17
Erie Hill	690	40	55	6-12
Talla Cleuch Head	690	41	56	5-1
Ballencleuch Law	689	42	57	8-7
Gathersnow Hill	688	43	58	4-3
Loch Fell	688	44	59	7-1
Rodger Law	688		60	8-8
Laird's Cleuch Rig	684		61	6-14
Blacklorg Hill	681	45	62	9-9
Garelet Hill	680		63	6-21
Capel Fell	678	46	64	7-7
Andrewhinney Hill	677	47	65	7-13
Dun Law	677	48	66	8-14
Larg Hill	676	49	67	10-4
Stob Law	676	50	68	5-21
Black Cleuch Hill (Blackhouse Heights)	675		69	5-18
Cardon Hill	675		70	4-8
Curleywee	674	51	71	10-6
Wedder Law	672	52	72	8-4
West Knowe	672		73	7-2
Andrew Gannel Hill	670		74	2-5
Drumelzier Law	668	53	75	5-12
Gana Hill	668	54	76	8-3
Din Law	667		77	6-9
Bodesbeck Law	665	55	78	7-10
Wind Fell	665	56	79	7-3
Uamh Bheag	664	57	80	1-1

Name	Height (metres)	Hill No.	Top No.	Ref. in Table 4
Scaw'd Law	663	58	81	8-6
Birkscairn Hill	661	59	82	5-22
Cairnsgarroch	659	60	83	10-24
Shalloch on Minnoch - North Top	659		84	10-14
Windlestraw Law	659	61	85	3-1
Windlestraw Law SW Top	657		86	3-2
Knee of Cairnsmore	656		87	10-1
Millfore	656	62	88	10-7
Hillshaw Head	652	63	89	4-2
Blackhope Scar	651	64	90	3-5
Moorbrock Hill	650	65	91	9-3
King's Seat Hill	648	66	92	2-6
Comb Law	645	67	93	8-9
Craignaw	645	68	94	10-15
Tarmangie Hill	645	69	95	2-7
Smidhope Hill	644		96	7-8
Greenside Law	643	70	97	5-5
Meikledodd Hill	643		98	9-8
Whitewisp Hill	643		99	2-8
Alhang	642	71	100	9-6
Clockmore	641		101	5-2
Coomb Hill	640		102	4-4
Hunt Law	639		103	5-6
The Law	638		104	2-4
Croft Head	637	72	105	7-6
Whitehope Heights	637	73	106	6-7
Taberon Law	636		107	5-10
Coomb Dod	635		108	4-1
Hopetoun Craig	632		109	7-4
Beinn nan Eun	631	74	110	1-4

Name	Height (metres)	Hill No.	Top No.	Ref. in Table 4
Blairdenon Hill	631	75	111	2-1
East Mount Lowther	631	76	112	8-11
Deer Law	629		113	5-15
Alwhat	628		114	9-7
Cold Moss	628		115	8-10
Trowgrain Middle	628		116	7-14
Beinn Odhar	626		117	1-3
Bowbeat Hill	626	77	118	3-4
Hudderstone	626	78	119	4-5
Conscleuch Head	624		120	5-16
Bell Craig	623	79	121	7-12
Coran of Portmark	623	80	122	10-26
Dundreich	623	81	123	3-6
Whitehope Law	623	82	124	3-3
Ben Ever	622		125	2-2
White Shank	622		126	7-9
Meall Clachach	621		127	1-2
Dungeon Hill	620	83	128	10-16
Tarfessock - South Top	620		129	10-11
Cauldcleuch Head	619	84	130	11-1
Windy Gyle	619	85	131	11-2
Louise Wood Law	618	86	132	8-15
Mid Rig	616		133	7-11
Herman Law	614	87	134	7-15
Bow	613		135	10-25
Glenleith Fell	612		136	8-5
Meikle Mulltaggart	612		137	10-3
Earncraig Hill	611	88	138	8-2
Keoch Rig	611		139	9-4
Innerdownie	610	89	140	2-9

Index of Donald's List of 2000ft Hills

Name	Section Reference	Name	Section Reference
Alhang	9-6	Dundreich	3-6
Alwhat	9-7	Dungeon Hill	10-16
Andrew Gannel Hill	2-5	Dun Law	8-14
Andrewhinney Hill	7-13	Dun Rig	5-19
Ballencleuch Law	8-7	Earncraig Hill	8-2
Beinn nan Eun	1-4	East Mount Lowther	8-11
Beinn Odhar	1-3	Erie Hill	6-12
Bell Craig	7-12	Ettrick Pen	7-5
Ben Cleuch	2-3	Falcon Craig	6-3
Ben Ever	2-2	Fifescar Knowe	5-7
Beninner	9-2	Firthhope Rig	6-17
Benyellary	10-8	Gana Hill	8-3
Birkscairn Hill	5-22	Garelet Dod	6-11
Black Cleuch Hill	5-18	Garelet Hill	6-21
Blackcraig Hill	9-10	Gathersnow Hill	4-3
Blackhope Scar	3-5	Glenleith Fell	8-5
Blackhouse Heights	5-18	Glenrath Heights	5-20
Black Law	5-17	Great Hill	6-10
Blacklorg Hill	9-9	Green Lowther	8-13
Blairdenon Hill	2-1	Greenside Law	5-5
Bodesbeck Law	7-10	Hart Fell	6-6
Bow	10-25	Herman Law	7-15
Bowbeat Hill	3-4	Hillshaw Head	4-2
Broad Law	5-3	Hopetoun Craig	7-4
Cairn Hill - West Top	11-3	Hudderstone	4-5
Cairnsgarroch	10-24	Hunt Law	5-6
Cairnsmore of Carsphairn	9-1	Innerdownie	2-9
Cairnsmore of Fleet	10-2	Keoch Rig	9-4
Cape Law	6-8	King's Seat Hill	2-6
Capel Fell	7-7	Kirriereoch Hill	10-10
Cardon Hill	4-8	Knee of Cairnsmore	10-1
Carlavin Hill	6-13	Laird's Cleuch Rig	6-14
Carlin's Cairn	10-22	Lamachan Hill	10-5
Carrifan Gans	6-15	Larg Hill	10-4
Cauldcleuch Head	11-1	Law, The	2-4
Chapelgill Hill	4-7	Lochcraig Head	6-18
Clockmore	5-2	Loch Fell	7-1
Cold Moss	8-10	Louise Wood Law	8-15
Comb Law	8-9	Lowther Hill	8-12
Conscleuch Head	5-16	Meall Clachach	1-2
Coomb Dod	4-1	Meaul	10-23
Coomb Hill	4-4	Meikledodd Hill	9-8
Coran of Portmark	10-26	Meikle Millyea	10-18
Corserine	10-21	Meikle Mulltaggart	10-3
Craignaw	10-15	Merrick	10-9
Cramalt Craig	5-4	Middle Hill	5-11
Croft Head	7-6	Mid Rig	7-11
Culter Fell	4-6	Milldown	10-19
Curleywee	10-6	Millfire	10-20
Deer Law	5-15	Millfore	10-7
Din Law	6-9	Molls Cleuch Dod	6-19
Dollar Law	5-8	Moorbrock Hill	9-3
Drumelzier Law	5-12	Mullwharchar	10-17

Name	Section Reference	Name	Section Reference
Nether Coomb Craig	6-1	Tarmangie Hill	2-7
Nickies Knowe	6-20	Tinto	4-9
Notman Law	5-9	Trowgrain Middle	7-14
Pykestone Hill	5-13	Uamh Bheag	1-1
Queensberry	8-1	Under Saddle Yoke	6-5
Rodger Law	8-8	Wedder Law	8-4
Saddle Yoke	6-4	West Knowe	7-2
Scaw'd Law	8-6	White Coomb	6-16
Scrape, The	5-14	Whitehope Heights	6-7
Shalloch on Minnoch	10-13	Whitehope Law	3-3
Shalloch on Minnoch - North Top	10-14	White Shank	7-9
Smidhope Hill	7-8	Whitewisp Hill	2-8
Stob Law	5-21	Wind Fell	7-3
Swatte Fell	6-2	Windlestraw Law	3-1
Taberon Law	5-10	Windlestraw Law SW Top	3-2
Talla Cleuch Head	5-1	Windy Gyle	11-2
Tarfessock	10-12	Windy Standard	9-5
Tarfessock - South Top	10-11		

PART 4

The Grahams

A Complete List of Scottish Hills between 2000 and 2499 feet high

Compiled by
Alan Dawson

From original lists by
Alan Dawson
and
Fiona Torbet (née Graham)

Introduction

There is a long tradition of climbing hills over 2500 feet high in Scotland, and hills over 2000 feet in England and Wales, but for some reason most Scottish hills between 2000 and 2500 feet have been overlooked. The Grahams fill this gap. A Graham is a hill between 610 metres and 761 metres high (2000-2499 feet), with a drop of at least 150 metres all round. The list of hills in this category was first published in *The Relative Hills of Britain* (Alan Dawson, Cicerone Press, April 1992), which lists all the British Marilyns, ie hills of *any height* with a drop of at least 150 metres all round. Originally, Scottish hills in this height range were referred to as Elsies (short for Lesser Corbetts). They have since been renamed Grahams in memory of the late Fiona Torbet (née Graham), who published her own list of such hills in November 1992. Her initial list omitted all hills in Southern Scotland and about a dozen in the Highlands, but included several hills with less than 150 metres drop. To avoid having two conflicting lists, it was agreed to use the existing list published in *The Relative Hills...* (with a few name changes), but to refer to the hills as Grahams. The task of compiling and updating this consolidated list has been undertaken by Alan Dawson and the results were first published in 1995 in *The Grahams and the New Donalds* (TACit Press, 138 West Stirling Street, Alva, Clackmannan, FK12 5EN). We are grateful to TACit Press and Alan Dawson for their agreement to the reproduction of the list of Grahams here.

There are 224 Grahams, distributed as follows: Highlands south of the Great Glen 92, Highlands north of the Great Glen 84, Central and Southern Scotland 23, Skye 10, Mull 7, Harris 3, Jura 2, Arran 1, Rum 1, South Uist 1.

NOTES ABOUT THE LIST

Hills are grouped into geographical regions. Most regions are subdivided into sections. Each region is given a descriptive heading, to provide a general idea of its location, and a more detailed summary of its boundaries. Hills are listed in height order within each section. The information is laid out in the following columns:

Section

Section numbers 1 to 17 correspond loosely to those used in *Munro's Tables*. Additional sections are used to cover those areas which do not contain Munros, but these sections follow a different nomenclature to that used in Corbett's Tables.

Name

Most names are taken from the relevant 1:50,000 map. If a hill is not named on this then the name shown on a larger scale map is used. Like spot heights, names on different maps do not always coincide. Where a hill has a general name *and* a summit name, the general name is given, as this tends to be more commonly used. Maps do not always show the general name at the summit, so close attention to the grid reference is required in many cases.

Height

This column gives the height of the hill above sea level in metres. All Ordnance Survey 1:50,000 maps now show metric contours and spot heights. The contours are very accurate, but spot heights are not generally as accurate as those on larger scale maps. However, it is not possible to rely solely on larger scale maps, as metric versions are not available for all areas. Also, numerous spot heights are shown on 1:50,000 maps but omitted from the 1:25,000 or 1:10,000 maps. In cases where differing heights for the same point are given on different maps, the following order of precedence is used: metric 1:10,000; metric 1:25,000; 1:50,000; non-metric 1:10,000 or 1:25,000.

O. S. Map Sheet

This column gives the sheet number(s) of the Ordnance Survey Landranger 1:50,000 series on which the summit of the hill is to be found.

Map Reference

Each map reference pinpoints the location of the summit of a hill to within 100 metres. Details of how to use grid references are given on all Landranger maps. Where a hill has more than one top, or the true summit can not be positively identified on the ground, knowing the correct grid reference can be extremely useful. It may be that not all Grahams have summit cairns.

Drop

This column refers to the *relative height* of the hill; ie the height difference (in metres) between the summit and the col connecting the hill to the nearest peak with a 150-metre drop of its own on all sides. If there is more than one col, the highest col is used. If there is no spot height for the col shown on any metric map, the drop is estimated from the position of contour lines; this is indicated by a c in the *drop* column. It should be accurate to within two or three metres. The resulting figure gives an indication of how isolated a hill is (in height) from its neighbours. No account, however, is taken of distance or topographical merit.

TABLE 6. The Grahams by Region

REGION 1
Firth of Clyde to Strath Tay

Crianlarich; A85 and A827 to Killin; Loch Tay and River Tay to Perth; A85 to Crieff and Comrie; Glen Artney and the Highland boundary fault to Loch Lomond; River Leven to Dumbarton; coast to Arrochar; A83 to Inveraray; A819 and A85 to Crianlarich.

Sect.	Name	Height (metres)	O.S. Map Sheet	Map Reference	Drop (metres)
1A	Shee of Ardtalnaig	759	51,52	NN729351	c224
1A	Beinn na Gainimh	730	52	NN837344	288
1A	Meall Buidhe	719	51	NN576275	c232
1A	Creag Ruadh.	712	51	NN674292	c196
1A	Meall Dearg	690	52	NN886414	c173
1A	Creag Each	672	51	NN652263	c216
1A	Creag Gharbh.	637	51	NN632327	c151
1A	Meall nan Caorach.	623	52	NN928338	159
1A	Meall Reamhar.	620	52	NN922332	156
1B	Beinn Dearg	706	57	NN696197	351
1B	Sgiath a'Chaise.	645	57	NN583169	304
1B	Mor Bheinn.	640	51,52,57	NN716211	327
1C	The Stob	753	51	NN491231	228
1C	Meall Mor	747	50,56	NN383151	c262
1C	Ben Venue.	729	57	NN474063	c504
1C	Stob Breac	688	57	NN447166	c243
1C	Creag Mhor.	658	57	NN510185	293
1C	Cruinn a'Bheinn.	632	56	NN365051	177
1D	Meall nan Gabhar	744	50	NN235240	265
1D	Beinn Damhain.	684	50,56	NN282173	220
1D	Meall Odhar	656	50	NN298298	183
1D	Fiarach.	652	50	NN344261	181
1D	Beinn Bhalgairean	636	50	NN202241	c209
1E	Doune Hill	734	56	NS290971	190
1E	Beinn Chaorach	713	56	NS287923	362
1E	Beinn a'Mhanaich	709	56	NS269946	358
1E	Beinn Eich.	703	56	NS302946	159
1E	Cruach an t-Sidhein	684	56	NS275965	169
1E	Beinn Bhreac.	681	56	NN321000	322
1E	Beinn Dubh.	657	56	NS321962	430
1E	Tullich Hill	632	56	NN293006	273

REGION 2
Loch Rannoch to Loch Tay

Rannoch Station; B846 and Loch Rannoch to Kinloch Rannoch; River Tummel, River Tay and Loch Tay to Killin; A827 and A85 to Tyndrum; railway to Rannoch Station.

Sect.	Name	Height (metres)	O.S. Map Sheet	Map Reference	Drop (metres)
2	Meall a'Mhuic.	745	42,51	NN579508	235

REGION 3
Loch Leven to Connel Bridge and Glen Lochy

Kinlochleven; River Leven, Blackwater Reservoir, Black Water and railway to Rannoch Station; railway to Tyndrum; A85 to Taynuilt; Loch Etive and coast to Kinlochleven.

Sect.	Name	Height (metres)	O.S. Map Sheet	Map Reference	Drop (metres)
3A	Pap of Glencoe	742	41	NN125594	156
3A	Stob na Cruaiche	739	41	NN363571	350
3B	Beinn Bhreac.	726	50	NN008408	c161
3B	Beinn Mheadhonach	715	50	NN019369	409
3B	Beinn Molurgainn	690	50	NN019400	c151
3B	Meall Mor	676	41	NN106559	c301
3B	Sgorr a'Choise	663	41	NN084551	c288
3C	Beinn nan Lus.	709	50	NN130375	c240
3C	Meall Garbh	701	50	NN168367	257
3C	Beinn Suidhe	676	50	NN211400	c267
3C	Meall Tairbh	665	50	NN251375	c253
3C	Beinn Donachain	650	50	NN198316	375
3C	Beinn na Sroine	636	50	NN233289	c221

REGION 4
Fort William to Loch Ericht

Fort William; River Lochy to Gairlochy; River Spean to Spean Bridge; A86 to Kingussie; A9 to Dalwhinnie; Loch Ericht and River Ericht to Loch Rannoch; B846 to Rannoch Station; railway, Black Water, Blackwater Reservoir and River Leven to Kinlochleven; Loch Leven and Loch Linnhe to Fort William.

Sect.	Name	Height (metres)	O.S. Map Sheet	Map Reference	Drop (metres)
4A	Cnap Cruinn.	742	41	NN302774	245
4A	Beinn na Cloiche	646	41	NN284648	194
4A	Creag Ghuanach.	621	41	NN299690	212
4A	Tom Meadhoin	621	41	NN087621	155
4A	Beinn na Gucaig.	616	41	NN062653	c451
4B	Binnein Shuas.	747	34,42	NN463826	c362
4B	Binnein Shios	667	34,42	NN492857	c282
4B	Meall nan Eagan.	658	42	NN596874	c166

REGION 5
Loch Ericht to Glen Tromie and Glen Garry

Kingussie; Glen Tromie to Gaick Lodge; Gaick pass and Edendon Water to Dalnacardoch Lodge; River Garry and River Tummel to Loch Rannoch; River Ericht, Loch Ericht and A9 to Kingussie.

Sect.	Name	Height (metres)	O.S. Map Sheet	Map Reference	Drop (metres)
5	Creag Ruadh...................	658	42	NN685882	197
5	Creag a'Mhadaidh	612	42	NN634650	156

REGION 6
Forest of Atholl to Braemar and Blairgowrie

Braemar; A93 to Blairgowrie; River Ardle, River Isla, River Tay, River Tummel and River Garry to Dalnacardoch Lodge; Edendon Water, Gaick pass and Glen Tromie to Kingussie; River Spey, River Feshie, Geldie Burn and River Dee to Braemar.

Sect.	Name	Height (metres)	O.S. Map Sheet	Map Reference	Drop (metres)
6	Blath Bhalg	641	43	NO019611	265

REGION 7
Braemar to Montrose

Braemar; River Dee to Aberdeen; coast to Montrose; River South Esk to Brechin; Strathmore and River Ardle to Blairgowrie; A93 to Braemar.

Sect.	Name	Height (metres)	O.S. Map Sheet	Map Reference	Drop (metres)
7	Mount Blair....................	744	43	NO167629	c369
7	Badandun Hill	740	44	NO207678	c154
7	Hunt Hill.....................	705	44	NO380805	181
7	Duchray Hill..................	702	43	NO161672	264
7	Hill of Wirren	678	44	NO522739	311
7	Cat Law......................	671	44	NO319611	c296
7	Corwharn	611	44	NO288651	154

REGION 8
The Cairngorms

Aviemore; River Spey to Grantown-on-Spey; A939 to Ballater; River Dee to Braemar and Linn of Dee; Geldie Burn, River Feshie and River Spey to Aviemore.

Sect.	Name	Height (metres)	O.S. Map Sheet	Map Reference	Drop (metres)
8	Geallaig Hill..................	743	37,44	NO297981	312
8	Cnap Chaochan Aitinn	715	36	NJ145099	c151
8	Creag Bhalg	668	43	NO091912	159

REGION 9
Spean Bridge to Elgin

Inverness; coast to Spey Bay; River Spey to Kingussie; A86 to Spean Bridge; River Spean to Gairlochy; Great Glen to Inverness.

Sect.	Name	Height (metres)	O.S. Map Sheet	Map Reference	Drop (metres)
9A	Carn Glas-choire	659	35,36	NH891291	c251
9A	Carn nan Tri-tighearnan	614	27	NH823390	c332
9B	Creag Dhubh	756	35	NN678972	c391
9B	Creag Liath	743	35	NH663007	188
9B	Carn na h-Easgainn	618	27	NH744320	174
9C	Leana Mhor	684	34,41	NN284878	169
9C	Leana Mhor	676	34,41	NN317879	c158
9C	Creag Dhubh	658	34,41	NN322824	c332
9C	Creag Ruadh.	622	35	NN558913	c314

REGION 10
Glen Shiel to Glenfinnan

Shiel Bridge; Glen Shiel and Glen Moriston to Invermoriston; Great Glen to Fort William; Loch Eil and A830 to Lochailort; coast to Shiel Bridge.

Sect.	Name	Height (metres)	O.S. Map Sheet	Map Reference	Drop (metres)
10A	Beinn a'Chapuill.	759	33	NG835148	258
10A	Druim Fada	713	33	NG894083	c486
10A	Biod an Fhithich.	644	33	NG950147	c153
10A	Beinn Clachach.	643	33	NG885109	228
10B	Slat Bheinn	700	33	NG910027	267
10B	Meall nan Eun	667	33	NG903052	174
10C	Sgurr Choinich.	749	34	NN127949	277
10C	Glas Bheinn	732	34	NN171919	292
10C	Meall Blair	656	33	NN077950	c341
10D	Druim Fada	744	41	NN087824	c516
10D	Mullach Coire nan Geur-oirean . . .	727	41	NN049892	191
10D	An Stac	718	40	NM866889	c223
10D	Meith Bheinn	710	40	NM821872	c308
10D	Meall Onfhaidh	681	41	NN010840	299
10D	Aodann Chleireig.	663	40	NM994825	316
10D	Glas-charn.	633	40	NM846837	c328

REGION 11

Loch Duich to Loch Ness, South of Loch Mullardoch

Shiel Bridge; Loch Duich, Loch Long and Glen Elchaig to Carnach; pass to Glen Cannich and A831 to Drumnadrochit; Loch Ness to Invermoriston; Glen Moriston and Glen Shiel to Shiel Bridge.

Sect.	Name	Height (metres)	O.S. Map Sheet	Map Reference	Drop (metres)
11A	Carnan Cruithneachd	729	25,33	NG994258	221
11A	Beinn a'Mheadhoin	610	25	NH218255	242
11B	Carn a'Chaochain.	706	34	NH235177	c208
11B	Meall Fuar-mhonaidh	699	26	NH457222	c204
11B	Meall a'Chrathaich.	679	26	NH360220	c184
11B	Carn Mhic an Toisich.	678	34	NH310185	c180
11B	Glas-bheinn Mhor	651	26	NH436231	c156

REGION 12

Lochalsh to Inverness, North of Loch Mullardoch

Kyle of Lochalsh; coast to Strathcarron; railway to Garve; A832 to Beauly; Beauly Firth to Inverness; Great Glen to Drumnadrochit; A831 to Cannich; Glen Cannich, Loch Mullardoch and pass to Carnach; Glen Elchaig, Loch Long and Loch Alsh to Kyle of Lochalsh.

Sect.	Name	Height (metres)	O.S. Map Sheet	Map Reference	Drop (metres)
12A	Beinn na Muice.	695	25	NH218402	c160
12A	Meall na Faochaig	680	25	NH257525	c272
12A	Carn na Coinnich.	673	26	NH324510	c265
12A	Beinn Mheadhoin.	665	25	NH258477	c218
12A	Creag Dhubh Mhor	612	25	NG982404	c169
12B	An Cruachan	706	25	NH093358	c238
12B	Carn na Breabaig	678	25	NH066301	c176
12B	Carn Gorm	677	26	NH328355	c191

REGION 13

Loch Carron to Loch Maree

Poolewe; Loch Maree to Kinlochewe; A832 to Achnasheen; A890 to Loch Carron and coast to Poolewe.

Sect.	Name	Height (metres)	O.S. Map Sheet	Map Reference	Drop (metres)
13A	Beinn a'Chearcaill	725	19	NG931637	c368
13A	An Ruadh-mheallan.	672	19,24	NG836615	c201
13B	Beinn na h-Eaglaise	736	25	NG908523	c303
13B	Sgurr a'Gharaidh	732	24	NG884443	c331
13B	Carn Breac	678	25	NH045530	c276
13B	Beinn a'Chlachain	626	24	NG724490	c373
13B	Beinn na Feusaige	625	25	NH093542	223

REGION 14
Loch Maree to Loch Broom and Garve

Ullapool; Loch Broom and A835 to Garve; A832 to Kinlochewe; Loch Maree and coast to Ullapool.

Sect.	Name	Height (metres)	O.S. Map Sheet	Map Reference	Drop (metres)
14A	Meall Mheinnidh	722	19	NG955748	c227
14A	Beinn a'Mhuinidh	692	19	NH032660	c378
14A	Beinn a'Chaisgein Beag	682	19	NG965821	c177
14A	Beinn Ghobhlach	635	19	NH055943	254
14B	Groban	749	19	NH099709	277
14B	Beinn nan Ramh	711	19	NH139662	c386
14B	Meall a'Chaorainn	705	19	NH136604	c190
14B	Beinn Bheag	668	19	NH086714	196

REGION 15
Ullapool to the Moray Firth

Ullapool; A835 to Ledmore; A837 and River Oykel to Bonar Bridge; Dornoch Firth and coast to Inverness; Beauly Firth to Beauly; A832 to Garve; A835 and Loch Broom to Ullapool.

Sect.	Name	Height (metres)	O.S. Map Sheet	Map Reference	Drop (metres)
15A	Meall Doire Faid	730	20	NH221792	c175
15A	Carn a'Choin Deirg	701	20	NH397923	319
15A	Meall Dubh	667	20	NH225886	158
15A	Meall a'Chaorainn	632	20	NH360827	157
15B	Beinn nan Eun	743	20	NH448759	c255
15B	Meall Mor	738	20	NH515745	263
15B	Beinn Tharsuinn	710	20	NH412829	176
15B	Carn Loch nan Amhaichean	697	20	NH411757	c202
15B	Beinn Tharsuinn	692	21	NH606792	353
15B	Carn Salachaidh	647	20	NH518874	234

REGION 16
The Far North

Ullapool; coast to Cape Wrath, Wick, Dornoch Firth, River Oykel and A837 to Ledmore; A835 to Ullapool.

Sect.	Name	Height (metres)	O.S. Map Sheet	Map Reference	Drop (metres)
16B	Carn an Tionail	759	16	NC392390	c214
16B	Sabhal Beag	732	9	NC373429	169
16B	Beinn Direach	688	16	NC406380	150

REGION 16 (continued)

Sect.	Name	Height (metres)	O.S. Map Sheet	Map Reference	Drop (metres)
16C	Morven	706	17	ND004285	c351
16C	Scaraben	626	17	ND066268	c328
16D	Creag Mhor.	713	16	NC698240	251
16D	Ben Armine.	705	16	NC695273	243
16D	Beinn Dhorain	628	17	NC925156	c249
16E	Meallan a'Chuail	750	15	NC344292	c204
16E	Ben Stack.	721	9	NC269423	532
16E	Meall an Fheur Loch	613	16	NC361310	c165
16F	Ben Mor Coigach	743	15	NC094042	c198
16F	Suilven	731	15	NC153183	c496
16F	Sgurr an Fhidhleir	705	15	NC094054	160
16F	Beinn an Eoin	619	15	NC105064	c178
16F	Stac Pollaidh.	612	15	NC107106	441

REGION 17

Skye, Rum and Mull

Three large islands in the Inner Hebrides.

Sect.	Name	Height (metres)	O.S. Map Sheet	Map Reference	Drop (metres)
17A	The Storr (Skye).	719	23	NG495540	230
17A	Hartaval (Skye)	669	23	NG480551	180
17B	Marsco (Skye)	736	32	NG507252	413
17B	Beinn Dearg Mhor (Skye).	731	32	NG520285	316
17B	Belig (Skye)	702	32	NG544240	246
17C	Sgurr na Coinnich (Skye).	739	33	NG762222	c161
17C	Beinn na Caillich (Skye)	732	32	NG601233	175
17C	Beinn na Caillich (Skye)	732	33	NG770229	c154
17C	Beinn Dearg Mhor (Skye).	709	32	NG587228	152
17C	Ben Aslak (Skye)	610	33	NG750191	c216
17D	Trallval (Rum)	702	39	NM377952	c189
17E	Beinn Talaidh (Mull)	761	49	NM625347	337
17E	Sgurr Dearg (Mull)	741	49	NM665339	c246
17E	Ben Buie (Mull)	717	49	NM604270	c464
17E	Corra-bheinn* (Mull)	704	48	NM573321	c316
17E	Beinn Fhada (Mull).	702	47,48	NM540349	c174
17E	Creach Beinn (Mull)	698	49	NM642276	c551
17E	Cruach Choireadail (Mull).	618	48	NM594304	194

* Cruachan Dearg (NM568331) is also 704m. It is a significant peak with a drop of about 130m between it and Corra-bheinn.

REGION 18
Ardnamurchan to Loch Linnhe

Fort William; Loch Linnhe and coast to Ardnamurchan Point and Lochailort; A830 and Loch Eil to Fort William.

Sect.	Name	Height (metres)	O.S. Map Sheet	Map Reference	Drop (metres)
18A	Beinn Gaire	666	40	NM781748	c230
18A	Croit Bheinn	663	40	NM810773	c227
18B	Sgurr a'Chaorainn	761	40	NM895662	205
18B	Beinn Bheag	736	40	NM914635	200
18B	Druim na Sgriodain	734	40	NM978656	436
18B	Meall nan Damh	723	40	NM919745	c238
18B	Stob Mhic Bheathain	721	40	NM914713	c215
18B	Sgurr nan Cnamh	701	40	NM886643	157
18B	Sgorr Mhic Eacharna	650	40	NM928630	168
18B	Glas Bheinn	636	40	NM938758	c151
18C	Beinn Mheadhoin	739	49	NM799514	c484
18C	Beinn na Cille	652	49	NM854542	c193

REGION 19
Oban to Dunoon and the Mull of Kintyre

Oban; coast to Taynuilt; A85 and A819 to Inveraray; A83 to Arrochar; Loch Long and coast to Oban.

Sect.	Name	Height (metres)	O.S. Map Sheet	Map Reference	Drop (metres)
19	Cnoc Coinnich	761	56	NN233007	c273
19	Beinn Mhor	741	56	NS107908	423
19	Stob an Eas	732	56	NN185073	248
19	Beinn Lochain	703	56	NN160006	c197
19	Beinn Ruadh	664	56	NS155883	499
19	Stob na Boine Druim-fhinn	658	56	NN168025	c152
19	Creag Tharsuinn	643	56	NS088913	c394
19	Beinn Bheag	618	56	NS125932	300
19	Cruach nam Mult	611	56	NN168055	282
19	Cruach nan Capull	611	63	NS095795	286

REGION 20
Jura and Arran

Two large islands off the Argyll coast.

Sect.	Name	Height (metres)	O.S. Map Sheet	Map Reference	Drop (metres)
20	Beinn Shiantaidh (Jura)	757	61	NR513747	303
20	Beinn a'Chaolais (Jura)	733	60,61	NR488734	359
20	Beinn Bharrain (Arran)	721	62,69	NR901427	326

REGION 21
Strathspey to Aberdeen

Fraserburgh; coast to Aberdeen; River Dee to Ballater; A939 to Grantown-on-Spey; River Spey to Spey Bey; coast to Fraserburgh.

Sect.	Name	Height (metres)	O.S. Map Sheet	Map Reference	Drop (metres)
21A	Cook's Cairn	755	37	NJ302278	c210
21A	Mona Gowan	749	37	NJ336058	c191
21A	Creagan a'Chaise	722	36	NJ104241	191
21A	The Buck	721	37	NJ412233	c256
21A	Carn a'Ghille Chearr	710	36	NJ139298	179
21A	Ladylea Hill	610	37	NJ343168	202
21B	Pressendye	620	37	NJ490089	c255

REGION 22
Western Isles

The Outer Hebrides.

Sect.	Name	Height (metres)	O.S. Map Sheet	Map Reference	Drop (metres)
22	Uisgnaval Mor (Harris)	729	13,14	NB120085	375
22	Tirga Mor (Harris)	679	13,14	NB055115	c436
22	Oreval (Harris)	662	13,14	NB083099	c419
22	Beinn Mhor (South Uist)	620	22	NF808310	c323

REGION 23
Central Scotland from Dumbarton to Montrose

Dumbarton; River Leven to Loch Lomond; Highland boundary fault and Glen Artney to Comrie; A85 to Perth; River Tay, Strathmore and River South Esk to Montrose; coast to Firth of Forth; Forth & Clyde Canal to Glasgow; River Clyde to Dumbarton.

Sect.	Name	Height (metres)	O.S. Map Sheet	Map Reference	Drop (metres)
23	Ben Cleuch	721	58	NN902006	452
23	Uamh Bheag*	664	57	NN691118	323

* Uamh Bheag has an East Top at NM696119 that is also 664m, though it looks less significant. The drop between the two is 21m.

REGION 24
South-West Scotland

Glasgow; River Clyde to Abington; A74 to Gretna; Solway Firth and coast to Firth of Clyde and Glasgow.

Sect.	Name	Height (metres)	O.S. Map Sheet	Map Reference	Drop (metres)
24A	Tinto	711	72	NS953343	425
24B	Lamachan Hill	717	77	NX435769	310
24B	Cairnsmore of Fleet	711	83	NX501670	489
24B	Mullwharchar	692	77	NX454866	187
24B	Millfore	657	77	NX478754	250
24B	Craignaw	645	77	NX459833	151
24C	Green Lowther	732	71,78	NS900120	c307
24C	Blackcraig Hill	700	71,77	NS647064	214
24C	Windy Standard	698	77	NS620014	212
24C	Queensberry	697	78	NX989997	c212
24C	Ballencleuch Law	689	78	NS935049	c204

REGION 25
Firth of Forth to the English Border

Edinburgh; coast to Berwick; English border to Gretna; A74 to Abington; River Clyde to Glasgow; Forth & Clyde Canal to Firth of Forth and Edinburgh.

Sect.	Name	Height (metres)	O.S. Map Sheet	Map Reference	Drop (metres)
25A	Windlestraw Law	659	73	NT371431	c290
25A	Blackhope Scar	651	73	NT315483	c282
25B	Culter Fell	748	72	NT052290	c270
25B	Dun Rig	744	73	NT253316	243
25B	Ettrick Pen	692	79	NT199076	173
25B	Gathersnow Hill	688	72	NT058257	c210
25B	Capel Fell	678	79	NT163069	159
25B	Andrewhinney Hill	677	79	NT197138	c192
25B	Croft Head	637	79	NT153056	194
25B	Cauldcleuch Head	619	79	NT456006	183

Highest Grahams

These are the top twenty-two Grahams in terms of height above sea level.

Sect.	Name	Height (metres)	O.S. Map Sheet	Map Reference	Drop (metres)
17E	Beinn Talaidh (Mull).	761	49	NM625347	337
18B	Sgurr a'Chaorainn	761	40	NM895662	205
19	Cnoc Coinnich	761	56	NN233007	c273
1A	Shee of Ardtalnaig	759	51,52	NN729351	c224
10A	Beinn a'Chapuill.	759	33	NG835148	258
16B	Carn an Tionail.	759	16	NC392390	c214
20	Beinn Shiantaidh (Jura)	757	61	NR513747	303
9B	Creag Dhubh	756	35	NN678972	c391
21A	Cook's Cairn.	755	37	NJ302278	c210
1C	The Stob	753	51	NN491231	228
16E	Meallan a'Chuail	750	15	NC344292	c204
10C	Sgurr Choinich.	749	34	NN127949	277
14B	Groban	749	19	NH099709	277
21A	Mona Gowan	749	37	NJ336058	c191
25B	Culter Fell.	748	72	NT052290	c270
1C	Meall Mor.	747	50,56	NN383151	c262
4B	Binnein Shuas.	747	34,42	NN463826	c362
2	Meall a'Mhuic.	745	42,51	NN579508	235
1D	Meall nan Gabhar	744	50	NN235240	265
7	Mount Blair.	744	43	NO167629	c369
10D	Druim Fada	744	41	NN087824	c516
25B	Dun Rig.	744	73	NT253316	243

PART 5

A Gaelic Guide

Translations and Pronunciations for the Munros, Tops and Corbetts

Compiled by
Iseabail C. MacLeod
Iain A. MacLeod
Domhnall Uilleam Stiùbhart

Introduction

The vast majority of Scottish mountain names are Gaelic or at least based on Gaelic. In the list (p.148) we attempt to give those with no knowledge of the language some idea of the meaning and pronunciation of the names of Munros, Tops and Corbetts. Certainty is not always possible: some words have several different meanings and some also vary in meaning from district to district. Others are so old and their forms have changed so much over the centuries that one can only put forward a theory as to their meaning. Many of the explanations given here are from the standard work on Gaelic place-names, W J Watson's *The History of the Celtic Place-Names of Scotland* (see list of sources, p.147).

Many of the translations may sound rather strange. This is sometimes because the Gaelic has a connotation which cannot be conveyed in English. For example 'big hill' for Beinn Mhór (Ben More) does not give the idea of the hill being the most prominent of the local hills. We would be grateful for any suggestions for improvements in the translations.

A simplified pronunciation scheme is included (see p.146) but it is not intended to be definitive. For example the pronunciation of *beinn* (a hill) is given as [bYn] although you will also hear [bayn] used by Gaelic speakers and [ben] is the commonest pronunciation by non-Gaelic speakers.

We would like to thank many friends and colleagues whose help and advice has been invaluable. We are especially grateful to:

Iain A Fraser, of the Place-Name Survey, School of Scottish Studies, University of Edinburgh;

Professor Donald Meek, of the Department of Celtic, Aberdeen University;

Dr John MacInnes, School of Scottish Studies, University of Edinburgh

Adam Watson, whose book *The Place-Names of Upper Deeside* gives readers more detailed information on that area.

For information on particular areas we would like to thank:

Mervyn Browne of Ardtalnaig, Loch Tay; Jean Lindsay of Dundonell; Iain MacKay of Beauly; Margaret MacKay of Newtonmore; John MacLeod of Breakish, Skye; Charles Rose of Torridon.

Iseabail C. MacLeod
Iain A. MacLeod
Domhnall Uilleam Stiùbhart
June 1997

Grammar

Detailed discussion of the complexities of Gaelic grammar is beyond the scope of this guide, but a few sample words are given in various forms to give some idea of why words are found in different spellings.

Initial, internal and ending changes are all used in Gaelic to indicate plural, feminine, genitive case etc. Thus:

Noun	Singular	Plural	Genitive singular	Genitive plural
càrn *masc.*	**an càrn** (the cairn)	**na cùirn** (the cairns)	**a' chùirn** (of the cairn)	**nan càrn** (of the cairns)
coire *masc.*	**an coire** (the corrie)	**na coireachan** (the corries)	**a' choire** (of the corrie)	**nan coireachan** (of the corries)
beinn *fem.*	**a' bheinn** (the hill)	**na beanntan** (the hills)	**na beinne** (of the hill)	**nam beann** (of the hills)
creag *fem.*	**a' chreag** (the rock)	**na creagan** (the rocks)	**na creige** (of the rock)	**nan creag** (of the rocks)

Note:

(1) noun with adjective
masculine - **càrn mór** big cairn
feminine - **beinn mhór** big hill

(2) In Gaelic the adjective usually comes after the noun, but you will find quite a few exceptions to this among hill names.

Glossary

In order to give some help with the translation of other hill-names, we have compiled a short and therefore highly selective list of common place-names elements, classified into groups. These appear in maps and other sources in many different forms. Some are variant Gaelic spellings but many are produced by different levels of anglicization; we have included, in brackets, a very few of the more widely-used of these variations. We have also given a few plural and genitive forms which are quite different from the nominative.

Types of hill and other hill names

Gaelic has many words for different types of hill, some of which require an English phrase to translate them - see **meall**, **màm**, **stob** etc. below. In the list of names we have rendered most of them as 'hill' or 'peak'.

aonach a mountain ridge; a hill, a moor.
beinn (ben) a hill, a mountain.
binnean, binnein a high, pointed hill; a peak.

càrn (cairn) a cairn, heap of stones; a hill of this shape.

cnap a little hill (literally, a knob, a lump).

cnoc (knock) a hillock, smallish hill.

creag (craig) a rock; a crag.

cruach a stack-shaped hill (literally, a heap, stack).

màm a large, rounded hill (literally, a breast).

meall a rounded hill (literally, a lump).

monadh (mon, mont, mount, mounth) a hill, mountain; a moor; a range.

sàil a rounded hill (literally, a heel).

sgòr(r), **sgùr(r)** a sharp, rocky hill or rocky peak (of Norse origin).

stac a steep, conical hill (of Norse origin).

stob a pointed hill (literally, a stake, pointed stick).

stùc(hd) a little hill jutting out from a larger hill; a peak; a cliff; a precipice; a steep, conical rock (of Norse origin).

tom a small, rounded hill; a piece of rising ground.

tòrr a steep, conical hill or mountain; a prominent, steep rock.

tulach a hillock, smallish hill.

Other features

achadh (ach) a field.

allt (ault) a burn, stream, small river.

bàrr a top, summit.

bealach a pass.

bidean a peak, summit.

blàr a plain.

bràigh an upper part; a slope, brae, top.

bruach a bank (of a river, etc.); a slope; a border; an edge.

cadha a narrow pass; a narrow ravine; a steep hill; a steep place.

clach a stone.

coire a corrie (literally, a cauldron, kettle).

dìollaid a saddle.

druim a ridge (literally, a back (of a person or animal).

eas a waterfall (note: *easan* may mean either 'waterfalls' or 'a little waterfall').

gleann a glen, a narrow valley.

làirig a pass.

leac a flat stone, slab.

leitir a steep slope; the side of a hill (usually one sloping down to the sea or to a loch).

linne a pool.

mullach a summit, top.

sloc(hd) a hollow, a pit.

spidean = **bidean**.

sròn a jutting ridge; a peak; a headland (literally, a nose).

toll a hole; a hollow; a crevice.

uamh a cave.

Colours

Gaelic divides the colour spectrum differently from English. For instance the same word **gorm** is used to describe both grass and the sky; it is usually translated as blue. Similarly **glas** is sometimes translated as grey, sometimes as green.

bàn white, light-coloured; fair (of hair or complexion).
buidhe yellow.
dearg (scarlet or blood) red.
donn (dark) brown.
dubh black.
fionn white, pale-coloured.
geal white.
glas grey, greenish-grey, green.
gorm blue; (of grass, foliage, etc.) green.
liath grey, bluish-grey.
odhar fawnish brown (usually translated as dun-coloured)
riabhach brindled, greyish.
ruadh red, brownish red, red-brown.
uaine green.

Other adjectives

àrd high.
beag (beg) small.
bòidheach beautiful
breac spotted, speckled.
cam crooked.
caol narrow.
ceathach misty.
cruinn round.
eagach notched, indented.
fada long.
garbh rough.
geàrr short.
leathann broad.
maol bald, bare.
mór big.
tarsuinn transverse, (a)cross.

Other common elements
Animals and birds

agh (plural **aighean**) a hind; a heifer.
bò a cow.
calman a dove.

crodh cattle.
cù (plural and genitive singular **coin**) a dog.
damh a stag; an ox.
each (plural and genitive singular **eich**) a horse.
eilid a hind.
eun (plural and genitive singular **eòin**) a bird.
fiadh a deer.
fitheach a raven.
gabhar, gobhar a goat.
iolair an eagle.
laogh a calf; a deer-calf.
madadh a dog; a wolf; a fox.
muc a pig.
sionnach a fox.

Plants

beithe birch.
caorann rowan, mountain ash.
còinneach moss.
darach oak.
fraoch heather.
giuthas Scots pine.
iubhar yew.
raineach fern, bracken.

Miscellaneous

àiridh a shieling, summer pasture.
bodach an old man.
cailleach an old woman.
coille a wood.
crìoch a boundary.
deas south.
doire a thicket; a clump of trees.
ear east.
frìth a deer-forest, i.e. a stretch of land reserved for deer-stalking, not usually tree-covered.
fuaran a well; a spring.
gaoth wind.
iar west.
meadhon middle.
sìdh, sìth (shee) a fairy hill.
tuath north.
uisge water.

Phonetic Key

The phonetic script used here is based on English spelling and it is therefore impossible to give more than a very rough approximation of the Gaelic sounds, which are quite different from those of English. But it should enable users to pronounce the names in such a way that they would at least be understood by a Gaelic speaker.

Gaelic pronunciation differs from area to area and it is not possible to cover regional variations here. Therefore you may hear quite different pronunciations in some places as well as anglicized versions. The more common of the latter we give as 'usually pronounced...'; see, for example, Braeriach.

Note that the key is based on standard Scottish pronunciation and not on standard South-Eastern English. For example, 'day' and 'road' have simple vowels and not diphthongs. Note also that 'r' is always pronounced.

Bold type indicates the stressed syllable.

Where there might be confusion we have used a hyphen to separate syllables, and a colon indicates the lengthening of the preceding vowel.

Vowels

ə	(technically, a 'schwa') is pronounced as in less**e**r
a	as in t**a**p
aa	as in f**a**ther
ay	as in d**ay**
e	as in r**e**d
ee	as in d**ee**d, w**ea**k
i	as in t**i**p
Y	as in b**y**
o	as in t**o**p
u	as in b**u**t
oa	as in r**oa**d
aw	as in b**aw**l
oo	as in p**oo**l
ow	as in **ow**l
oi	as in b**oi**l
oe	approximately the sound in French o**eu**f or German **Ö**sterreich

Consonants

Most of the consonants represent *approximately* the same sounds in English. Note the following:

g	as in **g**et
s	as in **s**it
y	as in **y**et

ch   as in lo**ch**; this is pronounced by putting the tip of your tongue on the back of your lower teeth, narrowing the gap at the back of your throat using your tongue and exhaling through this gap to make a sound without using your vocal chords.

gh has no equivalent in English; it is a voiced ch (i.e. it is pronounced like 'ch', but using the vocal chords).

d and t are pronounced with the tip of the tongue touching the back of the lower teeth (and not the teeth ridge as in English).

b is often transcribed as p although the sound is actually somewhere between these two sounds in English, but somewhat closer to p: similar d is often transcribed as t and g as k.

A small y (ʸ) indicates a nasal y as in million.

Sources

1. Books on place-names

Drummond, P. *Scottish Hill and Mountain Names*, Scottish Mountaineering Trust 1991

Ellice, E. C. *Place-Names of Glengarry and Glenquoich and their associations*, London 1931

Forbes, A. R. *Place-Names of Skye and adjacent islands*, Paisley 1923

Gillies, H. C. *Place-Names of Argyll*, London 1906

Johnston, J. B. *The Place-Names of Scotland*, Edinburgh 1903, 1978

MacBain, A. *Place-names, Highlands and Islands of Scotland*, Stirling 1922

Mackay, W. *Gaelic Place Names of Upper Strathglass*, 1968

MacKenzie, W. C. *Scottish Place-Names*, London 1931

Nicolaisen, W. F. H. *Scottish Place-Names*, London 1976, 1986

Place names on maps of Scotland and Wales, Ordnance Survey 1968, reprinted with corrections 1981

Stewart, T. F. *Hill Names of Perthshire*, 1974

Watson, A. and Allan, E. *The Place-Names of Upper Deeside*, Aberdeen 1986

Watson, W. J. *The History of the Celtic Place-Names of Scotland*, Edinburgh 1926, 1993

Watson, W. J. *Place-Names of Ross and Cromarty*, 1904, reprinted 1976, 1996

2. Dictionaries

Dwelly, E. *The Illustrated Gaelic-English Dictionary*, 1901-1911, now published by Gairm Publications, Glasgow

Macbain, A. *An Etymological History of the Gaelic Language* 1896, now published by Gairm Publications, Glasgow

MacLennan, M. *Gaelic-English and English-Gaelic Dictionary*, Edinburgh 1925, reprinted 1979 by Acair, Stornoway and Aberdeen University Press

The Meaning and Pronunciation
of the Munros, Tops and Corbetts

The names are quoted mainly in the spelling in this present edition of *Munro's Tables* and, where relevant, we have also given the Gaelic on which these are based (and in rarer cases, the common anglicized version where the Tables use the original Gaelic). Many names in the lists are not in their correct Gaelic form and in these cases the correct version is also given. If a name begins with **An** or **A'** (meaning 'the' in Gaelic), it is entered under the next word, e.g. **Teallach, An** .

We have translated most names for hill simply as 'hill' or 'peak' although in many cases the words have a more specific meaning – see first section of the glossary (p.142).

Ainshval [**ayn**shəval] from Old Norse *ass-fjall* rocky-ridged peak.
Airgiod Bheinn [arəkyit vYn] silver hill.
Aonach air Chrith [oenoch ər **chree**] ridge of trembling.
Aonach Beag [oenoch **bayk**] little ridge.
Aonach Buidhe [oenach **boo**yə] yellow hill.
Aonach Eagach [oenoch **ay**goch] notched ridge.
Aonach Meadhoin [oenoch **mee**-onʸ] middle ridge.
Aonach Mór [oenoch **moar**] big ridge.
Aonach Shasuinn [oenach **has**Ynʸ] ridge of England.
Arkle probably Old Norse *ark-fjall*, ark hill.
Askival [**ask**ival] probably from Old Norse *askr-fjall* ashwood peak.
Auchnafree Hill Gaelic *achadh na frìthe* [**ach**əgh nə **free**hə] field of the deer forest.
Bac an Eich [bachk ən **yaych**] hollow of the horse.
Basteir, Am [əm **bast**yərʸ] meaning obscure; not likely to be from *am bàsadair*, the
    executioner; maybe, however, the baptiser.
Baosbheinn [**baosh**vYn] explained locally as **Bathais-bheinn** [**ba**heesh vYn]
    meaning hill of the forehead - it has a long slope.
Bàthach, Am [əm **baa**hoch] the byre.
Beinn a'Bha'ach Ard properly **Beinn a'Bhàthaich Àird** [bYn ə vaaheech **aard**ʸ] hill
    of the high byre.
Beinn a'Bheithir [bYn ə **vay**heerʸ] hill of the thunderbolt, or hill of the bear.
Beinn a'Bhùird [bYn ə **voo:**rsht] hill of the table.
Beinn a'Bhùiridh [bYn ə **voo:**ree] hill of the bellowing (of stags).
Beinn a'Chàisgein Mór properly **Beinn a'Chàisgein Mhór** [bYn ə chaaskinʸ **voar**]
    possibly big hill of the tuft (*cèasg*), hence long grass.
Beinn a'Chaisteil [bYn ə **chash**tyilʸ] hill of the castle.
Beinn a'Chaorainn [bYn ə **choer**Ynʸ] hill of the rowan.
Beinn a'Chlachair [bYn ə **chla**cheerʸ] hill of the stonemason.
Beinn a'Chlaidheimh [bYn ə **chl**Yəv] hill of the sword.

Beinn a'Chléibh [bYn ə **chlayv**] hill of the creel or chest.

Beinn a'Chochuill [bYn ə **cho**cheel^y] hill of the cowl.

Beinn a'Choin [bYn ə **chon**^y] hill of the dog.

Beinn a'Chreachain [bYn ə **chre**chYn^y] scallop-shaped (that is, bare, dome-shaped) hill.

Beinn a'Chroin [bYn ə **chroan**^y] probably *beinn a'chròthain*, hill of the sheepfold.

Beinn a'Chrùlaiste [bYn ə **chroo:**lashtyə] hill of the rocky hill.

Beinn a'Chuallaich [bYn ə **choo**uleech] hill of the herding.

Beinn a'Chùirn [bYn ə **choo:rn**^y] hill of the cairn.

Beinn a'Ghlo [bYn ə **ghlaw**] hill of the hood or veil.

Beinn Achaladair [bYn acha**lad**ər^y] hill of the field by the hard water.

Beinn Àirigh Chàrr [bYn aaree **chaar**] hill of the bogland shieling.

Beinn Alligin properly **Beinn Àiliginn** [bYn **aa**leegin] derived from the River Alligin, a name either from *àilleag*, a jewel, or else connected with Old Irish *ail*, rock.

Beinn an Dòthaidh [bYn ən **daw**hee] hill of scorching.

Beinn an Eòin [bYn ən **yaw**een^y] hill of the bird.

Beinn an Lochain [bYn ə **loch**Yn^y] hill of the little loch.

Beinn an Òir [bYn ən **awr**^y] hill of gold.

Beinn Bhàn [bYn **vaan**] white hill.

Beinn Bheòil [bYn **vyaw**eel^y] hill of the mouth.

Beinn Bheula [bYn **vee**ulə] hill of mouths.

Beinn Bhreac [bYn **vrechk**] speckled hill.

Beinn Bhreac-liath [bYn **vrechk** lyee-ə] grey-speckled hill.

Beinn Bhrotain [bYn **vroh**tYn^y] the hill of (the mastiff) Brotan.

Beinn Bhuidhe [bYn **voo**yə] yellow hill.

Beinn Chabhair [bYn **chav**ər^y] probably hill of the hawk.

Beinn Chaorach [bYn **choe**roch] hill of sheep.

Beinn Cheathaich properly **Beinn a'Cheathaich** [bYn ə **che**heech] hill of the mist.

Beinn Chùirn properly **Beinn a'Chùirn** [bYn ə **choo:rn**^y] hill of the cairn.

Beinn Damh [bYn **dav**] stag hill.

Beinn Dearg [bYn **dye**rek] red hill.

Beinn Dearg Bheag [bYn dyerek **vayk**] little red hill.

Beinn Dearg Mhór [bYn dyerek **voar**] big red hill.

Beinn Dòrain properly **Beinn Dòbhrain** [bYn **doar**Yn^y] probably hill of the streamlet, rather than hill of the otter.

Beinn Dronaig [bYn **dron**ək^y] hill of the little ridge of hump.

Beinn Dubhchraig [bYn **doo**chrayk] hill of the black rock.

Beinn Each [bYn **yech**] hill of the horses.

Beinn Éibhinn [bYn **ay**veen^y] delightful hill.

Beinn Eighe [bYn **ay**-ə] file hill.

Beinn Enaiglair properly **Beinn Eunacleit** [bYn **ayn**əklaytsh] from Old Norse *enni-klettr* brow cliff.

Beinn Eunaich [bYn **ee**uneech] fowling hill.

Beinn Fhada [bYn **at**ə] (sometimes spelt **Ben Attow**) long hill.

Beinn Fhionnlaidh [bYn **yoo**nlY] Finlay's hill, said to be called after a gamekeeper of Mackenzie of Kintail, known for his violent behaviour.

Beinn Ghlas [bYn **ghlas**] grey-green hill.

Beinn Heasgarnich [bYn **hes**karneech] sheltering hill, from *seasgairneach*.

Beinn Iaruinn [bYn **ee**urYn^y] iron hill.

Beinn Ìme [bYn **ee**:m∂] hill of butter; at one time butter was made at hill shielings (summer pastures).

Beinn Iutharn Bheag [bYn yoo∂rn **vayk**] probably little sharp-ridged hill.

Beinn Iutharn Mhór [bYn yoo∂rn **voar**] probably big sharp-ridged hill.

Beinn Làir [bYn **laar**^{y}] mare hill.

Beinn Leòid [bYn **lyawt**^{y}] hill of the slope.

Beinn Liath Mhór [bYn lyee-∂ **voar**] great grey hill.

Beinn Liath Mhór a'Ghiuthais Lì [bYn lyee-∂ **voar** ∂ yooeesh **hlee**] big grey hill of the colourful pine.

Beinn Liath Mhór Fannaich [bYn lyee-∂ voar **fan**eech] the big grey hill of (Loch) Fannaich. Fannaich (from Loch Fainich), may mean stormy.

Beinn Luibhean [bYn **lY**van] hill of the little plants, or small grass.

Beinn Maol Chaluim properly **Beinn Mhaol-Chaluim** [bYn **voel** chal∂m^y] Malcolm's hill.

Beinn Mhanach [bYn **va**noch] monks' hill.

Beinn Mheadhoin [bYn **vee**on^y] middle hill.

Beinn Mheadhonach [bYn **vee**onoch] middle hill.

Beinn Mhic Ceididh [bYn veechk **kay**tee] possibly hill of the son of Katie or Kitty.

Beinn Mhic Chasgaig [bYn veechk **cas**kayk] MacCasgaig's hill.

Beinn Mhic-Mhonaidh [bYn veechk **vo**nee] literally, hill of the son of the moor.

Beinn Mholach [bYn **vol**och] rough or hairy hill.

Beinn na Caillich [bYn n∂ **kal**yeech] hill of the old woman.

Beinn na h-Eaglaise [bYn n∂ **hyuk**leesh∂] hill of the church.

Beinn na h-Uamha [bYn n∂ **hoo**av∂] hill of the cave.

Beinn na Lap [bYn n∂ **lahp**] dappled hill.

Beinn na Socaich [bYn n∂ **soch**keech] hill of the snout.

Beinn nam Fuaran [bYn n∂m **foo**uran] hill of the springs.

Beinn nan Aigheanan [bYn n∂n **Y∂**nan] hill of the hinds.

Beinn nan Caorach [bYn n∂n **koe**roch] hill of the sheep.

Beinn nan Eachan [bYn n∂n **yech**an] hill of the little horses.

Beinn nan Imirean [bYn n∂n **yee**m∂r∂n] hill of the rigs (cultivated ridges of land).

Beinn nan Oighreag [bYn n∂n **Y**rak] hill of the cloudberries.

Beinn Narnain probably *beinn bheàrnan* [bYn **vyaa**rn∂n] hill of the notches.

Beinn Odhar [bYn **oa**-∂r] dun-coloured hill.

Beinn Odhar Bheag [bYn **oa**-∂r **vayk**] little dun-coloured hill.

Beinn Resipol [bYn **resh**∂pol] Gaelic *beinn* hill, and probably Old Norse *hróss* horse and *bólstathr* farm.

Beinn Sgritheall [bYn **sgree**h∂l] maybe scree hill.

Beinn Sgulaird [bYn **skool**∂rt] hat-shaped hill.

Beinn Spionnaidh [bYn **spyoo**nee] hill of strength, or, just possibly, of plucking.

Beinn Tàlaidh [bYn **taa**lee] probably pleasant hill.

Beinn Tarsuinn [bYn **tars**Ynᵞ] transverse hill.

Beinn Teallach [bYn **tya**loch] forge hill.

Beinn Tharsuinn [bYn **hars**Ynᵞ] transverse hill.

Beinn Trilleachan [bYn **tree**lyochan] hill of sandpipers.

Beinn Tulaichean [bYn **too**leechən] hill of hillocks.

Beinn Ùdlaidh [bYn **oo:**dlee] gloomy hill.

Beinn Udlamain [bYn **oot**ləmənᵞ] jointed hill, or unsteady hill.

Ben Vuirich Gaelic **Beinn a'Bhùirich** [bYn ə **voo:**reech] hill of howling.

Ben Aden Gaelic **Beinn Aodainn** [bYn **oet**Ynᵞ] hill of the face.

Ben Alder properly **Beinn Eallar** [bYn **ya**lar] hill of rock and water.

Ben Arthur (The Cobbler) Gaelic **Beinn Artair** [bYn **arsh**tarᵞ] possibly after King Arthur. **The Cobbler** from the shape of the middle peak, like a cobbler bent over his work (Gaelic **An Greusaiche Crom** [ən **gree**əseechə **crowm**] the stooping cobbler).

Ben Attow see **Beinn Fhada**.

Ben Avon Gaelic **Beinn Athfhinn** [bYn **aan**] from the river name, probably Gaelic *athfhionn* the bright one.

Ben Challum properly **Beinn Chaluim** [bYn **chal**Ymᵞ] Calum's hill.

Ben Chonzie locally pronounced [ben **hon**zay] but sometimes known as **Ben-y Hone** [ben ee **hoan**] probably *beinn a'chòinnich*, mossy hill, in a Scotticized spelling.

Ben Cruachan or **Cruachan Beann** [**kroo**əchan **byown**] heaped hill.

Ben Donich [bYn **do**neech] possibly from Gaelic *dona* bad, evil.

Ben Gulabin from Old Irish *gulban* a beak.

Ben Hee Gaelic **Beinn Shìth** [bYn **hee**] fairy hill.

Ben Hope hill of the inlet or bay, from Old Norse *hóp*.

Ben Klibreck Gaelic **Beinn Chlìbric** [bYn **chlee:**breechk] hill of the speckled cliff, or of the cliff slope, from Old Norse *klif brekka*.

Ben Lawers Gaelic **Beinn Labhair** [bYn **la**vərᵞ] hill of the Labhair (loud) stream.

Ben Ledi [**le**ddy] Gaelic **Beinn Lididh** [bYn **lee**dee] probably from *leathad* [**lyee**-at] a slope.

Ben Lomond Gaelic **Beinn Laomainn** [bYn **loe**mənᵞ] probably beacon hill.

Ben Loyal properly **Beinn Laghail** [bYn **loe**ghəl] legal hill (it was used as a judgement place).

Ben Lui maybe from Gaelic *laogh*, calf or fawn, but more likely from **Beinn Luaidhe** [bYn **loo**-əyə] lead hill.

Ben Macdui probably **Beinn MhicDhuibhe** [bYn **veechk ghoo**yə] MacDuff's hill, rather than *beinn na muice duibhe*, hill of the black pig.

Ben More Assynt properly **Beinn Mhór Asainte** [bYn **voar a**səntyə] big hill of Assynt, from Old Norse *ass* ridge, and *endi* an end.

Ben More properly **Beinn Mhór** [bYn **voar**] big hill.

Ben Nevis Gaelic **Beinn Nibheis** [bYn **neev**əsh] obscure; maybe venomous hill, or cloudy hill.

Ben Oss [bYn **os**] elk hill, or hill of the loch outlet.

Ben Rinnes properly **Beinn Rinneis** [bYn **ree**ny∂sh] from *rinn* a point, promontory.

Ben Starav [bYn **sta**rav] maybe hill of rustling.

Ben Tee probably from Gaelic **Beinn an t-Sìthein** [bYn ∂n **tshee**hin] hill of the fairy hill.

Ben Tirran possibly from Gaelic *tuireann*, lightning.

Ben Vane probably from Gaelic *beinn mheadhoin* [bYn **vee**-oin^y] middle hill.

Ben Vorlich Gaelic **Beinn Mhùrluig** (bYn **voo**:rooloog^y] hill of the sack-shaped bay (*muir-bhalg*).

Ben Vrackie Gaelic **Beinn Bhràgaidh** [bYn **vraa**gee] probably speckled hill.

Ben Wyvis [ben **wi**vis] locally [ben **wee**vis]; Gaelic **Beinn Uathais** [bYn **oo**-∂th∂sh] possibly from Gaelic *fuathas* meaning terror, or, more likely, from *uamhas*, terrible, or majestic, hill.

Bhuidheanach Bheag, A' [∂ vooy∂noch **vayk**] the little yellow place.

Bidean an Eòin Deirg [beedyan ∂n yaween^y **dye**r∂k] peak of the red bird (probably grouse).

Bidean nam Bian properly **Bidean nam Beann** [beedyan n∂m **byown**] pinnacle of the hills.

Bidein a'Choire Sheasgaich [beedy∂n ∂ chor∂ **he**skeech] pinnacle of the corrie of the farrow cattle.

Bidein a'Ghlas Thuill properly **Spidean a'Ghlas-Tuill** [speedyan ∂ **ghlas** til^y] pinnacle of the grey-green hollow.

Binnein an Fhìdhleir [**been**y∂n ∂n yee:l∂r^y] peak of the fiddler.

Blà Bheinn [**blaa**vYn] Old Norse *blà* and Gaelic *beinn*, blue hill.

Bodach, Am [∂m **bo**toch] the old man.

Brack, The from Gaelic *breac* [brechk] spotted, speckled.

Braeriach [bray**ree**∂ch] but locally [brY**ree**ach]; Gaelic **Am Bràigh Riabhach** [∂m brY **ree**∂voch] the brindled upland.

Bràigh Coire Chruinn-bhalgain [brY kor∂ **chr**Yn val∂geen^y] height of the corrie of the round blisters.

Bràigh nan Uamhachan [brY n∂n **oo**uvoch∂n] brae of the caves.

Broad Law Scots *law* a rounded hill (of Old English origin).

Bruach na Frìthe [broo-uch n∂ **free**:h∂] slope of the deer forest.

Buachaille Etive Beag Gaelic **Buachaille Éite Beag** [boo-ucheely∂ ay:ty∂ **bayk**] little herdsman of Etive.

Buachaille Etive Mór Gaelic **Buachaille Éite Mór** [boo-ucheely∂ ay:ty∂ **moar**] big herdsman of Etive.

Bynack More probably *binneag mhór* larger little hill, or large cap.

Cabar, An [∂n **ca**bar] here, the top of a hill - literally rafter, or else antler.

Cac Càrn Beag probably **Cadha a'Chùirn Bhig** [kaa ∂ choorn **veek**] pass of the small cairn.

Cac Càrn Mór probably **Cadha a'Chùirn Mhóir** [kaa ∂ choorn **voar**^y] pass of the big cairn.

Cairn Bannoch probably *càrn beannach* peaked hill.

Cairn Gorm Gaelic **Càrn Gorm** [kaarn **go**rom] blue peak.

Cairn Lochan Gaelic **Càrn an Lochain** [kaarn ə loch**Yn**ʸ] cairn of the little loch.

Cairn of Claise usually pronounced [kayrn ə **gla**shə]; Gaelic **Càrn na Claise** [kaarn nə **kla**shə] peak of the hollow, or ditch.

Cairn of Gowal known locally as **Cairn o the Gowal**; from Gaelic *càrn a'ghobhail* [kaarn ə **ghoa**-eelʸ] peak of the fork.

Cairn Toul usually pronounced [kayrn **tool**]; Gaelic **Càrn an t-Sabhail** [kaarn ən **tow**əl] peak of the barn.

Cairnsmore of Carsphairn from Gaelic *càrn mór* [kaarn **moar**] big peak, Scots *carse* a stretch of low riverside land, and Gaelic *feàrna* alder.

Cairnwell, The Gaelic **Càrn Bhalg** [kaarn **va**lag] peak of bags, baggy peatbanks.

Caisteal Abhail [kastyal **a**veelʸ] castle of the apple tree.

Caisteil, An [ən **cash**tyal] the castle.

Cam Chreag [**kowm** chrayk] crooked rock.

Canisp Gaelic **Canasp** [**kan**asp] perhaps Old Norse *can*, can-shaped and *ups*, eaves or roof.

Càrn a'Chlamain properly **Càrn a'Chlamhain** [kaarn ə **chla**veenʸ] peak of the kite.

Càrn a'Choire Bhòidheach properly **Càrn a'Choire Bhòidhich** [kaarn ə chorə **vaw**yeech] peak of the beautiful corrie.

Càrn a'Choire Ghairbh [kaarn ə chorə **ghe**rev] peak of the rough corrie.

Càrn a'Chuilinn [kaarn ə **choo**leenʸ] holly peak.

Càrn a'Gheòidh [kaarn ə **yaw**ee] peak of the goose.

Càrn a'Mhàim [kaarn ə **vYm**] peak of the large rounded hill.

Càrn an Fhìdhleir [kaarn ən **yee**:lər] peak of the fiddler.

Càrn an Rìgh [kaarn ə **ree**:] peak of the king.

Càrn an t-Sagairt Mór [kaarn ən tagərsht **moar**] big peak of the priest.

Càrn an t-Sagairt Beag [kaarn ən tagərsht **bayk**] little peak of the priest.

Càrn an Tuirc [kaarn ən **toohrk**] peak of the wild boar.

Càrn Aosda [kaarn **oes**tə] ancient peak.

Càrn Ballach [kaarn **ba**loch] spotted peak.

Càrn Bàn [kaarn **baan**] light-coloured, or white, peak.

Càrn Bàn Mór [kaarn baan **moar**] big white peak.

Càrn Bhac [kaarn **vachk**] peak of peatbanks.

Càrn Bhinnein properly **Càrn a'Bhinnein** [kaarn ə **vee**nyən] peak of the little pinnacle.

Càrn Chuinneag [kaarn **choo**nyak] peak of churns, or milk-pails.

Càrn Cloich-mhuilinn [kaarn kloich **voo**leenʸ] peak of the millstone.

Càrn Dearg [kaarn **dye**rek] red peak.

Càrn Dearg Meadhonach [kaarn dyerek **mee**-onoch] middle red peak.

Càrn Dearg Mór [kaarn dyerek **moar**] big red peak.

Càrn Ealar [kaarn **ya**lar] see **Càrn an Fhìdhleir**.

Càrn Ealasaid [kaarn **ya**ləsatʸ] Elizabeth's peak.

Càrn Eas [kaarn **yes**] peak of waterfalls.

Càrn Eighe [kaarn **ay**ə] file peak.

Càrn Etchachan probably **Càrn Eiteachain** [kaarn **ay**tyochən^y] maybe peak of the burnt heather roots or, more probably, of juniper.

Càrn Ghluasaid [kaarn **ghloo**-asət^y] peak of movement.

Càrn Gorm [kaarn **go**rom] blue peak.

Càrn Liath [kaarn **lyee**-ə] grey peak.

Càrn Mairg [kaarn **mar**ək] probably peak of rust.

Càrn Mór [kaarn **moar**] big peak.

Càrn Mór Dearg [kaarn moar **dye**rek] large red peak.

Càrn na Caim [kaarn nə **kYm**] peak of the curve.

Càrn na Coire Mheadhoin [kaarn nə korə **vee**-on^y] peak of the middle corrie.

Càrn na Con Dhu [kaarn nə kon **doo**] probably *càrn nan con dubh*, peak of the black dogs.

Càrn na Crìche [kaarn nə **kree**:chə] peak of the boundary.

Càrn na Drochaide [kaarn nə **tro**chatyə] peak of the bridge.

Càrn na Fhreiceadain probably *càrn an fhreiceadain* [kaarn ə **ray**katyən^y] peak of the watch.

Càrn na Nathrach [kaarn nə **na**roch] peak of the adder.

Càrn na Saobhaidhe [kaarn nə **soe**veeyə] peak of the fox's den.

Càrn nam Fiaclan [kaarn nəm **fee**-ochklən] peak of the teeth.

Càrn nan Gabhar [kaarn nən **gow**ər] peak of the goats.

Càrn nan Gobhar [kaarn nən **gow**ər] peak of the goats.

Càrn Sgùlain [kaarn **skoo**:lən^y] probably peak of the basket.

Ceann Garbh [kyown **gar**av] rough head.

Ceann na Baintighearna [kyown nə **ban**tyeeərnə] head of the lady.

Cearcallach, An [ən **kyer**kaloch] the rounded (area).

Chailleach, A' [ə **chal**yoch] the old woman or witch.

Chìoch, A' [ə **chee**oach] the breast.

Chnò Dearg properly **Cnoc Dearg** [krochk **dye**rek] red hill.

Chòinneach, A' [ə **chawn**yoch] the moss.

Chràlaig, A' [ə **chraal**ək^y] the basket.

Cìr Mhór [keer **voar**] big comb.

Ciste Dhubh [keeshtyə **ghoo**] black chest.

Clach Leathad [klach **lyee**hat] stone of the slope.

Clisham properly **An Cliseam** [ən **klee**sham] possibly from Old Norse *klif hamarr*, rocky slope or outcrop.

Cnap a'Chléirich [krahp ə **chlay**reech] lumpy hill of the priest.

Cnap Coire na Spréidhe [krahp korə nə **spray**-yə] lumpy hill of the corrie of the cattle.

Coileachan, An [ən **ko**lochan] the little cock.

Còinneach Mhór [kawnyoch **voar**] big moss.

Cona' Mheall [konə **vyal**] adjoining hill.

Conachraig possibly from Gaelic *cona-chreag* [konə **chrayk**] 'linking' rock.

Conival see **Cona' Mheall**.

Corrag Bhuidhe [korak **voo**yə] yellow finger.

Corriehabbie Hill origin unknown; first element from Gaelic *coire*, a corrie.

Corrieyairack Hill from **Coire Ghearrag** [corə **ya**rak] probably corrie of the leverets, young hares.

Corserine from Scots *corse* a cross and Gaelic *rinn* a ridge.

Craig a'Chaorainn properly **Creag a'Chaorainn** [krayk ə **choe**rYnʸ] rock of the rowan.

Craig an Loch properly **Creag an Locha** [krayk ə **loch**ə] rock of the loch.

Craig Coire na Fiar-Bhealaich [krayk korə nə **fee**-ər vyaleech] rock of the corrie of the slanting pass.

Craig of Gowal probably Gaelic *creag a'ghobhail* [krayk ə **ghoa**-eelʸ] rock of the fork.

Cranstackie possibly from Gaelic *càrn stacach*, the rocky, or stacky, peak.

Creach Bheinn [**krech** vYn] plunder hill.

Creag a'Ghlas-uillt [krayk ə **ghlas** əltʸ] rock of the greenish-grey burn.

Creag a'Mhàim [krayk ə **vYm**] rock of the large rounded hill.

Creag an Dail Bheag [krayk ən daal **vayk**] little rock of the river-meadow.

Creag an Dàil Mhór [krayk ən daal **voar**] big rock of the river-meadow.

Creag an Dubh-Loch [krayk ən **doo** loch] rock of the black loch.

Creag an Fhithich [krayk ən **yee**-eech] rock of the raven.

Creag an Leth-choin [krayk ə **lye**chonʸ] rock of the lurcher, usually called in English Lurcher's Crag.

Creag Coire nan Each [krayk korə nən **yech**] rock of the corrie of the horses.

Creag Dubh properly **Creag Dhubh** [krayk **ghoo**] black rock.

Creag Ghorm a'Bhealaich [krayk ghorom ə **vya**leech] blue rock of the pass.

Creag Leacach [krayk **lyech**koch] slabby rock.

Creag Liath [krayk **lyee**ə] grey rock.

Creag MacRanaich properly **Creag MhicRanaich** [krayk veechk**ra**neech] MacRanaich's rock (named after a local robber).

Creag Meagaidh [krayk **me**gee] possibly bogland rock.

Creag Mhór [krayk **voar**] big rock.

Creag na Caillich [krayk nə **ka**lyeech] rock of the old woman.

Creag nan Damh [krayk nən **dav**] rock of the stags.

Creag nan Ghabhar properly **Creag nan Gobhar** [krayk nən **gow**ər] rock of the goats.

Creag Pitridh [krayk **pee**tree] possibly from Pictish *pit*, a hollow, rather than Petrie's rock, from the surname.

Creag Rainich [krayk **ran**yeech] fern or bracken rock.

Creag Uchdag [krayk **oochk**ak] rock, or cliff, of steep sides.

Creagan a'Choire Etchachan properly **Creagan a'Choire Eiteachain** [kraykən ə chorə **ay**tyochənʸ] maybe rocks of the corrie of burnt heather roots or, more probably, of juniper.

Creagan na Beinne [kraykan nə **bYn**yə] little rock of the hill.

Creise [**kray**shə] possibly from *créis*, a narrow defile.

Crow Craigies from Scots *craigies*, little rocks.

Cruach Àrdrain [kroo**ə**ch **aar**drənʸ] stack of the high region.

Cruach Ìnnse [krooach **ee:n**shə] probably stack of the pasture.

Cuidhe Crom [koeyə **krowm**] crooked wreath (of snow).

Cùl Beag [kool **bayk**] little back.

Cùl Mór [kool **moar**] big back.

Culardoch from Gaelic *cùl* back of, and possibly *fàrdach* [**faar**doch] dwelling-place.

Derry Cairngorm Gaelic **Càrn Gorm an Doire** [kaarn gorom ən **dir**ə] blue peak of the (oak) thicket.

Devil's Point, The euphemism for the Gaelic **Bod an Deamhain** [bot ən **dye**veenʸ] the demon's penis.

Dìollaid a'Chàirn [dyee-əlatʸ ə **chaarn**ʸ] saddle of the peak.

Driesh Gaelic *dris* [dreesh] a thorn-bush.

Drochaid an Tuill Easaich [drochatʸ ən tYl **e**seech] bridge of the hollow of the waterfall.

Drochaid Ghlas [drochatʸ **ghlas**] grey bridge.

Druim Mór [drim **moar**] big ridge.

Druim nan Cnàmh [drim nən **kraav**] ridge of the bones.

Druim Shionnach [drim **hin**och] ridge of foxes.

Druim Tarsuinn [drim **tar**sYnʸ] transverse ridge.

Dùn, An [ən **doo:n**] the fort.

Dùn da Ghaoithe [doon də **goey**ə] fort of two winds.

East Meur Gorm Craig [mayr **gor**om] east blue finger rock.

Eididh nan Clach Geala [aytyee nən klach **gyal**ə] web of the white stones.

Fafernie [fə **fer**nay] Gaelic *féith feàrnaidh* bog of the alder place.

Faochagach, Am *looks as if from Gaelic faochag a whelk, but properly* **Am Fraochagach** [əm **froe**chakoch] the heathery place.

Faochaig [**foe**chak] looks as if from Gaelic *faochag* a whelk, but properly **Fraochag** [**froe**chak] little heathery hill.

Fara, The probably from Gaelic *fàradh* [**faar**əgh] a ladder.

Farragon Hill probably named after St Fergan, a seventh-century abbot of Iona.

Fasarinen, Am [əm **faas**rinən] said locally to mean a path, pass, way through difficult ground.

Fionn Bheinn [**fyoon** vYn] white hill.

Foinaven properly **Foinne-Bheinn** [**foy**nyə vYn] hill of the warts.

Fraoch Bheinn [**froech** vYn] heather hill.

Fraochaidh [**froe**chee] probably heathery (hill).

Fuar Bheinn [**foo**-ər vYn] cold hill.

Fuar Tholl [**foo**ər howl] cold hole.

Gairbeinn possibly *garbh-bheinn* [**ga**rav vYn] rough hill.

Gàirich [**gaa**reech] roaring.

Ganu Mór possibly from Gaelic *ceann mór* [kyown **moar**] big head.

Gaor Bheinn [**goer** vYn] usually called **Gulvain** [**gool**vən]; either from *gaorr* filth, faeces, or *gaoir* noise.

Garbh Bheinn [**ga**rav vYn] rough hill.

Garbh Chìoch Bheag [garav cheech **vayk**] little rough place of the breast.

Garbh Chìoch Mhór [garav cheech **voar**] big rough place of the breast.

Garbhanach, An [ən **ga**ravanoch] the rough one.

Geal Chàrn [**gyal** chaarn] white peak.

Geal-chàrn Mór [gyal chaarn **moar**] big white peak.

Gearanach, An [ən **gyar**ənoch] the complainer.

Ghlas-bheinn, A' [ə **ghlas**vYn] the grey-green hill.

Glàmaig [**glaa**mak^y] gorge hill.

Glas Bheinn Mhór [glas vYn **voar**] big grey-green hill.

Glas Bheinn [**glas** vYn] grey-green hill.

Glas Leathad Beag [glas lyeehət **bayk**] little greenish-grey slope.

Glas Leathad Mór [glas lyeehət **moar**] big greenish-grey slope.

Glas Maol properly **Glas Mheall** [**glas** vyal] grey-green hill.

Glas Mheall Liath [glas vyal **lyee-ə**] greenish-grey hill.

Glas Mheall Mór [**glas** vyal **moar**] big greenish-grey hill.

Glas Tulaichean [**glas** tooleechən] grey-green hillocks.

Gleouraich [**gloe**reech] roaring noise.

Goatfell Gaelic is **Gaoda-bheinn** [**goe**də vYn] probably an adaptation of Old Norse *geitar-fjall* goat peak.

Gulvain see **Gaor Bheinn**.

Hart Fell Scots, stag hill.

Inaccessible Pinnacle / Sgùrr Dearg [skoor **dye**rek] red peak.

Ladhar Bheinn [**loe**-ər vYn] hoof hill.

Leabaidh an Daimh Bhuidhe [lyebee ən dev **vooy**ə] bed of the yellow stag.

Leathad an Taobhain [**lyee**hət ən **toe**vYn^y] slope of the ribbed side.

Leth-chreag, An [ə **lye** chrayk] the half rock; may refer to one of a pair of rocks.

Leum Uilleim [lyaym **ool**yəm] William's leap.

Liathach [**lyee**-əhoch] locally [**lyee**-əghoch] the grey one.

Little Wyvis [**wi**vis, locally **wee**vis] possibly from Gaelic *fuathas* meaning terror, or, more likely, from *uamhas*, terrible, or majestic (hill).

Lochnagar Gaelic **Lochan na Gàire** [lochan nə **gaa:r**ə] little loch of laughter, or noise; properly **Beinn nan Cìochan** [bYn nən **kee:**chən] hill of the paps.

Luinne Bheinn [**loo**nyə vYn] probably swelling hill.

Lurg Mhór [**loo**roog **voar**] big shank.

Màm na Gualainn [maam nə **goo**əleen^y] large rounded hill of the shoulder.

Màm nan Càrn [maam nən **kaarn**] large rounded hill of the cairns.

Màm Sodhail properly **Màm Sabhail** [maam **soa**al] or [maam **sool**] large rounded hill of the barns.

Maoile Lunndaidh [moelə **loon**dee] bare hill of the wet place.

Maol Chean-dearg [moel chyən **dye**rek] bald red head.

Maol Chinn-dearg [moel chyən **dye**rek] bald red head.

Mayar [may**ə**r] maybe *magh àrd* high plain.

Meall a'Bhàrr [myowl ə **vaar**] maybe hill of the summit, but probably hill of the cream.

Meall a'Bhuachaille [myowl ə **voo**-ucheelyə] hill of the cowherd.

Meall a'Bhùiridh [myowl ə **voo:**ree] hill of the bellowing (of stags).

Meall a'Choire Léith [myowl ə chorə **lyay:**] hill of the grey corrie.

Meall a'Chrasgaidh [myowl ə **chra**skee] hill of the crossing.

Meall a'Churain [myowl ə **choo**rəny] hill of the carrot.

Meall a'Ghiubhais [myowl ə **yoo**eesh] hill of the pine tree.

Meall a'Phubuill [myowl ə **foo**beely] hill of the tent.

Meall an Fhuarain Mhóir [myowl ən oo-arəny **voar**] hill of the great spring.

Meall an Fhùdair [myowl ən **oot**əry] hill of the powder.

Meall an t-Seallaidh [myowl ən **tya**lee] hill of the view.

Meall an t-Snaim [myowl ən **tnYm**] hill of the difficulty, or knot.

Meall Buidhe [myowl **boo**yə] yellow hill.

Meall Chuaich [myowl **choo**-Ych] hill of the quaich, or shallow cup.

Meall Coire Choille-rais [myowl korə chilyə **rash**] hill of the corrie of the wooded promontory.

Meall Coire na Saobhaidhe [myowl korə nə **soe**veeyə] hill of the corrie of the den.

Meall Corranaich [myowl **ko**raneech] probably crooked hill, rather than hill of lamentation.

Meall Cruidh [myowl **kroo**ee] cattle hill.

Meall Cuanail [myowl **koo**əneel] hill of flocks.

Meall Dearg [myowl **dye**rek] red hill.

Meall Dubh [myowl **doo**] black hill.

Meall Dubhag [myowl **doo**-ak] hill of the little dark one (probably the name of a cow).

Meall Garbh [myowl **ga**rav] rough hill.

Meall Ghaordaidh [myowl **ghoer**dee] maybe hill of the shoulder.

Meall Glas [myowl **glas**] grey-green hill.

Meall Glas-Choire [myowl **glas** chorə] hill of the grey corrie.

Meall Gorm [myowl **go**rom] blue hill.

Meall Greigh [myowl **gray**] hill of horse studs (horses were pastured there at one time); but also known as **Meall Gruaidh**, cheek hill.

Meall Horn possibly from Gaelic *meall fhìr-eòin* [myowl **ee:**rəny] eagle's hill.

Meall Liath [myowl **lyee**-ə] grey hill.

Meall Lighiche properly **Meall an Lighiche** [myowl ə **lyee**-eechə] hill of the doctor.

Meall Luaidhe [myowl **loo**Yə] lead hill.

Meall Mór [myowl **moar**] big hill.

Meall na Dìge [myowl nə **dyee:**gə] hill of the ditch or moat.

Meall na Feàrna [myowl nə **fyaar**nə] hill of the alder.

Meall na h-Aisre [myowl nə **hash**rə] probably hill of the path or defile.

Meall na Leitreach [myowl nə **lyay**troch] hill of the slope.

Meall na Meòig (of **Ben Pharlagain**) [myowl nə **myaw**eeky] whey hill; Pharlagain may be from *feur-lagain* [**fayr**lagəny] grassy hollow.

Meall nan Aighean [myowl nən **Y**ən] hill of the heifers, or hinds.

Meall na Teanga [myowl nə **tyoe**ghə] hill of the tongue.

Meall nam Peithirean [myowl nəm **pay**ərən] hill of the gamekeepers or foresters, or perhaps hill of the thunderbolts.

Meall nan Ceapraichean [myowl nən **keh**preechən] hill of the stubby hillocks.

Meall nan Eun [myowl nən **ee**-un] hill of the birds.

Meall nan Subh [myowl nən **soo**] hill of the berries (probably raspberries).

Meall nan Tàrmachan [myowl nən **taar**mochan] hill of the ptarmigans.

Meall Odhar [myowl **oa**-ər] dun-coloured hill.

Meall Tàirneachan [myowl **taar**nyochan] hill of thunder.

Meallach Mhór [myaloch **voar**] great lumpy hill.

Meallan Liath Coire Mhic Dhùghaill [myalan **lyee-**ə korə veechk **ghoo**eel^y] little grey hill of the corrie of Dougall's son (or of MacDougall's corrie).

Meallan nan Uan [myalan nən **oo**un] little hill of the lambs.

Merrick from Gaelic *meurach* [**may**roch] branched, fingered.

Mhaighdean, A' [ə **vY**tyan] the maiden.

Mharconaich, A' [ə **vark**əneech] the place of horses.

Monadh Mór [monəgh **moar**] big hill.

Monamenoch Gaelic *monadh meadhonach* [monagh **mee**onoch] middle hill.

Morrone from Gaelic *mór-shròn* [**moar** hrawn] big nose or promontory.

Móruisg [**moar**ishk] big water.

Morven from Gaelic *mór-bheann* [**moar**vyən] big hill.

Mount Battock probably from Gaelic *monadh badach* [monəgh **ba**toch] tufted hill.

Mount Keen Gaelic **Monadh Caoin** [monəgh **kYn**^y] gentle hill.

Mullach an Rathain [mooloch ə **rah**ən^y] summit of the pulley, or row of pinnacles.

Mullach Cadha Rainich [mooloch caa **ran**yeech] summit of the narrow pass of bracken.

Mullach Chlach a'Bhlàir [mooloch chlach ə **vlaar**^y] summit of the stone of the plain, or of the battlefield.

Mullach Coire Mhic Fhearchair [mooloch korə veechk **er**əchar^y] summit of the corrie of Farquhar's son.

Mullach Coire nan Nead [mooloch korə nən **nyet**] summit of the corrie of the nests.

Mullach Fraoch-choire [mooloch **froech** chorə] summit of the heathery corrie.

Mullach na Dheireagain probably originally *mullach nan deireagan* [mooloch nən **dye**rakan] summit of the kestrels.

Mullach nan Coirean [mooloch nən **kor**ən] summit of the corries.

Mullach Sìthidh [mooloch **shee:**hee] fairy summit.

Na Gruagaichean [nə **groo**əkeechən] the maidens.

Puist Coire Àrdair [poosht korə **aard**ər] posts of the high corrie; the name may refer either to the great snow-filled gullies, the Posts, at the head of Coire Àrdair, or to the fence-posts on the plateau at the head of the corrie.

Quinag Gaelic **A'Chuinneag** [ə **choon**yak] the milk-pail.

Riabhachan, An [ən **ree**əvochan] the grey or streaked one.

Rois-Bheinn [rosh **vYn**] from Old Norse *hróss* a horse and Gaelic *beinn* a hill.

Ruadh Stac Mór [rooəgh stachk **moar**] big red stack.

Ruadh-stac, An [ə **roo**əgh stachk] the red stack.

Ruadh-stac-Beag [rooəgh stachk **bayk**] little red stack.

Saddle, The for Gaelic **An Dìollaid** [ən dyeeəlat^y].

Sàil Chaorainn [saal **choer**Yn^y] hill (literally, heel) of the rowan tree.

Sàil Gharbh [saal **ghar**av] rough hill (literally, heel).

Sàil Gorm properly **Sàil Ghorm** [saal **ghor**om] blue hill (literally, heel).

Sàil Liath [saal **lyee-**ə] grey hill (literally, heel).

Sàil Mhór [saal **voar**] big hill (literally, heel).

Sàileag [**saal**ak] little hill (literally, heel).

Schiehallion Gaelic **Sìth Chailleann** [shee: **chal**-yan] fairy hill of the Caledonians.

Seana Bhràigh [**shen**ə vrY] old height.

Sgàirneach Mhór [sgaarnyoch **voar**] big scree.

Sgarsoch, An [ən **skar**soch] the place of the sharp rocks.

Sgiath Chùil [skee-ə **choo:l**^y] back wing, so sheltering spot.

Sgòr an Iubhair [skor ən **yoo-**ər^y] peak of the yew tree.

Sgòr an Lochain Uaine [skor ə lochYn^y ** oo**anyə] peak of the little green loch.

Sgòr Chòinnich [skor **chawn**yeech] mossy peak.

Sgor Éilde Beag [skor ay:ltyə **bayk**] little peak of the hind.

Sgòr Gaibhre [skor **gY**rə] peak of the goat.

Sgòr Gaoith [skor **goe**-ee] windy peak.

Sgòr Iutharn [skor **yoo**ərn] maybe peak of hell, but probably peak of the sharp ridge, from *fiubharainn* an edge point.

Sgor Mór (Glen Dee) [skor **moar**] big peak.

Sgòr na h-Ulaidh [skor nə **hoo**lee] peak of the treasure.

Sgoran Dubh Mór [skoran doo **moar**] big black pinnacle.

Sgòrr, An [ən **skawr**] the peak.

Sgòrr Bhàn properly **Sgòrr Bàn** [skor **baan**] white peak.

Sgòrr Craobh a'Chaorainn [skor kroev ə **choer**Yn^y] peak of the rowan tree.

Sgòrr Dhearg [skor **yer**ek] red peak.

Sgòrr Dhònuill properly **Sgòrr Dhòmhnaill** [skor **ghaw**eel^y] Donald's peak.

Sgòrr na Dìollaid [skor nə **dyee**əlid^y] peak of the saddle.

Sgòrr nam Fiannaidh [skor nəm **fee**ənee] peak of the Fingalians.

Sgòrr nan Lochan Uaine [skor nən lochan **oo**anyə] peak of the little green lochs.

Sgòrr Ruadh [skor **roo**əgh] red peak.

Sgùman Còinntich [skooman **kawn**tyeech] mossy, sack-shaped hill.

Sgùrr a'Bhac Chaolais [skoor ə vachk **choo**leesh] peak of the sandbank of the narrows.

Sgùrr a'Bhealaich Dheirg [skoor ə vyaleech **yer**ək] peak of the red pass.

Sgùrr a'Bhuic [skoor ə **vooy**chk] peak of the roe-buck.

Sgùrr a'Chaorachain [skoor ə **choe**rochən^y] probably peak of the torrent, from Gaelic *caoir*, rather than peak of the place of the rowan-berries; on old maps, however, it appears as **Sgùrr a'Chaoruinn**, peak of the rowan-tree.

Sgùrr a'Choire Ghlais [skoor ə chorə **ghlash**] peak of the grey-green corrie.

Sgùrr a'Choire-beithe [skoor ə chorə **beh**ə] peak of the birch corry.

Sgùrr a'Dubh Doire [skoor ə **doo** dirə] peak of the black thicket.

Sgùrr a'Fionn Choire [skoor ə **fyoon** chorə] peak of the pale-coloured corrie.

Sgùrr a'Ghreadaidh [skoor ə **ghre**dee] peak of torment, or conflict.

Sgùrr a'Mhadaidh [skoor ə **va**tee] peak of the fox.

Sgùrr a'Mhàim [skoor ə **vYm**] peak of the large rounded hill.

Sgùrr a'Mhaoraich [skoor ə **voe**reech] peak of the shellfish, but locally it is **Sgùrr a'Mhorair** [skoor ə **vor**ir^y] peak of the landowner.

Sgùrr a'Mhuilinn [skoor ə **voo**leen^y] peak of the mill.

Sgùrr Alasdair [skoor al*ə*stayr] Alasdair's peak; named after Alasdair MacNeacail, Sheriff Alexander Nicolson, a Skyeman, the first person known to have climbed it (1873).

Sgùrr an Airgid [skoor ən **ar**akyit^y] peak of silver; silver peak.

Sgùrr an Doire Leathain [skoor ən dirə **lye**hen^y] peak of the broad oak grove.

Sgùrr an Fhuarail [skoor ən **oo**-arəl] maybe peak of coldness, but probably **Sgùrr an Fhuar-thuill** peak of the cold hollow.

Sgùrr an Fhuarain [skoor ən **oo**ərYn^y] peak of the spring.

Sgùrr an Lochain [skoor ə **loch**Yn^y] peak of the little loch.

Sgùrr an Lochain Uaine [skoor ə **loch**Yn^y **oo**anyə] peak of the little green loch.

Sgùrr an Tuill Bhàin [skoor ən təl^y **vaa**n^y] peak of the white hollow.

Sgùrr an Ùtha [skoor ən **oo**:-ə] peak of the udder.

Sgùrr Bàn [skoor **baan**] light-coloured peak.

Sgùrr Breac [skoor **brechk**] speckled peak.

Sgùrr Chòinnich [skoor **chawn**yeech] mossy peak.

Sgùrr Chòinnich Beag [skoor chawnyeech **bayk**] small mossy peak.

Sgùrr Chòinnich Mór [skoor chawnyeech **moar**] big mossy peak.

Sgùrr Coire Chòinneachan [skoor korə **chawn**yochan] peak of the corrie of the mosses.

Sgùrr Còs na Breachd-laoidh [skoor kaws nə **brechk** lY] peak of the hollow of the speckled fawns (*breac-laoigh*).

Sgùrr Creag an Eich [skoor krayk ən **yaych**] peak of the rock of the horse.

Sgùrr Dearg [skoor **dye**rek] red peak.

Sgùrr Dhòmhnuill [skoor **ghaw**eel^y] Donald's peak.

Sgùrr Dubh [skoor **doo**] black peak.

Sgùrr Dubh Mór [skoor doo **moar**] big black peak.

Sgùrr Dubh an Dà Bheinn [skoor **doo** ən **daa** vYn] black peak of the two hills.

Sgùrr Éilde Mór [skoor ay:lty*ə* **moar**] big peak of the hind.

Sgùrr Fhuar-thuill [skoor **oo**ər hil^y] peak of the cold hollow.

Sgùrr Fhuaran properly **Sgùrr Ùrain** [skoor **oo**:rən^y] perhaps *sgùrr odhar-choin*, peak of the wolf; or, less likely, from *odharan*, cow-parsnip.

Sgùrr Fiona [skoor **fee**-ənə] either white peak, or wine peak.

Sgùrr Gaorsaic [skoor **goer**sik] probably after nearby Abhainn Gaorsaig, which may mean thrusting stream.

Sgùrr Ghiubhsachain [skoor **yoo**sochən^y] peak of the little pinewood.

Sgurr Ìnnse [skoor **ee**:nshə] probably peak of the pasture.

Sgùrr Leac nan Each [skoor lyechk nən **yech**] peak of the slab of the horses.

Sgùrr Mhic Bharraich properly **Sgùrr Mhic Mharais** [skoor veechk **va**reesh] peak of MacVarish (the son of Maurice).

Sgùrr Mhic Choinnich [skoor veechk **chun**yeech] MacKenzie's peak, named after the well-known Cuillins guide, Iain MacCoinnich, or John MacKenzie.

Sgùrr Mhurlagain [skoor **voo**roolagən^y] peak of the sea-inlet.

Sgùrr Mór [skoor **moar**] big peak.

Sgùrr na Bà Glaise [skoor nə baa **gla**shə] peak of the grey cow.

Sgùrr na Banachdich [skoor nə **ba**nachteech] either peak of smallpox, from its pitted appearance, or peak of the milkmaid.

Sgùrr na Càrnach [skoor nə **kaar**noch] rocky peak.

Sgùrr na Cìche [skoor nə **kee:**chə] peak of the breast.

Sgùrr na Ciste Duibhe [skoor nə **keesh**tyə **doe**yə] peak of the black chest.

Sgùrr na Fearstaig properly **Sgùrr nam Feartag** [skoor nəm **fyar**shtak] peak of the sea pinks.

Sgùrr na Forcan [skoor nə **fo**rakan] peak of the little fork.

Sgùrr na h-Aide [skoor nə **hat**yə] peak of the hat.

Sgùrr na Lapaich [skoor nə **lah**peech] peak of the bogland.

Sgùrr na Ruaidhe [skoor nə **roo**ᵞ-ə] peak of the redness.

Sgùrr na Sgìne [skoor nə **skee:**nə] peak of the knife.

Sgùrr nan Ceannaichean [skoor nən **kya**neechən] peak of the merchants or pedlars.

Sgùrr nan Ceathreamhnan [skoor nən **kay**rəvnən] peak of the quarters.

Sgùrr nan Clach Geala [skoor nən klach **gya**lə] peak of the white stones.

Sgùrr nan Coireachan [skoor nən **ko**rəchən] peak of the corries.

Sgùrr nan Conbhairean [skoor nən **ko**nəveran] peak of the hound keepers.

Sgùrr nan Each [skoor nən **yech**] peak of the horses.

Sgùrr nan Eag [skoor nən **yek**] peak of the notches.

Sgùrr nan Eugalt [skoor nən **ay**kalt] probably peak of the furrowed rocks (*eigeal*).

Sgùrr nan Fhir Dhuibhe properly **Sgùrr an Fhir Dhuibhe** [skoor ən yeer **ghoo**yə] peak of the dark man.

Sgùrr nan Gillean [skoor nən **geel**yən] peak of the young men, or, more probably, peak of the gullies.

Sgùrr nan Saighead [skoor nən **sY**ət] peak of the arrows.

Sgùrr nan Spàinteach [skoor nə **spaa**ntyoch] peak of the Spaniards; in memory of the 250 Spanish infantrymen who fought with the Jacobites at the Battle of Glenshiel in 1719.

Sgùrr Sgùmain [skoor **skoo:**mən^y] peak of the (boat) bailer.

Sgùrr Theàrlaich [skoor **hyaar**leech] Charles' peak; named after Charles Pilkington, a member of the Scottish Mountaineering Club.

Sgùrr Thormaid [skoor **ho**romat^y] Norman's peak; named after Norman Collie, a member of the Scottish Mountaineering Club who did much early mountaineering exploration in Scotland.

Sgùrr Thuilm [skoor **hoo**ləm] peak of the rounded hillock.

Shalloch on Minnoch possibly from Gaelic *seileachan* [**shay**lochan] related to *saileachaidh* a place of willows, and *meadhonach* [**mee**onoch] middle.

Sìdhean, An [ən **shee**han] fairy hill.

Slioch Gaelic **An Sleaghach** [ən **shlye**ghoch] the spear hill.

Socach, An [ən **soch**koch] the snout.

Sow of Atholl, The, or **Muc Athaill** [moochk aheelʸ] paired with the neighbouring **Boar of Badenoch**, or **Torc Bhàideanach** [torchk̬ **vaa**dyenoch]; its original name was **Meall nan Dobhraichean** [myowl nən **doh**reechən] hill of the watercresses.

Spidean a'Choire Léithe [speedyan ə chorə **lyay:**hə] peak of the grey corrie.

Spidean Còinnich [speetyan **kawn**yeech] peak of the moss.

Spidean Coire nan Clach [speedyan korə nən **klach**] peak of the corrie of stones.

Spidean Dhòmhnuill Bhric [speedyan ghawil **vreechk**] peak of spotted Donald.

Spidean Mialach [speedyan **mee**-uloch] peak of deer.

Sròn a'Choire Chnapanaich [strawn ə chorə **chrah**paneech] jutting peak (literally, nose) of the corrie with the little hillocks.

Sròn a'Choire Ghairbh [strawn ə chorə **ghe**rev] jutting peak (literally, nose) of the rough corrie.

Sròn a'Choire [strawn ə **cho**rə] jutting peak (literally, nose) of the corrie.

Sròn a'Ghearrain [strawn ə **yar**ənʸ] jutting peak (literally, nose) of the gelding.

Sròn an Isean properly **Sròn an Isein** [strawn ən **ee**shən] jutting peak (literally, nose) of the chicken.

Sròn Chona Choirein [strawn chonə **cho**rənʸ] jutting peak (literally, nose) of the meeting of the corries.

Sròn Coire a'Chriochairein [strawn korə ə **chree**-oachərənʸ] possibly jutting peak (literally, nose) of the corrie of the stonechat.

Sròn Coire na h-Iolaire [strawn korə nə **yoo**lərə] jutting peak (literally, nose) of the corrie of the eagle.

Sròn Garbh [strawn **ga**rav] rough jutting peak (literally, nose).

Sròn na Làirige [strawn nə **laa**rikə] jutting peak (literally, nose) of the pass.

Sròn nan Giubhas [strawn nən **gyoo**-as] jutting peak (literally, nose) of the Scots pines.

Sròn Riach [strawn **ree**-och] brindled, greyish jutting peak (literally, nose).

Stac, An [ə **stachk**] the stack, or steep hill.

Stacan Dubha [stachkən **doo**ə] black stacks.

Stob a'Bhruaich Léith [stob ə vroo-eech **lyay**] peak of the grey slope.

Stob a'Choin [stob ə **chon**ʸ] peak of the dog.

Stob a'Choire Dhomhainn [stob ə chorə **ghoa**-eenʸ] peak of the deep corrie.

Stob a'Choire Liath Mhóir [stob ə chorə lyee-ə **voar**ʸ] peak of the big grey corrie.

Stob a'Choire Mheadhoin [stob ə chorə **vee**onʸ] peak of the middle corrie.

Stob a'Choire Odhair [stob ə chorə **oa**ər] peak of the dun-coloured corrie.

Stob a'Ghlais Choire [stob ə **ghlash** chorə] peak of the grey corrie.

Stob an Aonaich Mor properly **Stob an Aonaich Mhóir** [**stop** ən oeneech **voar**ʸ] peak of the big ridge.

Stob an Cùl Choire properly **Stob a'Chùl-Choire** [stob ə **chool** chorə] peak of the back corrie.

Stob an Duine Ruaidh [stob ən dinyə **roo**Y] peak of the red (haired) man.

Stob an Fhuarain [stob ən **oo**-urənʸ] peak of the spring.

Stob an t-Sluichd [stob ən **tloo**-eechk] peak of the hollow.

Stob Bàn [stob **baan**] light-coloured peak.

Stob Binnein [stob **beeny**ən] probably conical peak.

Stob Cadha Gobhlach properly **Stob a'Chadha Ghobhlaich** [stob ə chaa **ghoa**leech] peak of the forked pass.

Stob Choire a'Mhàil [stob chorə ə **vaal**ʸ] perhaps peak of the corrie of the rent or tax.

Stob Choire Claurigh [stob chorə **klow**ree] perhaps the peak of the corrie of clamouring, or bellowing, from *clamhras*.

Stob Coir' an Albannaich [stob korə ən **al**əpaneech] peak of the corrie of the Scotsman.

Stob Coire a'Chàirn [stob korə ə **chaarn**] peak of the corrie of the cairn.

Stob Coire a'Chearcaill [stop korə ə **chyer**kilʸ] peak of the corrie of the circle.

Stob Coire Altruim [stob korə **altr**əm] peak of the corrie of nursing (deer).

Stob Coire an Lochain [stob korə ə **loch**Ynʸ] peak of the corrie of the little loch.

Stob Coire an t-Saighdeir [stob korə ən **tY**dyər] peak of the corrie of the soldier.

Stob Coire an Laoigh [stob korə ə **loe**-ee] peak of the corrie of the calf, or fawn.

Stob Coire an t-Sneachda [stob korə ən **tnech**kə] peak of the corrie of the snow.

Stob Coire Bhealaich [stob korə **vya**leech] peak of the corrie of the pass.

Stob Coire Cath na Sìne [stob korə ka nə **shee**:nə] peak of the corrie of the battle of the elements.

Stob Coire Dheirg properly **Stob a'Choire Dheirg** [stob ə chorə **yer**ək] peak of the red corrie.

Stob Coire Dhòmhnuill [stob korə **ghaw**eelʸ] peak of Donald's corrie.

Stob Coire Dubh properly **Stob a'Choire Dhuibh** [stob ə chorə **ghoo**-ee] peak of the black corrie.

Stob Coire Easain [stob korə **es**ənʸ] peak of the corrie of the little waterfall.

Stob Coire Etchachan properly **Stob Coire Eiteachain** [stob korə **ayt**yochənʸ] maybe peak of the corrie of burnt heather roots, or, more probably, of juniper.

Stob Coire Léith properly **Stob a'Choire Léithe** [stob ə chorə **lyay**hə] peak of the grey corrie.

Stob Coire Lochain [stob korə **loch**Ynʸ] peak of the corrie of the little loch.

Stob Coire na Ceannain [stob korə nə **kyan**ənʸ] probably peak of the corrie of the white-headed cow, from **ceann-fhionn**.

Stob Coire na Cloiche [stob korə nə **kloch**yə] peak of the corrie of the stone.

Stob Coire na Cràlaig [stob korə nə **kraal**əkʸ] peak of the corrie of the basket.

Stob Coire na Gaibhre [stob korə nə **gYr**ə] peak of the corrie of the goat.

Stob Coire nam Beith [stob korə nəm **bay**] peak of the corrie of the birches.

Stob Coire nan Dearcag [stob korə nən **dyer**kag] peak of the corrie of the little berries.

Stob Coire nan Lochan [stob korə nən **loch**an] peak of the corrie of the little lochs.

Stob Coire Raineach [stob korə **ran**yoch] peak of the corrie of bracken.

Stob Coire Sgreamhach properly **Stob a'Choire Sgreamhaich** [stob ə chorə **sgre**veech] peak of the dreadful corrie.

Stob Coire Sgrìodain [stob korə **sgree:d**Yn^y] peak of the corrie of the scree.
Stob Dearg [stob **dye**rek] red peak.
Stob Diamh properly **Stob Daimh** [stob **dev**] peak of the stag.
Stob Dubh [stob **doo**] black peak.
Stob Dubh, Beinn Ceitlein [stob **doo**, bYn **kayt**shlin^y] black peak, possibly of Caitlin's hill, or else derived from old Gaelic *céis* a sow.
Stob Fraoch Choire [stob **froech** chorə] peak of the heathery corrie.
Stob Garbh [stob **ga**rav] rough peak.
Stob Ghabhar [stob **ghow**ər] peak of goats.
Stob na Bròige [stob nə **broyg**ə] peak of the shoe.
Stob na Doire [stob nə **dir**ə] peak of the (oak) thicket.
Stob nan Clach [stob nən **klach**] peak of the stones.
Stob Poite Coire Àrdair [stob **pot**shə korə **aa:rd**ər] the peak of the pot of the high corrie.
Streap [strayhp] (the) climb.
Stùc, An [ə **stoo:chk**] the peak.
Stùc a'Choire Bhig [stoochk ə chorə **veek**] peak of the little corrie.
Stùc a'Chroin probably *stùc a'chròthain* [stoochk ə **chroa**-ən^y] peak of the sheepfold.
Stùc Bheag [stoochk **vayk**] little peak.
Stùc Mór properly **Stùc Mhór** [stoochk **voar**] big peak.
Stuchd an Lochain [stoochk ə **loch**Yn^y] peak of the little loch.
Teallach, An [ən **tya**loch] the forge, or hearth.
Tigh Mór na Seilge [tə moar nə **shayl**əkə] big house of the hunt.
Toll Creagach [towl **kray**koch] the rocky hollow.
Tolmount locally [toal**mun**] from old Gaelic *dol* a valley and *monadh* a hill.
Tom a'Choinich Beag properly **Tom a'Chòinnich Beag** [towm ə **chawn**yeech **bayk**] little hill of the moss.
Tom a'Choinich properly **Tom a'Chòinnich** [towm ə **chawn**yeech] hill of the moss.
Tom Buidhe [towm **boo**yə] yellow hill.
Tom Dubh [towm **doo**] black hill.
Tom na Gruagaich [towm nə **groo**əkeech] hill of the maiden.
Tom na Sròine [towm nə **straw**nyə] hill of the jutting peak (literally, nose).
Toman Còinich properly **Toman Còinnich** [toman **kawn**yeech] little mossy hill.
Tudair, An properly **An Tughadair** [ən **too**ədər] the thatcher.
West Meur Gorm Craig [mayr **go**rom] west blue finger rock.
White Coomb [koom] *coomb* a valley or hollow on the side of a hill, a corrie, from Old English *cumb* (compare Welsh *cwm*).
White Mounth, The usually pronounced [munth] from Gaelic *monadh* a hill

The Climber and the Mountain Environment

With increasing numbers of walkers and climbers going to the Scottish hills, it is important that all of us who do so should recognise our responsibilities to those who live and work among the hills and glens, to our fellow climbers and to the mountain environment in which we find our pleasure and recreation.

The Scottish Mountaineering Club and Trust, who jointly produce this and other guidebooks, wish to impress on all who use the information in these books that it is in everybody's interest that good relations are maintained between visitors and landowners, particularly when there may be conflicts of interest, for example during the stalking season. The description of a climbing, walking or skiing route in any of these books does not imply that a right of way exists, and it is the responsibility of climbers to ascertain the position before setting out. In cases of doubt it is best to enquire locally.

During the stalking and shooting seasons in particular, much harm can be done in deer forests and on grouse moors by people walking through them. Normally the deer stalking season is from 1st July to 20th October, when stag shooting ends. Hinds may continue to be culled until 15th February. The grouse shooting season is from 12th August to 10th December. These activities are important for the economy of many Highland estates. During these seasons, therefore, special care should be taken to consult the local landowner, factor or keeper before taking to the hills.

Climbers and walkers are recommended to consult the book *Heading for the Scottish Hills*, published by the Scottish Mountaineering Trust on behalf of the Mountaineering Council of Scotland and the Scottish Landowners Federation. It gives the names and addresses of factors and keepers who may be contacted for information regarding access to the hills.

It is important not to disturb sheep, particularly during the lambing season between March and May. Dogs should not be taken onto the hills at this time, and at all times should be kept under close control.

Always try to follow a path or track through cultivated land and forests, and avoid causing damage to fences, dykes and gates by climbing over them carelessly. Do not leave litter anywhere, but take it down from the hill in your rucksack.

The number of walkers and climbers on the hills is leading to increased, and in some cases very unsightly erosion of footpaths and hillsides. Some of the revenue from the sale of this and other SMC guidebooks is used by the Trust to assist financially the work being carried out to repair and maintain hill paths in Scotland. However, it is important for us all to recognise our responsibility to minimise the erosive effect of our passage over the hills so that the enjoyment of future climbers will not be spoiled by damage caused by ourselves.

As a general rule, where a path exists walkers should follow it and even where it is wet and muddy should avoid walking along its edges, the effect of which is to extend erosion sideways. Do not take shortcuts at the corners of zigzag paths. Remember that the worst effects of erosion are likely to be caused during or soon after prolonged wet weather when the ground is soft and waterlogged. A route on a stony or rocky hillside is likely to cause less erosion than on a grassy one at such times.

Although the use of bicycles can often be very helpful for reaching remote hills and crags, the erosion damage that can be caused by them when used 'off road' on soft footpaths and open hillsides is such that their use on such terrain must cause concern. It is the editorial policy of the Scottish Mountaineering Club that the use of bicycles in hill country may be recommended on hard tracks such as forest roads or private roads following rights of way, but is not recommended on footpaths and open hillsides where the environmental damage that may be caused is considerable. Readers are asked to bear these points in mind, particularly when the ground is soft and wet after rain.

The proliferation of cairns on hills detracts from the feeling of wildness, and may be confusing rather than helpful as regards route-finding. The indiscriminate building of cairns on the hills is therefore to be discouraged.

Climbers are reminded that they should not drive along private estate roads without permission, and when parking their cars should not block access to private roads and land, and should avoid causing any hazard to other road users.

Finally, the Scottish Mountaineering Club and the Scottish Mountaineering Trust can accept no liability for damage caused to property, nor for personal injury resulting from the use of any of their publications.

The Mountaineering Council of Scotland is the representative body for climbers and hillwalkers in Scotland. One of its primary concerns is the continued free access to the hills and crags that we now enjoy. Information about restrictions due to bird nesting, stalking and general access issues can be obtained from the Access and Conservation Officer of the MCofS at 4a St Catherine's Road, Perth, PH1 5SE (Tel: 01738 638 227)

SCOTTISH MOUNTAINEERING CLUB GUIDEBOOKS
Published by the Scottish Mountaineering Trust

District Guides

The Southern Uplands *Ken Andrew*	ISBN 0 907521 38 X	£16.95
The Southern Highlands *Donald Bennet*	ISBN 0 907521 34 7	£16.95
The Central Highlands *Peter Hodgkiss*	ISBN 0 907521 44 4	£17.95
The Cairngorms *Adam Watson*	ISBN 0 907521 39 8	£17.95
The Northwest Highlands *Donald Bennet and Tom Strang*	ISBN 0 907521 28 2	£17.95
The Islands of Scotland including Skye		
Derek Fabian, Graham Little and Noel Williams	ISBN 0 907521 23 1	£19.95

Hillwalkers Guides

The Munros *Edited by Donald Bennet*	ISBN 0 907521 31 2	£16.95
The Corbetts and other Scottish Hills		
Ed by Scott Johnstone, Hamish Brown and Donald Bennet	ISBN 0 907521 29 0	£16.95

General Guide

Scotland's Mountains *W.H.Murray*	ISBN 0 907521 15 0	£17.95

TACIT PRESS TABLES
Published by the TACit Press, 138 West Stirling Street, Alva, FK12 5EN

The Grahams and the New Donalds   *Alan Dawson*   20pp   ISBN 0 9522680 2 7   £1.70
   224 Scottish Hills of 2000ft to 2499ft with 150m drop, and 118 Scottish lowland hills over 2000ft

The Murdos   *Alan Dawson*   20pp   ISBN 0 9522680 3 5   £1.70
   444 Scottish Hills over 3000ft with 30m drop

World Tops and Bottoms   *Grant Hutchison*   28pp   ISBN 0 9522680 4 3   £2.00
   High and low points of all countries and their dependencies

The Hewitts and Marilyns of Wales   *Alan Dawson*   24pp   ISBN 0 9522680 6 X   £2.00
   137 Welsh hills over 2000ft with 30m drop, and 156 Welsh hills with 150m drop

The Hewitts and Marilyns of England   *Alan Dawson*   28pp   ISBN 0 9522680 7 8   £2.00
   178 English hills over 2000ft with 30m drop, and 178 English hills with 150m drop

The Hewitts and Marilyns of Ireland   *E.D.Clements*   48pp   ISBN 0 9522680 8 6   £3.70
   211 Irish hills over 2000ft with 30m drop, and 453 Irish hills with 150m drop